SEXUAL ATTRACTION AND LOVE

SEXUAL ATTRACTION AND LOVE

An Instrumental Theory

By

RICHARD CENTERS

Professor of Psychology
University of California, Los Angeles

CHARLES C THOMAS • PUBLISHER

Springfield • Illinois • U.S.A.

Published and Distributed Throughout the World by
CHARLES C THOMAS · PUBLISHER
Bannerstone House
301-327 East Lawrence Avenue, Springfield, Illinois, U.S.A.

© *1975 by* CHARLES C THOMAS · PUBLISHER

ISBN 0-398-03169-X

Library of Congress Catalog Card Number: 74 7191

With THOMAS BOOKS *careful attention is given to all details of
manufacturing and design. It is the Publisher's desire to present books
that are satisfactory as to their physical qualities and artistic possibilities
and appropriate for their particular use.* THOMAS BOOKS *will be true
to those laws of quality that assure a good name and good will.*

Printed in the United States of America
Y-2

Library of Congress Cataloging in Publication Data

Centers, Richard.
Sexual attraction and love; an instrumental theory.

1. Sex (Psychology) 2. Love. 3. Interpersonal attraction. 4. Need
(Psychology) I. Title.
[DNLM: 1. Interpersonal relations. 2. Love. 3. Sex
behavior. HQ64 C397s 1974]
BF692.C45   155.3   74-7191
ISBN 0-398-03187-8

PREFACE

A THEORY which lays emphasis upon man's use of woman and woman's use of man, as the instrumental theory advanced here does, is almost certain to strike some readers as either cynical or irreverent of humankind. But it is meant to be neither. It is meant simply to offer the most adequate understanding available of an area of human psychological functioning in terms of what ultimately determines the character of the interrelationships of the respective sexes, seeing their use of each other as neither good nor bad but as merely inevitable and necessary to the fulfillment and happiness of both. As pointed out in subsequent pages, only when the exchange of benefits is inequitable and one-sided can one of the parties to it be seen as having been a victim, and even then, in most cases, only when the inequity is flagrant and obvious to someone either in the relationship or outside it.

In our culture, as in others, folk wisdom concerning the relationship between the sexes, especially where marriage is involved, has long recognized the exchange aspect of it. People, for example, often explicitly ask one another what a given person for whom marriage is in prospect "has to offer" another. The instrumental theory presented here is in accord with this conception in that it is in a basic sense an exchange theory. The idea of exchange is integral to it and pervades the interpretation of the relationships dealt with in these pages. In making use of the exchange concept, however, the writer has exploited not only the long established common sense notion of exchange that may be said to exist in the common domain of contemporary thought, but has also made some use of the more systematized concepts of it as a process, i.e. those presented recently by social scientists Blau, Homans, and Thibaut and Kelley. Although adaptation is mainly that of employing simply the general idea common to all these theories rather than an adherence to any particular variant formulation, the concepts and terminology of the latter two

v

theorists have been employed more explicitly than any others, and seemingly make for a more complete and sophisticated presentation of exchange relationships than would otherwise be possible. That is perhaps all the affinity to any previously established exchange theory that can be either claimed or acknowledged, for no attempt is made to systematically test any particular hypothesis derived from any previously extant exchange theory. Rather, the writer has developed a more or less independent set of formulations concerning exchange at the level of motivational analysis and has systematically sought to test these.

In the theory advanced here, however, the idea of exchange is quite secondary to the recognition of the role of instrumentality, or instrumental need gratification. *It is what is exchanged and the means and mechanisms by which the exchange is accomplished that is conceived of as the key to understanding intersexual attraction.* In other words, if anything can be maintained to be basic, the reciprocal need gratification of lovers is surely to be regarded as the most basic of all. Here, again, is an idea not new but actually very ancient, traceable, if one is especially insistent in such matters, to such thinkers as Plato and Aristotle. Among more recent writers one finds it, along with the idea of complementarity of needs and other variables, more or less explicit in discussions and theories of intersexual relationships advanced by Ohman (1942), Dreikurs (1946), Reader and English (1947), Gray (1949), Cattell (1950), Winch (1958), etc.

Still, in these pages there are both things that are new and, hopefully, things that will prove to be true, but in the scientific endeavor the true is not always found to coincide with the new and the true itself is always considered more or less tentative, the accumulation of massive evidence in favor of an hypothesis usually being thought necessary for its being accepted as valid. Further research guided by alternate theories may either seriously question the adequacy of the interpretation of the phenomena dealt with in this work or reveal it to be only partially and unimportantly descriptive of the realities it seeks to understand. It is hence offered simply as this writer's best comprehension of intersexual attraction phenomena in terms of the data available at the time of this writing, and with the expectation that further efforts by himself and others will eventually afford a more complete and more precise knowledge of them. The very meagerness of previous serious study of intersexual attraction and love itself suggests that some years hence, if research in this area is much intensified, and information is duly accumulated, what is revealed here may prove to have been only a surface scratching enterprise. However, if this attempt proves to have been no more than an advance beyond what was previously known, that will have more than compensated this investigator for his effort.

Actually, much more research derived information explicative of intersexual attraction and love than that encompassed in this volume has been already accumulated by the writer himself, but could not be included because of such practical reasons as seeming interminability of length. In the interest of readability of what is inevitably a somewhat complex and technical body of material requiring a highly analytical presentation, a book longer than the present one seemed ill advised. With the incorporation of more theoretical ramifications and the data supporting them, the reader might well not have been able to see the wood because of all of the trees.

ACKNOWLEDGMENTS

A WORK OF THIS NATURE can not be carried out unless one is permitted to describe the research of others. The writer hereby expresses his special appreciation for the efforts of Allen L. Edwards and to the Psychological Corporation for their allowing him to reproduce materials from Edwards' *Manual of The Edwards Personal Preference Schedule*, 1959, to Robert F. Winch for permission to quote passages from his *Mate Selection*, (Harper and Bros. 1958) and to Elaine Walster, Vera Aronson, Darcy Abrahams, and Leon Rottman (as well as to The American Psychological Association) for permission to reproduce Table 1 of their article *Importance of Physical Attractiveness in Dating Behavior* which originally was published in Vol. 4 of the *Journal of Personality and Social Psychology*, 1966.

CONTENTS

Page

Preface v

Acknowledgments ix

Chapter

One. THE CONCEPT OF INSTRUMENTALITY IN INTERPERSONAL
RELATIONS AND SOME GENERAL THEORIES OF INTER-
PERSONAL ATTRACTION 3

Two. SOME SPECIFIC THEORIES OF INTERSEXUAL ATTRACTION . 14

Three. SOME ELEMENTS OF INSTRUMENTAL THEORY: A THEORY
OF LOVE, A THEORY OF INITIAL ATTRACTION AND A
THEORY OF SEXUAL ATTRACTION 35

Four. THE BASIC THESIS OF THE INSTRUMENTAL THEORY AND
A THEORY OF THE ORDER OF PRIMACY OF PARTICULAR
NEEDS IN INTERSEXUAL ATTRACTION AND LOVE . . . 62

Five. MECHANISMS OF INTERPERSONAL NEED GRATIFICATION:
THE THEORY OF INTERMOTIVATIONAL MECHANICS . . 89

Six. SUBJECTS AND METHOD 144

Seven. EVALUATION OF THE THEORY OF AN ORDER OF PRIMACY
OF LOVE'S DETERMINANTS AND THE THEORY OF
INTERMOTIVATIONAL MECHANICS 152

Eight. PREPARATIONS FOR A THEORY OF INTERMOTIVATIONAL
DYNAMICS: INTERPERSONAL ATTRACTION AND
REPULSION AS A PARTIAL FUNCTION OF THE GENERAL
AND COMMON PROPERTIES OF NEEDS 178

Nine. THE THEORY OF INTERMOTIVATIONAL DYNAMICS . . . 201

Ten. PREDICTIONS DERIVED FROM THE THEORY OF INTER-
MOTIVATIONAL DYNAMICS AND THEIR OUTCOMES . . 232

xi

Eleven. Evaluation of Instrumental Theory as a Whole and of the Theory of Intermotivational Dynamics in Particular 255

Twelve. Male-Female Complementarity and the Role of Self-Esteem in Intersexual Love 279

Thirteen. Summary and Conclusions 304

References 313

Index 323

SEXUAL ATTRACTION AND LOVE

THE CONCEPT OF INSTRUMENTALITY IN INTERPERSONAL RELATIONS AND SOME GENERAL THEORIES OF INTERPERSONAL ATTRACTION

INSTRUMENTALITY

PROMINENT AND PERVASIVE, but only occasionally made explicit in the thinking of mankind with respect to how humans relate to each other is the idea that people sometimes use one another. And often, when it is observed to be a very selfish and one-sided manipulation, a friend or other concerned person may attempt to obstruct its continuance by informing the exploited one of its existence, cautioning him that he is "being used." There is intended the discrediting and condemnation of the user in such a remark; the moral and ethical values of our society and those of most others deny the rightness and legitimacy of one man making another his instrument. Unselfish devotion to the needs and welfare of others is what is held up, typically, as the noblest of virtues.

Yet, we, almost at all times, are the instruments of each other; we cannot gain the satisfactions of life or gratify most of our manifold needs without using another. Only in our extero-personal transactions with the physical environment, as in sowing a field and reaping its yield for our sustenance, are we making nature, rather than others, our instrument in the satisfaction of our needs. Even there we may use another if we can.

Although we commonly and typically define our goals with reference to one another in terms which imply denial, all social interaction and interpersonal behavior, stabilized patterns which are spoken of as "relationships," may be conceived of as processes wherein we seek to use each other as instruments for self-gratification. Our needs or mo-

3

tives are themselves very numerous and varied. They wax and wane in their individual determinance over our interaction goals with respect to each other. This they do not only in accordance with the degree of deprivation or satiation but also with the opportunity, i.e. the properties of a particular situation confronting us at a particular time.

Transient and temporary needs born of circumstances, such as an instance wherein we have lost our way in a strange city and accost the nearest passerby for information and reorientation, are not what we have in mind here: nor are a myriad of routinely occurring life-maintenance needs, those pertaining to food, clothing, shelter, transportation, and professional services. These largely determine our interaction goals in many brief, routine, and largely impersonal encounters and transactions with others. Rather, it is the other long-enduring needs, which are of such central importance that large segments of our behavior are dominated and determined by them, that give, in seemingly casual ways, structure and organization to our personalities. We are concerned, in short with those needs which motivate responses leading to less incidental and more lasting interactions and associations between ourselves and others.

The cataloging of man's needs is possibly, at this stage of development of psychology, far from complete. Yet, the list, since the early formulations of Freud and McDougall, has grown increasingly long. Murray's 1938 compilation, which seemed to many psychologists at the time to be overelaborate, has already been revealed, on the contrary, to require much supplementation. For instance, the one need other than sex and affectionate intimacy, that is seen in this work as most determinative in intersexual attraction, that of generic identity and role maintenance, has, until now, been practically ignored in psychological observation and research. Much, much more will be said concerning this need later. The point upon which stress must be placed is that we cannot wait upon a complete and certain cataloging of needs when seeking self-understanding. It is acknowledged that we do not, as yet, know all of man's needs and precisely how they function in psychological processes. Yet, it is believed that through understanding of intrapersonal and interpersonal need mechanics and dynamics an explanation of interpersonal relations, at a true depth level, is to be found. Enough is now known of needs to permit such an understanding to be arrived at, even if regarded as tentative and subfinal.

Association and interaction with others, for periods ranging from minutes to lifetimes and involving groups ranging from two to an indefinite number, *is engaged in for the purpose of gratifying these needs.* It is proposed that we can understand much, although not necessarily all, of the various phenomena associated with interpersonal interaction in terms of the mechanics and dynamics of intrapersonal and interpersonal motivations of participants and the behaviors instigated by them in their interactions with each other. The development of interpersonal attraction, power relations, and status differentials are seen as dependent upon these psychological forces.

Concern in the present work is not, however, inclusive of the entire range of phenomena with which the *instrumental theory of interpersonal relations* is ultimately engaged. It is focused essentially on attraction, love, and dyad formation between persons of opposite sex. Intersexual dyad formation, however, is regarded simply as a particular and special case of dyad formation. Dyad formation, in turn, is merely a particular and special case of group formation. Thus, what principles are found to govern or account for the one part may also be applicable to, although certainly not entirely sufficient for, understanding the whole.

In the most broad and general terms the propositions employed as the working hypotheses and conceptual framework for what is to be presented here are the following:

1. Human groups are originally established as a consequence of human interdependency for the gratification of biological drives: especially those for sexual satisfaction, nourishment, and survival support (protection against predators, provision for the dependent young, etc., provision of food, shelter, etc. in infancy).

2. As groups expand and become stably institutionalized as societies, rules and norms of behavior become established as means of insuring their continuation.

3. Social motivation and interpersonal needs of all sorts are consequents of continued human interaction in groups and the institutionalization of a host of behavioral interrelations norms, including those of reciprocity (reciprocal obligation, fair exchange, etc.).

4. Interpersonal needs, themselves developing as consequents of

these processes, and being only gratifiable by human association, interaction, and interchange, become at a more evolved stage of human existence an additional basis for the establishment and maintenance of all groups of whatever kind. The intersexual dyad and marital union is simply the most necessary and important kind of group so originating. Friendship and larger recreational, economic, political, religious, and other types of affiliation are all need instigated and need gratification based associations, each given its particular character in terms of the kinds of needs for which its existence serves as the vehicle of gratification.

5. Explanation and understanding of interpersonal and group relations, including attraction and repulsion, superordination and subordination, (status and power relationships) and other phenomena are to be found in the principles of intermotivational mechanics and dynamics that are instrumental in the reciprocal need gratifications of persons.

6. Social interaction and interpersonal behavior may be conceived of as an exchange process wherein individuals seek to use and do use each other for the gratifications of their needs. When there is a mutually gratifying use of each other (positive exchange) the result is attraction, liking, and love. When there is either mutual or one-sided frustration of needs (negative exchange) the result is repulsion and hate. Where no exchange of gratifications or frustrations results from our encounters we experience merely disinterest and apathy.

In the effort to validate, more intricately develop, and expand this instrumental explanation of interpersonal relations, it may be reiterated that the most fitting point at which to begin is in an examination of the beginning. The beginning was, of course, the intersexual dyad.

SOME GENERAL THEORIES OF INTERPERSONAL ATTRACTION

It is curious that although all of us are more or less continuously concerned with interpersonal relationships and often anxious about whether we are loved or hated by others, psychologists and other behavioral scientists have until quite recently done little to advance our insight and understanding into such matters. Slow beginnings, to be sure, are to be found in the work in Sociometry instigated by Moreno as far back as 1934 (Moreno, 1934). This work (e.g., Bonney, 1947, Jennings, 1950), is focused primarily upon the patterns of attraction and repulsion obtaining in groups of several to many persons in size rather than upon dyadic relations. It bypasses almost completely the dynamics of intersexual attraction, but has contributed valuable empirical data as to the traits and characteristics of persons associated with popularity, leadership, rejection, and isolation in our society. Lewin's study of group dynamics in the early forties, using more experimental procedures, often with contrived groups of various sorts, measurably added to the fund of understanding. This, however, was largely in respect to the individual's attraction to the group, rather than to another individual. Not until the early fifties did anything with enough sophistication to be called a theory of *interpersonal* attraction emerge. Newcomb (1956, 1961) carried out laborious studies at the University of Michigan which more or less clearly established what most people had always known: we like those who agree with us. His work also revealed, that liking for another whose attitudes are similar, takes time to develop, requiring a fairly extended period of at least moderately intensive interaction.

He predicted that as strangers in a new group undergo interaction with each other, gaining information concerning the other's attitudes, strong bonds of attraction would come to be formed most strongly between those who held similar attitudes towards objects of mutual importance and common relevance. The prediction was tested with the use of two groups of male college students who were initially total strangers to one another and who were recruited to the experiment with the inducement of free quarters in a house provided by the investigator. Their attitudes and beliefs toward a wide variety of objects, including each other, as well as the patterns of attraction that developed, were measured at frequent intervals during a sixteen-week semester.

Generally, the results confirmed expectations. Preacquaintance similarities in attitudes, beliefs and values, as determined by questionnaire responses, were found to be related to patterns of attraction at a late stage of acquaintance, although not so at an early stage. Inasmuch as the attitudes, beliefs and values did not themselves change appreciably over the semester's time, it seems a reasonable conclusion that as persons get to know each other's attitudes, attraction develops along the lines of similarity in these respects. This tendency was especially strong with reference to attitudes toward, or beliefs about, *persons*. That is, when two persons had similar feelings and beliefs about themselves and toward other members of the group they were especially likely to be attracted to each other. Also, as length of acquaintance increased, agreement between members of a pair in attitude toward other group members also increased, with there being a concomitant increase in liking for each other.

Another significant finding was the close association between liking oneself and belief that one is liked by others. A person was found to like those who had the same feelings toward him as he had toward himself. The relationship between being attracted to a person and the perceiving of him as having similar attitudes was also true for perceptions and cognitions about the other's impressions. Each subject was asked to describe himself by checking a series of adjectives and then to use the same checklist to describe himself as he thought each of the other house members would. A close association was found between liking and agreement on this sort of self-description. This association was present for unfavorable traits and characteristics as well as for favorable ones. A person was thus attracted to individuals whom he saw as judging him the way he saw himself, for faults as well as favorable attributes.

Various studies have confirmed Newcomb in showing that attraction is affected by both actual and perceived similarity in attitudes and characteristics (Tagiuri, 1958; Backman and Secord, 1959, 1962; Broxton, 1963). On the whole evidence suggests that the *belief* that another person is similar to oneself is a more significant determinant of attraction than whether or not the person is actually similar (Neugarten, 1946; Davitz, 1955; Preston, Peltz, Mudd and Froscher, 1952; Snucker, 1960; Broxton, 1963).

Sullivan (1947) called attention to a motivational process, *consensual validation*, which functions first as a need to validate one's thoughts and feelings, and second, one's evaluation of one's own self-worth, by seeking and finding agreement with others. Festinger (1950, 1954), somewhat later in his theory of social comparison processes, also posited a drive on the part of the individual to determine whether his opinions were correct and his appraisal of his abilities was accurate. Newcomb, influenced by both Festinger and Heider (1944,

1958a), and in his earlier formulations, reinforcement theory as well, posited a drive or "strain" of the same sort.

In early presentations of his findings he accounted for attraction based upon similarity of attitudes as a function of the reciprocal rewards in the way of consensual validation and ego support that association with an agreeing other provides. As his theory has further developed he has also presented it in terms of Heider's (1958) balance theory, which, following Gestalt principles, holds that separate entities which are *similar* tend to be perceived as belonging together; as forming a unit. It is Heider's contention that people strive to make their sentiment relationships conform more or less closely to their perceptions of the unit relationships formed with regard to objects. According to balance theory, then, positive unit formation in terms of perceived similarity should induce a harmonious sentiment relationship of liking, or feeling of attraction. The reverse would also be expected. That is, liking for another, or being attracted to him (on what basis initially is not explained), would generate perceptions to the effect that the liked one is similar to oneself.

The cognitive aspect of Newcomb's theory is valuable, in making sense of the phenomena of the overestimations of similarity between mutually attracted people, as well as in revealing the balance-restoring cognitive maneuvers of such persons. It is also valuable in helping to understand certain processes of person perception and interpersonal influence. However, the main relevance of Newcomb's theorizing to the present subject lies in his highlighting of the role of similarity of beliefs and attitudes in the providing of *reciprocal gratifications* for the members of an attracted pair. Although in embracing cognitive balance theory he might seem to imply that he saw the more recent formulations as superior in explanatory value to the earlier need gratification explanation, there is no clear warrant for assuming any such thing as a repudiation of the reinforcement principle by him.

At any rate, Byrne's theory of interpersonal attraction, which also has focused mainly upon the similarities in attitudes and beliefs between persons, clearly asserts its allegiance to the reinforcement model, and is perhaps as systematic in its own way as is that of Newcomb (Byrne, 1961, 1964). The underlying assumption of Byrne's approach is that "attraction towards X is a function of the relative number of rewards and punishments associated with X." In a recent paper he and his associate, Nelson, have proposed as a tentative law of attraction the formula $A_s = mPR_x + k$, or, "attraction toward X is a positive linear function of the proportion of positive reinforcements received from X" (Byrne and Nelson, 1965, p. 662).

Byrne and Nelson compared, in an experiment, the effect upon attraction of the *proportion* of similar attitudes expressed by an anonymous other person with the effect of the *number* of similar attitudes expressed. Each subject in the experiment was asked to examine an attitude questionnaire purportedly answered by a person unknown to him. Following this, the subjects were asked to evaluate the stranger along a number of dimensions, including their degree of liking for him or attraction to him. The experimenters had composed the protocols to be read by the subjects in such a manner that the number of similar attitudes was varied parametrically. Crosscutting variation in number of such attitudes was parametric variation in the proportion of similar attitudes. The results indicated that attraction was significantly affected only by the proportion of similar attitudes. That is, the greater the proportion of similar, as opposed to dissimilar attitudes, the greater the liking for the fictitious person. Moreover, the findings also supported the hypothesis of a linearity of the functional relationship.

Subsequent studies carried out by Byrne and his associates have corroborated the above findings that interpersonal attraction is a positive linear function of the proportion of attitude statements attributed to a fictitious other which are in agreement with those of the subject (Byrne and Clore, 1966; Byrne and Griffitt, 1966). The explanation offered by Byrne is in familiar terms; those of consensual validation: ". . . any time that another person offers us validation by indicating that his percepts are congruent with ours, it constitutes a rewarding interaction, and, hence, one element in forming a positive relationship. Any time that another person indicates dissimilarity between our two notions, it constitutes a punishing interaction and thus one element in forming a negative relationship. Disagreement raises the unpleasant possibility that we are to some degree stupid, uninformed, immoral, or insane," (1961, p. 713).

Both Byrne's theory and Newcomb's (earlier) theory, then, are saying the same thing. Persons are mutually attracted to each other when they reciprocally gratify each other's need for consensual validation of beliefs, values and attitudes by virtue of the similarities of these variables between them. *Each person is, thus, of course, serving an instrumental role for the other in this process.* Byrne and New-comb have, in stressing the role of reciprocal gratifications of the need for consensual validation, anticipated in at least a segmental way something that is also basic in the formulation of instrumental theory, and to that extent the theories are essentially compatible or, in a very limited way, even identical. All employ a reinforcement concept as determinant and cause. Yet, as will be seen in the instrumental theory elaborated in later discussion, it attempts, as their formulations thus far have not, to indicate the *modus operandi* of reciprocally reinforc-ing (or gratifying) not merely a single need, but, many others not dealt with by them at all. The fault with them, is not seen in what is said, but rather what is left unsaid concerning what is necessary for a more complete understanding of interpersonal attraction in general and of intersexual attraction in particular. On the other hand, if it may be assumed that they are placing complete or even major reliance upon gratification of the need for consensual validation as causal and determinative (and this does often seem implied) then the theory to be advanced here must be viewed as much less cordial to their ideas.

The process we are concerned with is one of interchange, or ex-change of behaviors, or, more specifically an exchange of gratifica-tions and/or punishments, between persons. Hence, it articulates in-timately into the framework of conceptions and relational formula-tions of exchange theories of social interaction and interpersonal be-havior, such as those of Thibaut and Kelley (1959), Homans (1961) and Blau (1964). Each of these theories accounts for interpersonal attractions as a resultant of the mutually gratifying exchanges or re-wards accruing to the respective partners in a dyad. They are, like Byrne's and Newcomb's, reinforcement theories. The Thibaut and Kelley thesis, conceptualized within the framework of game theory, further specifies that for attraction to the dyadic relation to exist (they speak of attraction to the relation, not the *person*), the out-comes experienced by the parties to it must be above their respective comparison levels for outcomes. This comparison level, representing the person's minimal level of expectation or desserts for gratifications in a relationship of the kind he is involved in, is itself a product of several considerations. These are: (1) his past experience in the relationship, (2) his past experience in comparable relationships, (3) his judgment of what outcomes others like himself are receiving, and (4) his perceptions of outcomes available to him in alternative relations.

Although the Thibaut and Kelley formulation provides a useful way of describing exchange processes concerning rewards and costs, highlighting the fact that rewards and costs are not experienced in absolute, but rather, in relative terms, it has not as yet generated the kind of research studies that could directly validate its formulations by empirical test.* For this, and for demonstration of its predictive value, independent determination of the dimensions of the comparison levels of the respective partners in a dyad would be required. To date, a practical technique for accomplishing this appears wanting. Although the theory is one which implicitly assumes interpersonal attraction and repulsion to be a resultant of need satisfactions and frustrations (or rewards and costs), it deals most explicitly and expressly with the consequences of differentials in the exchanges of rewards and costs between partners in an ongoing and already established relationship. It fails to concern itself with the functional relationships between rewards and costs and the various needs of the respective partners. Nor does it address itself to an explanation of the mechanisms and dynamisms of the forces of attraction and repulsion and how these outcomes are engendered in interactions involving the need-activated behaviors of the respective partners in a relationship. Essentially it concerns itself with explication of the dynamics of dyadic and other interpersonal relationships *already in being*, without contributing much to an explanation of how or why the relationship came to be. How the exchanges of positive and negative reinforcements are related to interpersonal needs is also largely ignored. The Thibaut and Kelley analysis is, however, brilliantly insightful and especially useful in understanding the mechanisms and dynamisms of changes that occur in

---

*There have been published, to be sure, some studies which, while not involving the concept of or the measurement of comparison levels, do constitute tests of the Thibaut and Kelley formulations. An important prediction from the theory is that no matter where, or with what pattern, interaction between members of a dyad begins, it should always lead toward a final or stable pattern of interaction, wherein the outcomes (rewards) are high for both persons. However, several empirical studies involving game behavior (Bixenstine, Potash, and Wilson, 1963; Shaw, 1962; Willis and Joseph, 1959) have yielded results opposite to those predicted by the theory. That is, members of the interacting dyads tended to develop patterns of interactions in which the outcomes were low for both of them.

a relationship over time, accounting for these in terms of changes in the reward-cost outcomes of the interacting partners. Unfortunately, the level of analysis pursued largely bypasses the exploration of the systematic relationships between the behaviors of the participants in the interaction and their underlying motivational processes.

Although the instrumental theory is on the whole quite compatible with exchange theory in a general sense, it focuses primarily upon the analysis and understanding of motivational relatedness and the mechanics involved in the reciprocal gratification that it supposes to determine interpersonal attraction. In effect, it pursues what is considered to be a deeper level of analysis—that of involving the motivational basis underlying the rewarding and punishing behaviors of dyadic members. In this enterprise the theory is not seen as having either any special dependence upon or as having any particular one of the several exchange theories previously developed. Nevertheless, since what is being dealt with is an exchange process, some of the terminology of already existing exchange theory seems applicable and is frequently used.

Another formulation closely related to the instrumental theory is the theory of complementarity of needs as the basis of interpersonal attraction formulated by Winch (1958). It is one which also stresses reciprocal need gratification and pursues explanation through analysis of need relatedness. This theory, which asserts that the needs of attracted persons are different rather than similar, is quite clearly and saliently opposed by the data and interpretations offered here. Since Winch's theory has become so very strongly identified with specifically intersexual attraction and mate selection, discussion of its features is reserved for the following chapter wherein theories and ideas particularly germane to intersexual attraction are reviewed.

CHAPTER TWO

SOME SPECIFIC THEORIES OF INTERSEXUAL ATTRACTION

SOME ANCIENT PHILOSOPHICAL CONTRIBUTIONS

THE IDEA that people love those who are instrumental in the gratification of their needs is ancient in Western thought, manifesting itself at least implicitly in the earliest infancy of our heritage. Thus, Aristotle in his Rhetoric wrote in the fourth century B.C.

> . . . men love any one who has done good to them or to those for whom they are concerned . . .
> Further, men like those who are able and inclined to benefit them in a pecuniary way, or to promote their personal safety . . . those who are pleasant to live with, and to spend the day with; such are the good-tempered—people who are not given to catching up one's mistakes and are not pertinacious or crossgrained . . . Further, we like those who praise our good qualities, and especially if we are afraid we do not possess them . . . We like those who take us seriously—who admire us, who show us respect, who take pleasure in our society . . . We like those who do not frighten us, and in dealing with whom we do not lose our aplomb—for no one likes a person of whom he is afraid (Aristotle, translated 1932, pp. 203-106).

Much later, in the seventeenth century, that Euclid of the emotions, Spinoza, who saw the essence of man as *desire*, and who noted that man *could be either conscious or unconscious of his appetites*, defined love and hate in terms that can scarcely be improved upon today. "Love," he says, "Is nothing but pleasure accompanied by the idea of an external cause" (Spinoza, translated, 1936, p. 177). "Hatred," he says further on, "is nothing but pain accompanied by the idea of an external cause" (1936, p. 178). On love, he continues, "This definition explains sufficiently clearly the essence of love: the definition given by those who say that love is *the lover's wish to unite himself with the love object* expresses *a property*, but not *the essence* of love," (1936, p. 177).

14

Also appearing very early in the development of concepts of love, in that classic work on it by Plato, *The Symposium*, is the idea of complementariness. In this he has Aristophanes tell a story of an angry Zeus, who, in punishment for the insolence of men, originally of a single sex, cut them into two halves, fashioned two sexes of them, and condemned them forever to seek each other in order to be one again (Plato, translated, 1933). "Each of us when separated is but the indenture of a man—and he is always looking for his other half" (1933, p. 317).

FREUDIAN IDEAS

Philosophers seem, as have men everywhere, to have known of motivation, or at least to have known something of the role of desires and wishes in their lives, and Spinoza, as noted above, comes close to anticipating the place that psychologists assign them today. With increasing consensus since the time of those earliest theorists of human motivation, the great instinctivists McDougall and Freud, psychologists have come to see human needs as the prime movers in human interaction. Each of these earliest theorists in one way or another adumbrated in his writings the idea of attraction and love and repulsion and hate being based on motivational processes. McDougall (1908) emphasized the role of the gregarious instinct in accounting for human association, whereas Freud saw it as dependent upon the erotic instinct.

From his intimate clinical studies of neurotic persons Freud (1925) thought he could distinguish two kinds of love in people, an anlehnungstypus—or literally leaning-up-against type and a narcissistic or "egotistical" type. The first type is now often referred to as the anaclitic type, and Flugel (1921) in his treatment of Freud's distinctions refers to it somewhat more revealingly as the dependent type of love. Freud implied a kind of complementariness operating to produce attraction between persons with dependency needs on the one hand and ego-enhancement sorts of needs on the other. He depicted dependent love as being expressed in responses of reverence, admiration and submissiveness toward the loved one, who, as an egotistical narcissistic person, would derive gratification from the approval, applause, adulation and adoration of the other. In another work Freud (1922) indicated a completion principle, pointing out that one characteristically falls in love with a particular person because that individual is seen as representing a perfection which the loving one has striven to attain, but unsuccessfully so.

From these germinal ideas has sprung a proliferation of particular variant formulations which are to be found in the writings of various psychoanalytically oriented theorists (e.g., Benedek, 1946; Bergler, 1946; Flügel, 1921; Gray, 1949; Mittelman, 1944; Ohmann, 1942; Reik, 1944; Winch, 1958). Benedek, for example, has stressed the completion principle in her proposition that lovers offer each other "an exchange of ego-ideals." She conceives of love itself as an "emotional manifestation which grows out of the surplus excitation following satisfaction of the receptive needs" (1946, p. 12). Ohmann advances the general formulation that love between persons comes into being because of the specific needs obtaining in the two respective persons, and points out that lovers are attracted to and select each other in terms of each other's capacities to fulfill the needs of each other. He states: ". . . We fall in love with those whom we need to complete ourselves . . . whom we need to satisfy our feelings of ego deficiency" (1942, p. 15). Love, itself, he characterizes as "a feeling of need for another personality to complete, supplement or protect our own" (1942, p. 28).

Some support for Ohmann's proposition with regard to "ego deficiency" is found in a study by Martinson (1955), wherein he compared personality test scores of girls who had married within five years after their graduation from high school with those of matched socioeconomic status who were still single. He reports that "the single girls were more self-reliant, had a greater sense of personal freedom, showed less tendency to withdraw, were more appreciative of accepted social standards and were less likely to have anti-social tendencies" (1955, p. 162).

Reik's notions are somewhat similar to those of Benedek in stressing the completion principle and in his pointing out that we seek a love object which more or less compensates for our failure to attain our own ego ideal (Reik, 1944, p. 40). He emphasizes the projective aspect of this dynamic in asserting that persons "jump" into rather than just fall in love. He means more or less by this a conscious and unconscious seeking of the ego-ideal, the finding of which is, itself, such a powerful need that it distorts perceptions of the love object in the direction of conformity with the ideal. Time worn cliches, such as "love is blind," and "beauty is in the eye of the beholder" are possible consequents of this process.

THE COMPLETION THEORY

Cattell (1950) and Cattell and Nesselroade (1967) have more explicitly formulated the completion principle as "a desire to possess characteristics (by sharing them in the possessed partner) which are felt by the individual to be necessary to his self-concept or to his or her general life-adjustment in marriage . . . For example, a socially awkward person might especially value a partner who is socially adroit and poised" (1967, p. 351). Although the completion principle and the need-complementarity principle are overlapping concepts, the need-complementarity principle is bound up more with the idea of reciprocal gratification of disparate needs of two partners in an interplay of their behaviors in interpersonal interactions. The completion principle is distinct from it. It is concerned more specifically with the personal and social desirability of the behaviors, traits, and physical characteristics of the prospective partners. Cattell and Nesselroade further particularize it by stating "every person tends to seek in a partner much the same set of desirables—good looks, intelligence, emotional stability, etc.—but more so to the extent that he or she lacks them" (1967, p. 356).

Cattell and Nesselroade's own data failed to confirm or measurably support their theory in a study concerned with responses to tests of personality conducted by them wherein they compared response data of stably and unstably married couples. Some supportive evidence is found for the hypothesis, however, in studies of intrasexual friendship, wherein subjects have been asked to describe the personality characteristics of their friends (Reader and English, 1947; Thompson and Nishimura, 1952; Lundy, Katkovsky, Cromwell and Shoemaker, 1955; and Beier, Rossi and Garfield, 1961). In these, when subjects perceived their friends as different in characteristics from themselves the traits were typically ones which the subjects themselves admired, and wished they possessed, but felt they lacked to some degree.

In the most recent of such studies, that of Beier, Rossi and Garfield (1961), subjects were asked to respond to the Minnesota Multiphasic Personality Inventory in three different ways. First, they took the test themselves as subjects normally would, then responded to the items as they thought their best friend would, and finally as they thought their most disliked acquaintance would respond.

Beier, Rossi and Garfield predicted that subjects would: (1) project more of their own personal attributes onto friends than onto those they disliked; (2) project onto friends more socially desirable traits than they attributed to themselves; and (3) project more socially undesirable characteristics onto disliked persons than they attributed to themselves. The results confirmed each of their three hypotheses. Their subjects tended to perceive their friends as psychologically better adjusted and emotionally stronger than they themselves were. As Beier, Rossi and Garfield describe their findings, "The friend as compared with the self is seen as more social, less depressed, less susceptible to moods, less concerned with bodily functions, less incapacitated by feelings of inadequacy, and generally more active and realistic than oneself. If the individual doing the rating is a male, he sees his male friend as being more interested in masculine activities than himself" (1961, p. 7). Subjects perceived the person they disliked, on the other hand, as being more poorly psychologically adjusted and endowed with socially desirable characteristics than themselves. "The disliked person as compared to the self is seen as being more impulsive, more suspicious of others, with more idiosyncratic ideas, and also with more aggressiveness. The non-friend was attributed an excess of almost all the characteristics tapped by the MMPI, i.e., impulsiveness, moodiness, concern with bodily functions, feelings of inadequacy, depression, social isolation, idiosyncratic ideas, and manic activity" (1961, p. 7).

Bergler and Others: Projection and Complementary Neuroses

Bergler (1946) has also couched his conception of love in the language of projection, pointing out that ". . . love is a process of projection of one's own ego-ideal, based upon narcissistic attitudes. Ultimately the lover loves only himself in his love object" (1946, p. 32). It is also Bergler who has, along with various other psychoanalysts, stressed the idea of complementary neuroses in marriage, asserting that "the neurosis of the woman complements the neurosis of the man she chooses, and vice versa." The process is, of course, an unconscious one as he sees it, but as, nevertheless, inexorable as fate in a Greek drama. A masochistic woman is not conscious of a wish she has to be treated badly, nor is a castrating female conscious of her wish for an impotent male. Each of them will simply regard themselves as unlucky in their marital choice. However, Bergler insists, luck it not responsible for this outcome. Unconscious choice is (1954, pp. 92-93). Again, "All stories about a normal woman who becomes the prey of a neurotic man, and vice versa, or a normal man who falls in love with a highly neurotic woman, are literary fairy tales. Real life is less romantic; two neurotics look for each other with uncanny regularity. Nothing is left to chance, as far as emotional attachments are concerned" (1948, p. 11).

Clinical corroboration of the principle of complementary needs, especially in the form of complementary neuroses is rather abundant in the reports of psychiatrists, psychologists, and marriage counsellors, and makes quite fascinating reading. Mittleman (1956), for example, reports five types of neurotic relationships, the majority of which are to be regarded as complementary in pattern, which he claims to have observed in his practice:

1. A dominant and aggressive person married to a submissive person.
2. An emotionally detached person married to one who craves affection.
3. A pair engaged in continuous rivalry for aggressive dominance.
4. A helpless and dependent person married to an endlessly supportive mate.
5. A person who vacillates between self-assertion and dependency married to one who vacillates between unsatisfied need for affection and giving support and help (Mittleman, 1956, p. 98).

Sullivan

A survey of the writings of neo-Freudian theorists reveals no essentially new conceptions. Even Sullivan, one of the most original of them, simply echoes more or less the dominant idea of complementarity; emphasizing that a marital relationship requires an integration of complementary needs and reciprocal patterns of activity (Sullivan, 1953).

Jungians and Adlerians

Complementarity is not, of course, an exclusive property of Freudians. Both Jung and Adler suggested the same sort of phenomenon in their various works. Both have in their present-day advocates theorists who have sought to elaborate and extend their ideas of this sort in the realm of intersexual attraction. For example, Gray (1948, 1949) and Gray and Wheelwright (1949) in a series of papers explicated the Jungian theory of psychological types and developed tests for measuring them. They administered the latter to a sample of 271 married couples to test the hypothesis that in mate selection spouses are unconsciously attracted to each other, not by virtue of their possession of similar personality traits, but rather by complementariness of traits or "type." The traits, which combine to make up the typology are introversion-extroversion, sensation-intuition, and thinking-feeling. Gray concluded, against nonsignificant and inconsistent findings, that he had demonstrated the correctness of his theory. At most it can only be regarded as tentative, needful of additional research, and with more sophisticated technique.

The Adlerian conception of "life style" is difficult to characterize succinctly, but in essence it seems to blend the concept of interpersonal behavioral traits with interpersonal and metapersonal needs or wishes. Dreikurs, one of today's leading Adlerian advocates, maintains that people choose each other in terms of the congruity of their life styles. "We feel attracted," he says, "when we have met somebody who offers us through his personality an opportunity to realize our personal pattern, who responds to our outlook and conceptions of life, who permits us to continue or to revive plans which we have carried since childhood. We even play a very important part in evoking and stimulating in the other person precisely the behavior which we expect and need. In other company the same partner might behave altogether differently" (Dreikurs, 1946, pp. 68-69).

Attraction between two persons and congruity of their two life styles does not, he points out, mean identity, or *similarity*, of the life styles. "On the contrary, they demand complementary differences. Two individuals each of whom wants to be dominant hardly fit together. Neither would two martyrs. The distinction must be made, however, between psychologically insignificant qualities and the all-important life style. Husband and wife may both be ambitious or both resentful and yet may get long: their identical qualities may unite them more closely. But the decisive point is neither the qualities nor, we may add, the common interests, as many believe, but— the basic pattern of life, the method by which they strive for superiority or suffering, for success or security. This explains why so often an oldest child marries a youngest one; a dominant individual a submissive one; why the brute finds a saint, and the rogue his protective victim" (1946, pp. 83-84).

As can be seen from consideration of the foregoing discussion of the complementarity and completion concepts, there is remarkable consensus as to their focal importance in intersexual attraction. Yet relatively little, other than clinical observation, and the studies of Martinson, Cattell and Nesselroade and Gray employing more systematic and essentially psychometric data collection, can be found as evidence for evaluating them.

THE RISE AND FALL OF THE COMPLEMENTARITY THEORY

A major effort to test the complementarity theory, employing essentially clinical methods was that of Winch, who in 1950 conducted an intensive study of the need structures of 25 young married couples. Winch, together with his associates Ktsanes and Ktsanes, reported fragments of their data and its analysis in a series of papers beginning in the early fifties and eventually culminating in a book by Winch summarizing the whole in 1958 (Winch, Ktsanes and Ktsanes, 1954; Ktsanes, 1955; Winch, 1955a, 1955b, 1958). Since it represents by far the most ambitious and influential attempt, to date, to develop a coherent theory of intersexual attraction, but more particularly mate selection, it will be treated in some detail.

Winch maintained that *"In mate selection each individual seeks within his or her field of eligibles for that person who gives the greatest promise of providing him or her with maximum need gratification"* (Winch, 1958, pp. 88-89). He uses the phrase *field of eligibles* to acknowledge the well-documented fact that marital choice tends to occur within segments of the population which are more or less homogeneous with regard to such demographic variables as age (Glick and Landan, 1950; Bossard, 1951; Hollingshead, 1950; Thomas, 1951; Kennedy, 1952), socioeconomic status (Marvin, 1918-1919; Hunt, 1940; Nimkoff, 1943; Centers, 1949; Hollingshead, 1950), education (Landis and Day, 1945), previous marital status (Glick,

1949; Bowerman, 1953), and residential propinquity (Bossard, 1932; Davie and Reeves, 1939; Kennedy, 1943; Ellsworth, 1948; Clarke, 1952; Marches and Turbeville, 1953).

Within the field of eligibles an individual in our society, as well as in many others, is expected to choose his mate more or less strictly on the basis of reciprocal attraction and mutual love.

Winch's proposition of most central importance here is his assertion that the need strengths and structures of persons attracted to each other are *different and complementary rather than similar* (1958, p. 96).

Purposing "to obtain the smallest number of (hopefully crucial) variables which would cover the domain under study: the emotional and motivational elements involved in that special case of interpersonal attraction and dyad formation—mate selection" (1958, p. 89), Winch and his associates selected twelve needs and two general traits from the list proposed by Murray (1938). They added a third trait to this assortment, called *Vicariousness*. The chosen variables are displayed here with their definitions in Table I. Each one of them was assumed to have in the array one or more complements to itself, or more conventionally expressed, each of the thirteen variables or needs was presumed to be complementary to one or more of the others. In illustration of the meaning of complementarity Winch says, "As one speculates on the kind of person a highly hostile individual might be attracted to, one phrases the answer, 'one who enjoys receiving expression of hostility.' Such a person is one whose hostility—or at least a part of whose hostility—turns inward (masochistically) on himself. To denote this kind of need Murray offers the term *abasement*. Thus it seemed advisable to try to get some measure of each person's level of hostility and abasement, and furthermore we should reason that a highly hostile individual would seek to mate with a highly abasing person. Here we have an example of the sort of thing we mean by complementariness" (1958, pp. 89-91). He then goes on to present a rather startling theory of the need for affiliation: ". . . We may regard a need to be gregarious (our need approach and Murray's affiliation) as related to feelings of hostility in the sense that a person may seek the company of others to prove to himself that in the eyes of others he is not as hostile as he feels himself to be" (1958, p. 91). Even more arch-Freudian is his view of the achievement motive: ". . .

TABLE I

THE TWELVE NEEDS AND THREE GENERAL TRAITS
USED IN WINCH'S STUDY

Variable	*Definition*
	Needs
Abasement	To accept or invite blame, criticism or punishment. To blame or harm the self.
Achievement	To work diligently to create something and/or to emulate others.
Approach	To draw near and enjoy interaction with another person or persons.
Autonomy	To get rid of the constraint of other persons. To avoid or escape from domination. To be unattached and independent.
Deference	To admire and praise a person.
Dominance	To influence and control the behavior of others.
Hostility	To fight, injure, or kill others.
Nurturance	To give sympathy and aid to a weak, helpless, ill, or dejected person or animal.
Recognition	To excite the admiration and approval of others.
Status Aspiration	To desire a socioeconomic status considerably higher than one has. (A special case of achievement.)
Status Striving	To work diligently to alter one's socioeconomic status. (A special case of achievement.)
Succorance	To be helped by a sympathetic person. To be nursed, loved, protected, indulged.
	General Traits
Anxiety	Fear, conscious or unconscious, of harm or misfortune arising from the hostility of others and/or social reaction to one's own behavior.
Emotionality	The show of affect in behavior.
Vicariousness	The gratification of a need derived from the perception that another person is deriving gratification.

Adapted from Winch, R. F. Mate Selection, New York, Harper & Bros. 1958.

one may regard an achievement drive as a derivative (sublimation?) of a sexual or hostile need" (1958, p. 19). Status aspiration and status striving are described as "obvious middle-class applications of the achievement need." The latter statement, certainly, is plausible.

In a similar vein various possible complementary pairs such as achievement and vicariousness, succorance and nurturance, and dominance and deference are discussed; but, curiously, the sex drive is excluded from the purview of the study, on the grounds of its difficulty of conceptualization as a unidimensional need. One is left to wonder, if it had been included, just what other need might have been posited as complementary to it. Also, since the central hypothesis of the study was that the strengths of the needs of persons attracted to each other would be different rather than similar, one wonders whether Winch actually (supposing that the sex need could have been measured) would expect two persons of opposite sex, one high in sex drive and one low in sex drive, to be attracted to each other. This would seem to be a most bizarre and implausible, but yet, on the basis of the theory, necessary finding. As Winch conceived it, a negative correlation between the two spouses on the same need was evidence of complementarity of one sort, whereas a positive correlation between the two on any two different needs would be indicative of another variety of complementarity. Thus, as he saw it, his theory would be validated if one spouse, for example of the first type, were high on the need for dominance whereas the other was low on this need. This he said would be indicated by a negative correlation. For the second case of complementarity one spouse would be high on dominance whereas the other would be high on its assumed complement, deference. The correlation in this case, of course, would be positive between the two needs.

One reason given by him for the assumption that persons whose need strengths and structure being different are attracted to each other is that each member of a dyad finds interaction mutually or reciprocally rewarding because his needs are expressed in behavior that is rewarding to himself as well as the other. For example a dominant person behaves in a dominant way toward another person who has a strong need to be deferent. Both achieve gratification in such a case. Another reason, the theory underlying which he develops at some length, is vicarious gratification achieved through witnessing another being gratified. This is closely bound up with a process he describes in the life history of the individual as the adoption and abandonment of a succession of "ego-models." The ideal self, as Havighurst, Robinson and Dorr (1946) have portrayed its development, "commences in childhood as an identification with a parental figure. It moves during middle childhood and early adolescence through a stage of romanticism and glamour, and culminates in late adolescence as a composite of desirable characteristics which may be symbolized by an attractive, visible young adult, or may be simply an imaginary figure" (1946, p. 256). Winch notes that in early childhood there is "a tendency for most children to perceive the parent as omniscient, omnipotent, and perfect in all respects." But disillusionment is practically inevitable sooner or later, "and the child takes up a succession of other ego-models from the world of movies, television and sports, and still later the ego-model may be a business tycoon or a leading jurist, doctor, minister, or teacher" (1958, p. 80). There thus comes to be an incorporation into the ego-ideal and a subsequent abandonment as impractical a multitude of successive ego-models. Yet, Winch says, it seems probable that at least some of the abandoned ego-models "live on as nostalgic wishes which cause a person to respond positively to subsequent representatives" (1958, p. 81). Following Flügel (1945), he speaks of this as a "projection" of the ego-ideal.

Perhaps the point can best be explicated by one of Winch's own examples.

"To tie these ideas together, let us dream up a little boy, Herbert, whose mother demanded 'model' behavior and gave him to understand that neither she nor anyone else would ever have anything to do with him unless he did as she said. Let us imagine that little Herbert was frightened and conformed but realized that occasionally he had impulses to be 'bad.' Let us assume that he was worried about those impulses and subsequently became a very 'good' and 'controlled' boy—a bit of a sissy and not very popular. One of his ego-models—taken up, cherished, and abandoned—would probably be a swash-buckling exemplar of der-ring-do, mobilized at all times to run his sword through anyone who might cross his path. And as Herbert became an adult, we might expect that he would be attracted to expressive people, to people who talk back and don't take nonsense from others. This is something we might feel sure that he would wish he could do —just feel some aggression well up in his veins. We might expect him to draw vicarious gratification from seeing other people 'blow their tops.' We might even expect that he would marry a girl who would blow her top regularly' (1958, p. 87).

It is by such means as this that Winch appears to suppose that what he identifies as complementariness among some needs or pairs of needs obtains. Although he does not say so, it would seem that he has sought to fuse the Freudian idea of characterological perfection or self completion with that of complementarity of needs.

"We may," he says, "summarize our two types of complementariness as follows:

Type I: The same need is gratified in both A and B but at very different levels of intensity. A negative interspousal correlation is hypothesized.

Type II: Different needs are gratified in A and B. The interspousal correlation may be hypothesized either to be positive or negative, contingent upon the pair of needs involved" (1958, pp. 94-95).

Winch continues, being more specific in revealing the logic of his theoretical processes, as follows:

> There remains the task of trying to indicate the procedure by which specific hypotheses were developed to the effect that certain pairs of needs were complementary. For example, we hypothesized that persons high on the achievement need would mate with persons high on the deferent need. Can such a hypothesis be deduced from the theoretical exposition to this point? More generally and more formally the question may be asked: If A is a $+X$ (high on any specified need), does the theory—or any other set of considerations—lead us to the conclusion that because of this fact A will be attracted to and will be found attractive by a B with a $+Y$ or a $-Y$ (where Y is either the same as or different from X)?
>
> From our definition of complementariness we can see that there are at least two pairs of needs which are complementary by definition: hostility with abasement and nurturance with succorance. (There is still the empirical question as to whether or not these pairs of needs are complementary in fact, i.e., whether or not our theory and definitions correspond to 'reality'). With the addition of Freudian, Freudian-derived, and commonsense ideas some other pairs seemed very plausible: e.g., dominance-deference, recognition-abasement, and achievement-vicariousness. But these pairs are not deducible in any rigorous way from the theory here presented. Rather the intellectual operation involved was to ask ourselves the following questions: (1) In what sort of behavior would a $+X$ (say, highly nurturant) person

engage? and then (2) To a person with what sort of needs would +X behavior be gratifying?

In this fashion my associates and I came forth with numerous specific hypotheses as to how our variables (needs and general traits) should pair up. As foreshadowed in the remarks on Type I complementariness, we hypothesized for everyone of our fifteen variables that a person high with respect to that variable would select a mate who was low on that variable (1958, pp. 95-96).

Winch has been quoted at some length here because in explicating his deductive processes with regard to complementarity it is clear that he is implicitly defining complementarity to refer to any and all sorts of reciprocally gratifying exchanges of behaviors instigated in the interacting persons by any needs whatever. As will be noted in subsequent discussions, this robs the concept of complementary needs of any distinctive meaning as a mechanism of instrumental need gratification, leading to misunderstanding and confusion.

The sample of subjects employed in the Winch study consisted of 25 married couples drawn from the undergraduate population of Northwestern University. At least one spouse in each couple was a student. All had been married less than two years, were childless, middle class, non-Jewish, white and native born. They were paid a "token" fee for participating: $7.50 per couple.

Three types of data were secured in the study. Winch specifically rejected any "paper and pencil" tests of needs to tap the kind of data he sought (1958, p. 108) in favor of a case-history interview, an eight card Thematic Apperception Test, and what he calls a "need interview." This latter was something like an intensive interview or depth interview procedure, for which a list of open-ended questions was formulated and systematically used. "For example, to tap the intensity and mode of expression of aggression, the subject was asked how he felt when someone stepped in front of him in a queue in a crowded restaurant; and on the variable recognition, how he felt when he saw his name in print. The subject was encouraged to give a full reply and to describe instances. If the subject had not met with the situation, the interviewer would recast the question in the light of the subject's experiences. Forty-five such questions were compiled to cover our variables in a two to three hour session. . ." (1958, p. 108-109).

A content analysis of the need interview data was performed in-

dependently by two members of his staff, who decided, after studying each subject's response to each question, to which variable or
variables it related and assigned a rating to it on the basis of a five-
point scale. Inter-rater reliability was indicated by a correlation of
.75. There was no basis upon which to estimate the reliability of the
subject's responses. Variables were, further, dichotomized or double
dichotomized in terms of whether the need was expressed within
and/or without the marital relationship and whether it was expressed
overtly and/or covertly. This resulted in 388 separate predictions,
which were tested in various ways.

Using Murray's (1938) own method of measuring the needs, the
Thematic Apperception Test (TAT), the correlations of the ratings
derived from it were, more often than chance, contrary to Winch's
hypotheses. Moreover barely half of the correlations based on case-
history data were in the predicted direction. Only when Winch and
his associates made what he refers to as a " 'global' or 'molar' or 'clinical' or 'projective' or 'holistic' " analysis (1958, p. 110) were a significant number of correlations in the direction required. Of 44 Type
I correlations, 35 were found to be in the predicted direction (approximately 80 percent) and of these, eight were significantly so (approximately 18 percent). Of the 344 Type II correlations predicted
to be positive in direction, 221 or approximately 64 percent were so
found, with 71 of these significant at the .05 level. This is again about
18 percent (Winch, 1955, 1958). In the other direction, against the
theory, 12 of the 123 negative correlations were significant (about
10 percent). Winch concluded that he had substantially validated
the theory of complementariness of needs in mate selection.

Other behavioral scientists have not agreed. Attempts to independently sustain the complementarity theory have met with uniform failure. Bowerman and Day (1956), for example, examined the
need complementarity hypothesis with a sample of 60 college student couples, 37 of whom were engaged, the other 23 "going steady."
Bowerman and Day employed as a measure of needs, the Edwards
Personal Preference Schedule, which was designed to measure fifteen
of the needs described by Murray in 1938 (Edwards, 1959). Ten of
the variables included in the schedule are practically identical in definition and meaning to the ones used by Winch, which he also adapted
from Murray. The 15 EPPS need variables and their abbreviations are

as follows: abasement; n aba, achievement; n ach, affiliation; n aff, aggression; n agg, autonomy; n aut, change; n chg, deference; n def, dominance; n dom, endurance; n end, exhibition; n exh, intraception; n int, nurturance; n nur, order; n ord, sex; n sex, and succorance; n suc.

In their study, testing for Type I complementarity, only two of the correlations on the same need were negative, and neither of these significantly so. On the other hand, four of their positive correlations on same needs were significant at the .05 level, showing a tendency toward homogamy rather than complementarity in their data. In testing for Type II complementarity, they were able to compare correlations on 16 of the 24 pairs of needs employed in the Winch research. Since each member of the couple was scored on both needs of the pair, this provided 32 correlations which could be compared with those in the other study. Since the number of correlations which was found in the hypothesized direction was less than would be expected by chance, Bowerman and Day concluded that their results were not in accord with the general theory of complementary needs. Moreover, little evidence for homogamy of needs could be found by them. It is their opinion that "It is very unlikely that any theory of mate selection which is stated in terms of a uniform direction of relationship between needs in general will be substantiated" (1956, p. 605).

Winch, in commenting upon the Bowerman and Day study, faulted it as a replication because of its use of a non-married sample, whereas his own work had been based on married couples (Winch, 1958, p. 108). Although this would seem to be a rather weak point, inasmuch as he has presented the complementarity theory as a general theory of dyad formation, it would also seem to have been adequately countered by a study conducted by Schellenberg and Bee (1960). In this, both married and premarried samples of subjects were employed to test the hypothesis, and the data for these two groups were separately analyzed. A total of 64 recently married couples, with a median length of marriage of less than two years and 36 premarried couples, 18 engaged and 18 "going steady" were included. Like Winch's, these were also student couples, most between 20 and 25 years of age, all caucasian in race, 85 percent Protestant in religion and most (75 percent) were of urban middle class background. The sample, except for the fact that it was a University of Kansas, rather than a Northwestern University one, seems highly similar to that employed in the Winch research.

Schellenberg and Bee computed for each couple a "convergence score," "which measures the extent to which the characteristics (in this case, patterns of manifest needs) of the two members of a couple are similar" (1960, p. 228). In contrast to what was predicted by the theory of complementary needs, the results obtained by them tended slightly in the direction of *homogamy*. In all, 69 of the 100 couples showed *positive* correlations of need patterns, including 73 percent of the married sample and 61 percent of the premarried sample. The average of need convergence scores for married couples was 112.4, for premarried, 106.9 (a convergence score above 100 is interpreted as indicative of homogamy rather than dissimilarity of need. A score of 200 represents a perfect positive correlation). The results for married couples differed significantly (.001 level) from chance, although the results for the premarried sample did not. When all 100 couples were considered together, the average convergence score for the aggregate was 110.4, which was statistically significant at the .001 level in the direction opposite to that predicted on the basis of the complementarity theory.

Schellenberg and Bee, following Winch's own emphasis as to which need combinations showed the highest degrees of complementariess, computed correlations between males and females of each of the respective samples on dominance, nurturance, male dom and female aba, male aba and female dom, m dom and f def, m def and f dom, m nur and f suc, and m suc and f nur. The results of this procedure were that ten of the 16 correlations were in the direction to be expected in terms of the theory, although none were statistically significant. Winch had complained that the Bowerman and Day study introduced sets of need variables his study had not included, hence could not be considered to have been a proper test of his hypothesis. Yet, when in the Schellenberg and Bee study attention was focussed upon only his most focal need variables the results again failed to confirm him.

Day (1961) in a study, wherein she compared the need patterns of courtship couples and the same sex friends of partners, discovered no systematic pattern of either similarity or complementarity in such pairings.

Murstein (1961) studied the need patterns and certain other variables in samples of both newlywed and nonnewlywed couples. Besides the Edwards Personal Preference Schedule (EPPS) he had his subjects respond to the Bass Famous Saying Test (Bass, 1958) and a marriage adjustment scale devised by Wallace (Locke and Wallace, 1959), thus securing scores on a total of 20 need or trait variables. In addition to the 15 EPPS needs, there were thus scores of marital adjustment, conventionality of morals, hostility, fear of failure and social acquiescence.

His samples consisted in part of student couples (20 out of a total of 68), with the remainder being recruited through religious associations. The newlywed couples were defined as those married less than two years who had no children. They were thus comparable to those used in Winch's study. The nonnewlywed couples had been married for an average period of 11 years and five months. Sixteen of the 20 correlations were positive in direction for the newlywed couples and 18 of the 20 for the nonnewlyweds. Murstein also computed correlations on all the variables for randomly constituted couples of both samples. His statistical comparisons for significance of differences in correlations between the veridical couples and randomly constituted ones revealed only two significant values in the correlations for the newlywed couples, one of them in accord with the complementarity hypothesis. For the nonnewlywed sample, five of the 20 sets of correlations were found to differ significantly; one favoring the complementarity theory, four opposing it. He sums up his findings by saying, "The data, while far from conclusive, favor a homogamous theory of need pattern choice for nonnewlyweds. The evidence for newlyweds is entirely inconclusive in the sense that neither the homogamous nor heterogamous theory is supported" (Murstein, 1961, pp. 196-197).

In a more elaborate sampling than any of the foregoing, Banta and Hetherington (1963) undertook to investigate complementarity and similarity of needs in both mate and friendship selection. The EPPS was administered by them to 29 clusters of six subjects each. A cluster consisted of an engaged couple and a male and female friend of each fiancé. Some evidence for similarity of needs in both mate selection and friendship choice was found, but none consistent enough to support the complementarity hypothesis. More specifically, engaged couples were alike—positively correlated—on 14 of the 15 EPPS needs, and 8 of these correlations were significant at the .05 level. Females, in friendship pairings with those of their own sex, tended to have friends whose need patterns were similar to their own, but males tended to have friends of their own sex whose needs were distinctly less similar. The male fiancé was found to have a female friend who was in many respects like the woman he was presently engaged to marry, but this was not true of the female fiancé. Her male friend was quite dissimilar to her future spouse in need structure. In addition to examining similarity-dissimilarity between pairs of subjects with regard to the *same* need, similarity-dissimilarity with regard to different needs was analyzed, but the cross-need correlations did not occur in any meaningful or systematic pattern that would support the hypothesis of complementarity of needs.

Becker (1964) examined the relationship between authoritarianism of personality and the needs for dominance and deference in relation to mate selection, hypothesizing complementarity for the personality trait and these needs. In general, very little support for the hypothesis was found.

Apparently the only data from mate selection research supportive of Winch and his associates' original findings comes from a study by Kerckhoff and Davis (1962) wherein the sample, measuring instruments and method of data analysis all differed from those in the pioneer investigation. Courting and steady dating couples were given the Farber Index of Consensus test as well as Schutz's FIRO-B Scales in abbreviated form (Schutz, 1958). Complementarity was equated with Schutz's concept of compatibility and measured by means of his formula for computing reciprocal compatibility indices on the FIRO need variables. The evidence was indicative of need compatibility being promotive of progress toward marriage only for couples who had gone together for more than 18 months, and similarity of values was found to be significantly related to progress toward a permanent union for couples who had been dating for less than 18 months.

Kerckhoff and Davis interpret their findings as indicative of a series of "filtering factors" operating in mate selection at different stages of the selection process. They suggest that demographic factors operate in the early stages, consensus on values somewhat later, and need complementarity (reciprocal compatibility) still later. This seems quite plausible, even if not compellingly indicated by their data.

Unfortunately, even the limited support of Kerckhoff and Davis study gives the Winchian formulations by translating his ideas of complementarity into Schutz's concept of reciprocal compatibility is of dubious value. A more recent study by Levinger, Senn, and Jorgensen (1970), which sought in two different but parallel efforts to replicate the Kerckhoff and Davis findings, failed to do so.

In their study, samples of "steadily attached" couples from two different state universities reported on their courting relationships in both the fall and the spring of the school year. Analyses of the response data from the 330 participating couples showed that, contrary to Kerckhoff and Davis' findings, progress toward permanence was not significantly predictable from their initial value consensus or "need complementarity" as Levinger, Senn and Jorgensen measured these variables. "Nor," finally, "did the length of the couples' relationship have the mediating effect suggested by the Kerckhoff and Davis theory of filtering factors" (1970, p. 436).

Practically coincident with the publication of the just reviewed study Centers and Granville (1971) also reported an investigation involving married couples and ones in various stages of courtship that is relevant to the Kerckhoff-Davis hypotheses. The findings of this research are also inconsistent with those of Kerckhoff and Davis.

The dearth of confirmatory data for either the complementarity or similarity hypotheses is discouraging, yet a modicum of support for each alternative is apparent, with this being somewhat the greater for similarity. Various reasons have been suggested for the discrepancies in the findings of the various studies, common ones being the differences in the nature of the samples and the differences in measures of the needs. Winch's original data was derived from a quasi-clinical procedure, whereas in all subsequent studies except the Kerckhoff and Davis one and ones attempting replication of it or related to it (Centers and Granville) the same needs have been measured by the EPPS. Samples have varied over a spectrum from couples going steady to those who have been married for several years. Winch has argued that none of the studies adequately replicates his own (Winch, 1958). Critics of Winch have argued that his method was highly subjective and his sample of dubious appropriateness. The answer to the riddle of the replicative failures, despite the search for it along the foregoing lines, has remained as elusive as of now as it was at the beginning of its quest. It is the view of this writer that it is not the studies themselves, the methods, nor the sampling that accounts for the inconsistency, but simply the inadequacy of the theory of complementarity of needs itself.

CHAPTER THREE

SOME ELEMENTS OF INSTRUMENTAL THEORY: A THEORY OF LOVE, A THEORY OF INITIAL ATTRACTION AND A THEORY OF SEXUAL ATTRACTION

THE NEED FOR A THEORY

As was seen in the preceding chapter, the complementarity theory of need relatedness in mate selection has consistently failed of validation, with the exception of the support given it in the Kerckhoff and Davis study noted above, and there the concept of complementarity was in effect redefined as *reciprocal compatibility*. This latter is a similar concept, it is true, but more research is required to demonstrate its equivalence to complementarity as conceived by Winch. Even the Kerckhoff and Davis support, however, seems of very questionable value, inasmuch as two separate studies attempting replication failed in this purpose.

If we abandon the complementarity principle, however, with what else may we supplant it if we are to have a principle that will account for the mutual choices of mates in terms of need relations? Should we now turn to a similarity principle? It appears to have little to recommend itself to us, for its efficiency as a dependable phenomenon is only a little less unimpressive than the complementarity factor. Yet, what else is there? It is the only clear alternative that has been seriously proposed and for which at least some supportive data can be found. Yet, do the findings themselves clearly indicate that a search for a more adequate theory must be sought between the alternatives traditionally presented, that is, between similarity on the one hand, and difference on the other? Does one have to choose between sayings like "birds of a feather flock together" and "opposites attract?" Actually a third one, equally hoary with wisdom and age is *"you scratch my*

back and I'll scratch yours." It is also more in keeping with the ideas
of the instrumental theory as they will be proposed here than either
the difference or similarity notions, which may well turn out to
both be true so far as they go. But neither of them can be properly
assessed as to their contribution until they are more adequately understood than they are at present. Both difference and similarity of
needs may be artifactual rather than causal in significance when examined more closely.

What, for instance, is similarity? At present it is simply an occasional empirical finding in search of a theory as to the *modus operandi* for its possibly resulting in mutual need gratification and the
attendant attraction phenomenon. No plausible reasons have been advanced that the writer is aware of that would explain the findings
with respect to similarity of needs in intersexual attraction, and similarity *in itself* explains nothing. It is a result, not a cause. One knows
no more in knowing it than he knows when he observes that two
objects are both the same color. To explain the fact that they are of
the same color requires identification of an underlying cause productive of this result. The phenomenon of similarity of needs in intersexual attraction has as yet gone unexplained.

ATTITUDES, BELIEFS AND NEEDS

Newcomb and Byrne, as has been noted, have each of them, proposed mechanisms which account for attitude similarities in people
who are friends. But attitudes are not needs and their principles are
not readily transferable for finding of either complementarity or
similarity of needs. Newcomb, has attempted, to relegate complementarity to a role making it merely a special case of similarity. He
has argued that although an assertive male and a receptive female
may be attracted to each other because of the complementarity of
their needs, this attraction may be seen as due to the similarity of their
shared attitude that one partner should be assertive and the other
receptive (1956). Such attitudes may commonly exist in our society,
but the argument borders so closely on circular reasoning that it is
felt that few would take it seriously. The theory of the author, moreover, is that attitudes and beliefs are in large part created out of needs
and exist to serve them. If a pair of persons, one receptive the other
assertive, find each other instrumental in the gratification of their
respective needs, their attitudes and beliefs concerning the fitting-

ness and rightness of such a relationship would undergo changes in the direction consonant to their experience, if they were not so to begin with.

It will be recalled that the found similarity in beliefs, values, and attitudes between attracted persons has been itself explained by both Newcomb and Byrne in terms of the gratification of a need, that of consensual validation for the correctness and worth of one's beliefs. It would almost certainly seem that this mechanism, to be effective in producing this result, would require that both partners possess the need for consensual validation in some considerable strength. That is, *that they be similar in it*. This would be indicated by a positive correlation of their scores on an appropriate measure of this need. Although, so far as is known at this writing no such measure has been developed. It is the writer's hypothesis that the above relationship would be found were the appropriate instrument available. Further, instead of attempting to account for either similarity or difference in need strengths between attracted persons as some sort of attitudinal phenomenon or effect, a more plausible explanation is one which reverses the direction of causality. That is, *similarities of attitudes, beliefs and values are most sensibly explained as due to people finding others who agree with them attractive because they both have similar strengths of need for consensual validation*. Moreover, it would follow that the lesser the magnitudes or strengths of this need in friends or lovers the less the similarity would be found to be in respect to beliefs and attitudes.

LIMITATIONS OF THE CONSENSUAL VALIDATION THEORY

Consensual validation is only one need of many that function in interpersonal attraction and repulsion, and important though it may be to many people, especially same sex friends, no one surely seriously entertains the idea that it is either an adequate and sufficient explanation for attraction between either same sex friends or lovers. Actually, before its true importance can be assessed, it is required that it be included as a motivational variable in company with other measures of needs of an interpersonal nature which may be compared with its determinative significance. At present its role in intersexual attraction, while remaining to be discovered in this sense, is not believed by the writer to be a truly important one. This will be explained in a later context.

GUIDELINES FOR DEVELOPING A THEORY OF INTERSEXUAL ATTRACTION

What appeared to the writer as required for solution of the problems of how needs function in relation to each other in intersexual attraction and love was a more penetrating and careful analysis of the underlying dynamics of need relatedness than any heretofore attempted. For this it was seen that a useful starting point would be the data already extant in studies of need relations which have used the need concepts of Murray and the EPPS as the instrument for measuring them. Analyses of the type envisioned are almost non-existent in these studies. The authors of them have characteristically contented themselves with a brief presentation of their data, indicating the extent to which it supported either the complementarity or the similarity principle, with little or no attempt to *explain* what was found. Banta and Hetherington (1963), for example, present fairly convincing and consistent evidence for similarity in the needs of fiancés; finding 14 of the 15 EPPS needs positively correlated, with eight of these significant at the .05 level and a ninth correlation only barely missing that level. Yet they make no attempt to explain why the similarity should be manifest. Apparently, like other researchers, the only important question to them was that as to whether needs would be found to be similar or different.

Whether there is similarity or difference in the need strengths of fiancés, although an interesting question is not one seen as having much explanatory significance. More important questions in such a sense are the following: (1) which interpersonal needs are of greatest determinative significance in intersexual attraction? (2) How can we account for the fact that samples of partners in a love relationship are revealed to be similar in certain needs, but different in others? (3) What are the general and specific gratifying and punifying* properties of the behaviors which arise from each of these needs. (4) How do these latter effect attraction or repulsion and to what de-

---

*This term is used in instrumental theory to mean exactly the opposite of gratify and may be used as verb (to punify), noun (punification), adverb (punifyingly), or, in short, in any form in which its opposite appears. Heretofore our language has had no word that fulfills the need for an exact opposite of gratification, etc., thus requiring use of inexact approximations such as frustration, costs, and others, all of which makes for cumbersomeness of expression and other difficulties which by use of this new term may be avoided.

gree? It was seen that the answers to each of these last two questions were in each case part of the answers to the other two as well.

In attempting to ascertain the underlying and causal basis for whatever systematic relationships of a correlational nature might be found to exist among the measured needs of fiancés in the investigation in prospect, it was necessary to realize several important limiting circumstances. First of all, one is dealing with a dependent variable, a response of loving, getting engaged to, making a marital choice of someone, which has already occurred. An analyst is thus disadvantaged as compared with the circumstances of a laboratory investigation. There he has artificially restricted or narrowed down the number of the known or presumed causal determinants, or independent variables, to only one or two which he deliberately manipulates to ascertain the affect on the response. This he also typically restricts by his instructions or by the tasks he sets, or by other means of one sort or another. In correlational studies, since perhaps a host of independent variables are involved in producing the effect, some or many of which may be unknown or unsuspected, his assignation of causal significance to his correlational findings is far more risky than in the laboratory situation and his interpretations are distinctly more vulnerable to alternative explanations. Until such time as love and engagement are producible under laboratory or observed conditions, however, correlational studies of the variables suspected to be significant in a causal sense are the analyst's only resource.

An analyst is further handicapped by the fact that it is not merely the response of a single individual for which an explanation is required, but two responses, of two people, of different sexes, with all of the complications that hinge on sex differences being present to further complicate an already complex state of affairs. One is, further, despite his being fully aware that many motives might have determined the reciprocal responses of the two people, limited circumstantially to employing only a sample of the possible ones. This, no matter how reasonably and wisely chosen, may have omitted particular ones of considerable determinative weight. He is going to attempt to put the puzzle picture together, on the gamble that no critically important pieces are missing. Also, there is the realization that the responses he is attempting to account for have arisen out of circumstances wherein each mate selector has made his choice, not in simple, strict and complete dictate of the concatenation of the needs he has, but also in terms of the bargaining power of the behavioral and other resources he possesses. These, in many cases at least, are not adequate to exchange for what his needs require. That means, obviously, that even if the would be theorist has all the "need pieces" for solving his picture puzzle, the resource pieces, *equally determinative of the reciprocal choices* (*bargain*) are being ignored. He is then confronted with the fact that the bargain struck (the mutual choice) between the two is one that has occurred in a love and mate market governed, like an economic or goods market is, by conditions of supply and demand. Not all, or perhaps only a few, of the opposite sex is able to supply the gratifications a given person, with the *deserts stance** taken by him. He takes what he can get as does the one who is the other party to the transaction.

Nevertheless, it was believed, even given these constraints, that within the sampling of needs in purview, a theoretical understanding of love and mating responses could be constructed. And the patterning of intercorrelations that could be found between the measured strengths of the two sets of 15 needs of a sample of fiancés could be predicted from it.

It was seen that in order to answer the four significant questions posed earlier in this section what would be required was to ask systematically, and to seek to answer with regard to each need, a set of questions constituted as follows:

1. To what degree does need X function in interpersonal interchange? Some needs, it must be recognized, do not motivate behaviors that are likely to engage persons in interchange. Order and Endurance, for example, have little or no engaging properties as compared to the behaviors instigated by Sex and Affiliation needs, which pervade the interchange process.

2. (a) What sorts of behaviors are likely to be motivated in M (the male) by need X?
    (b) What sorts of behaviors are likely to be motivated in F (the female) by need X?
    The importance of this pair of questions lies in the high prob-

---

*This term is a convenient one by which to refer to the individual's own estimate of his worth in the sex-love-mate market as well as to his feelings as to what he deserves in terms of the gratification values of potential partners.

ability that the behaviors instigated are by no means identical in the respective sexes. Nurturant behavior exhibited by a male will probably be somewhat different in its qualities from Nurturant behavior exhibited by a female. This is the phenomenon of *sexual style*.

3. (a) What kinds of stimulus value for F has behavior motivated in M by need X?

   (b) What kinds of stimulus value for M has behavior motivated in F by need X?

   Expressed somewhat differently, the question becomes: What meaning, significance or instigative value do the behaviors motivated by need X have for the other person? That is, what kinds of experience and/or behavior are likely to be evoked in M (or F) by F's (or M's) enactment of type X responses (responses motivated by need X)?

4. Are F's (or M's) behaviors thus elicited of such a character as to gratify a need or needs that M (or F) has at the same time that such behaviors are gratifying to the need X in M (or F)?

   The effects may be quite different in the respective cases. If M, instigated by a dominance need, emits dominant behavior toward F, and she has a deference need in some strength it may be activated, and deferential behavior toward M may be manifested. Both are gratified. Result. attraction. Suppose, on the other hand, it is F who is motivated by a dominance need and engages in dominating responses toward M. Even if he has a deference need of a strength identical with the F in the preceding example, this may quite possibly be differentiated in terms of gender, and mostly limited in its direction and expression toward other males. F's dominating behavior may anger and repell him. Neither is gratified, both are punified. Result repulsion.

5. What is the goal sought, or the gratifying condition, or state of affairs required for gratification of need X?

6. If these aforementioned differ with gender, then in what qualities?

7. If there are multiple goals or gratifications for need X, what do these consist of?

8. Does the behavior motivated in M by need X directly gratify

any obviously corresponding and measured need in F (or vice-versa), or is the gratification provided by M's behavior more likely to be for some other need in F that is not within the purview of present observation? This question became very quickly to be seen as an important one as analysis of need relationship along the lines of these questions proceeded. The 15 needs measured by the EPPS are only a sample of all the needs people may have, and many needs not included in the system may be operating to influence the correlations obtained. All the needs measured there, moreover, are needs for *emitting* various kinds of behavior. None of them (except Succorance) are needs for *receiving or consuming* the behavioral products of others. In the ideal matrix of needs, for this kind of research, each need included would have separate measures for both production and consumption, somewhat after the model of FIRO-B (Schutz, 1958).

9. In an interaction between M and F, apart from the direct gratification of the reciprocally instigating needs, what are some indirectly resulting or mediated gratifications which could result for one or both persons in the process?

10. What needs, if the above occurred, would be thus gratified?

11. What are the possible effects on M or F of either of them witnessing behaviors generated by given needs in the other in the other's interactions with third parties?

12. What are the effects on M or F of either of them witnessing behaviors generated by given needs in the other in the other's interactions with physical objects or animals or with regard to the execution of tasks and projects of one sort or another?

From these lucubrations gradually coalesced a theory to account for intersexual attraction and love, consisting of six major interrelated parts. These were: a theory of love, a theory of initial attraction, a theory of what is sometimes called physical attraction, or sexual attraction, and three interrelated theories concerning the significance of and manner of functioning of interpersonal needs, with particular attention in this being directed to the 15 measured by the EPPS. These latter were:

1. A theory of the relative significance of *particular needs* as de-

terminants of attraction and the particular patternings of the forces of attraction that would be created in the relationships among those identified as having major attractiveness power.

2. A theory of the nature of need mechanics, or the coinstrumentalities, by means of which the behaviors instigated by either the *same* need in both male and female or by a *different* one in the respective cases could result in either reciprocal gratification or punification in an interaction episode or in an enduring relationship between them.

3. A theory of the intermotivational dynamics in intersexual attraction and repulsion.

These latter, when understood and identified could be used in combination with the understanding of intermotivational mechanics. They could be employed to explain or account for both the direction and magnitude of relationships that should obtain between particular pairs of needs of a male and female in order to result in attraction between them.

Of the six major parts of the theory described above, three, although data for testing their various implications could not be acquired and included in this volume, will be presented in a somewhat informal way in order to give a certain completeness to the whole. This the writer believes will be of value, both for the purpose of revealing certain of his basic assumptions and possibly for its heuristic utility as well. The three untested theories are formulations concerning the nature of love, the theory of initial attraction, and the theory of sexual attraction.

Before describing these, however, certain basic assumptions must be made explicit, and certain conceptual difficulties of an obstructing character removed.

THE PSYCHOLOGICAL FUNCTIONS OF NEEDS

First, is the assumption as to the functions of needs. Living organisms keep living mainly, it is thought, because their precarious balance with respect to their environment requires for its maintenance a continuous interaction with it by the organism by virtue of the metabolic and other processes required for the continuance of its life itself. The requirements of food, oxygen, liquid, etc., the requirements of rest and sleep, and the built-in stimuli-producing mechanisms regulated by hormonal secretions of the endocrine glands all constitute drive-creating conditions. These, oriented toward the appropriate goals of food, water, etc., insure if effectively consummated, the survival of the organism and its "happiness," as well. Happiness is eating when you are hungry, drinking when you are thirsty, having sex when you are sexy. Unhappiness is not being able to do these things. Living, for many organisms, it appears, has little more to offer than this routine of biological tension arousal and tension reduction.

Man is infinitely more complex than even his nearest of kin. His long period of biological and social dependence upon others and the fact that he lives in a world contrived by others to embody a social order and cultural system creates for him a special condition. For him to survive happily, necessitates that he acquire and gratify a great many sociogenic and psychogenic motives. These, often referred to as secondary motivations, because their motivating properties seem to originate in the circumstances and conditions attendant upon the early routines of consummation of the "primary" or biogenic drives are, unlike the latter, highly variable. They differ with such circumstances or socialization practices and such subculture-creating conditions as racial or ethnic membership, religious affiliation of parents, and socio-economic status. Centers (1948, 1949a, 1949b) has shown that the different social strata and social classes have quite distinctive motivational patterns or life goals.

Drives, motives, needs, desires—the terms are interchangeable as they are used here—have many properties. Not all of them are interpersonal, in the sense that they require for their gratification the occurrence of more or less specific qualities of or kinds of behavior from others, but many are. All needs have goals of some sort, and the goals of interpersonal needs have the peculiar property just mentioned: the response of another. For one need a word of praise, for another a show of fear or embarrassment, for another a hug or kiss or genital coupling, for another a show of concern or sympathy or kindness, for another some word of advice—the examples are endless in supply.

A first proposition of the instrumental theory of interpersonal relations is *the postulate of interpersonal dependency for interpersonal need gratifications*: individuals are dependent upon each other for specific gratifications of certain motives, which for that reason are referred to as interpersonal needs.

A second proposition is *the postulate of gratification and punification as the functional antecedents (or causes) of attraction and repul-*

sion (effects). Because the behaviors devolving upon the interpersonal needs of one person directly or indirectly gratify or punify the needs of those persons (or gratify or punify the *persons*) with whom he interacts, feelings of attraction and liking or repulsion and disliking are produced toward or with reference to him as object.

A THEORY OF LOVE

We go about the business of living with a large part of our time devoted to the conscious and unconscious seeking and enjoying of interactions with people who will regularly produce the behaviors needed by us for the gratification of our needs. Those who reinforce us will, other things being equal, seem attractive to us and may become our friends. If the sexual need is involved, those who reinforce us in relation to that need may become our lovers. *Love on the part of one individual for another is the response or responses evoked in the first individual through his experiencing of rewards, pleasures, or need gratifications as products of his interactions with the other. If the gratifications experienced are sexual in nature, or, more specifically, if there is gratification of the sex need, then it is sexual love.*

Love has many forms and varieties: for example, parental, filial, fraternal, and platonic. Any attempt at differentiating among these varieties is futile without the kind of love object (whether child, same sex adult, etc.) being specified and the kind of need gratification involved being noted as well. The theory, in conceiving of love as a response process, is intended to apply to *any form of love* between humans, between organisms of any species, or between members of different species, for that matter. Further, the response is recurrent and hence love typically endures as a recurrent reaction to the other as a stimulus object. But the duration is variable. It may be very short or very long, contingent as it is upon the experiencing of gratification of a recurring and continuing nature from the other. It is facilitated in its enduringness when it is reciprocated. This requires that the other also be gratified in interactions with the first person. Both persons in order to continue receiving gratification from each other are typically motivated out of their expectations of more gratifications being forthcoming to continue to engage in behaviors that are gratifying to the needs of each other. So long as a reciprocally gratifying exchange of such behaviors obtains, love responses will continue to be made by each of them to the other as love object (in fact, stimulus object). When or if there is a diminution in the quality or quantity of the gratifiers exchanged then love responses will also undergo an attenuation, and with a cessation of the exchange of gratifiers there will also occur a cessation in love responses. However, these may continue to be made by a person *as memory responses* for an indefinite time where the cessation was occasioned by circumstancial separation, exile, or death.

Love is in this formulation not an all or none reaction. Love responses may be so lacking in intensity as to be subliminal, but they may, at the other extreme, be excruciating in strength. How strong or how weak the love responses become depends upon: (1) the strengths of the need or needs being gratified, (2) the magnitudes of the gratifications received, and (3) the frequency or frequencies with which the latter are delivered by the supplier (love object). All of these, in turn, are contingent upon many, many other variables both intrapersonal and interpersonal and situational as well. An attempt at a detailing of these must wait upon another time.

Primitively, love responses are essentially *affective in quality*. However, these affective reactions to the object stimulus are from their very incipience strongly conditioned to the accompanying perceptual reactions to the stimulus object. The result is that the affective and cognitive products and residues from the original and accompanying perceptual responses become partially fused and interdependent as a compound response process. Love responses are, thus, consequently characteristically experienced in awareness in this partially, but not entirely, fused form. In humans, who are highly reflective, and eternally seeking meaning and understanding, there are great possibilities for cognitive and affective response ramification in relation to the love object, with an important part of these latter consisting of evaluative reactions. These are usually, if love endures beyond the moment by virtue of reencounters and interactions, consonant with the already and originally aroused affective and cognitive components, but not entirely so. To the very person toward whom the love responses are felt and behaviorally expressed (perhaps only felt) there may be mingled some dislike, even a little hate, engendered by other, and nongratifying, effects of the interactive experience. The qualities of all these component and consequent reactions not only strongly determine the eventual *intensity* of love responses toward the object, but because of their complexity, often leave the individual a little bewildered or mystified as to the nature of his response. Love is commonly a mystery to him.

Affect enveloped in a cloak of cognition, as love responses come to be, have typically, occurring as they do in youth, when sexual and emotional motivations are of great intensity and commonly associated with intrapsychic conflict resolution, an extremely confusing character in many instances. With both attractive and repelling forces co-existing with respect to the stimulus person, as they often do, there is likely to be a behavioral vacillation between approach and avoidance in many instances. The evaluation and re-evaluation of the love object often observed in the verbalizations of persons in love is one result of this process. While a stable and positive evaluation of the loved one is eventually produced by it where love responses endure, this evaluation may typically contain a good many negative components within the, on the whole, positive product. Moreover, as research previously published by the writer has shown (Centers, 1971), the evaluation which eventually obtains will be one demonstrably congruent with the motivational dynamics of the evaluator.

Intersexual love is the response resulting from gratifications derived from interactions with a specific person of the opposite sex, with at least part of these gratifications being sexual in nature.

One could, and probably should, to please most or many people, qualify this further by indicating that the love object in each case be a socially acceptable one, which would, of course, exclude parents, siblings and close relatives as well as persons of one's own sex. There is no intention to do this. Such love is not excluded. It occurs, but it is of only peripheral concern in this volume, which focusses attention on the socially acceptable, normal, heterosexual variety of love relationships.

The theory, it will be noted, conceiving of love as a response and specifying sexual love as contingent upon the gratification of sexual motivation, is, when not deliberately and further applied to only persons of the opposite sex as objects, equally applicable, in its basic sense, to *intrasexual love* or homosexual love. In this work, however, this variant of sexual love is quite outside the compass of our survey.

It is intersexual love that is presumed existent as a mutual response on the part of two persons who are engaged to be married, and thus the essential subject of this study. However, the existence of the condition is and can be no more than an inference on our part from observed and presumed congruent behavior. Since only the existence of intimate association and mutual commitments made to be married to each other are observable and verifiable, it might be more appropriate to use the phrase *intersexual engagement*, as one denoting simply these observables. However, the inference that becoming engaged on the part of two people is equivalent to their being mutually attracted is such a little step that the phrase *intersexual attraction* seems quite acceptable as an alternative. It is a more conservative and literal phrase than *intersexual love* and because of that will often be used in place of the latter. But it should be explicitly acknowledged that in doing so the writer intends to imply that whatever is offered here as an explanation of intersexual attraction is also to be regarded as his explanation of intersexual *love*. Being engaged is an objective criterion commonly used to infer, at the minimum, mutual attraction, but more often love itself, and, indeed, love at maximum strength.

CONCEPTUAL CLARIFICATIONS

It is perhaps a minor point, but at this juncture not entirely inappropriate, to quarrel somewhat with the nomenclature and word usages that have developed with reference to the psychological variables being discussed here. The terms attraction, liking, and love have been undiscriminated in customary psychological usage and made, in effect, synonymous. Such imprecision commonly results in confusion, which is certainly not at all desirable in the context of science, if anywhere at all.

The terms *liking* and *loving* would be best reserved to refer to the responses resulting from the *experienced* gratifyingness of persons (or objects). Attraction, in distinction, should refer to the *perceived, subceived or imagined* gratifyingness of persons (or objects). In ordinary discourse concerning acquaintances, we use the term *attraction* to describe our feeling when we may scarcely know a person, but have experienced a desire for further contact and interaction with him. We may recognize this to be due to the perceived and implied potential gratifyingness inherent in his looks, dress, behavioral style, charm, apparent congeniality or what not. But often we will not explicitly do so, being fully aware only of our feeling and typically it is enough for us to say simply that we feel attracted to him or her or that he or she is attractive. Although our listener may now and then disagree because he feels differently, the communication of feeling is so sufficiently complete as to require no additional explanation. The listener is by no means likely to understand by it that we are *in love*. He will not confuse these or regard one as synonymous with the other. Liking or loving may or may not develop from such initial feelings, depending upon whether the outcomes of interactions with the person are gratifying or punifying to us. Attraction, followed by liking, then in turn, loving is the usual order of development of our feelings in intersexual relationships, and, of course, each of these has degrees of magnitude which we are accustomed to defining for both ourselves and others.

A THEORY OF INITIAL ATTRACTION

The data to be examined in the present work is primarily concerned with the functioning of needs in intersexual attraction and the theoretical development centers essentially on that problem. However, it is useful to establish a set of ideas that may at the outset be as inclusive as possible for understanding the range of phenomena encompassed within the area of interpersonal attraction, but especially of intersexual attraction. Hence some discussion of the phenomenon of *initial attraction* to one of the opposite sex is desirable.

Initial attraction to one of the opposite sex, including sexual attraction, physical attraction or, for that matter, simply attraction without involvement of sex impulses, is a resultant of the perceived, subceived, imagined or unconsciously anticipated gratifyingness of interaction with the other. Sexual attraction, in particular, mystifies and perplexes people principally because the processes of their psychological functioning are not well known to them. They typically do not know their own needs and motives for what they are. They are less mystified by their feelings of attraction when they do know their needs and can see that the object of their desire is that because he or she is perceived or imagined, conscious processes, both of them, as having the abilities, attributes or kinds of behavior that they need for their gratification. When they are less aware or totally unaware of their needs, as they often are, love, attraction, fascination—call it what you will—is the great mystery, the enigma, the unfathomable, the hidden, yes, even the arcane. It need not be a love that "cannot speak its name" for it may be based upon impulses which would be wholly acceptable to the individual if he could but identify them, give them labels. But, at least occasionally, the darkness of it all is born of the fact that the kind of gratification subceived by or redintegrated in him or her is shameful and sinful and totally disowned and hence hidden like a Medusa's head from the awareness, lest it destroy one's very conception of himself. Then is it a mystery, a puzzle, an arcane thing; perhaps often an anxiety arousing experience, even a terrifying one. Repression, a mechanism of emotional inhibition of thought, has blocked it from consciousness, and it may never come to be formulated in consciousness for what it is because it cannot be.

Freud's teachings, of course, are principally the source of such insights as the ones just mentioned, but Pavlov is perhaps equally to be cherished for his gifts. When the writer was very young and very new at the job of teaching and found his tales of Pavlov and his drooling dogs leaving his students unmoved and unprofited, he, in his desperate attempts to make the material more proceleusmatic to his charges, used to tell them: "If you want people to like you—and you do I'm sure—just become a conditioned stimulus." The very weirdness of the idea so intrigued them that in one rare moment of receptiveness he was able to make it all meaningful and worthwhile by going on to point out that all they had to do was be the stimulus associated with gratifying experiences for their potential friend. This they could do, it was explained, by saying and doing the things that would be rewarding or reinforcing to the target of their actions. He, the experiencer of the gratification would, it was pointed out, by a simple conditioning mechanism, that of association, come to like *the producer of it* too. This would be so because every time the producer occurred as a stimulus, some of or all of those previously experienced gratifications would be reexperienced, redintegrated, as simple conditioned responses. In other words, the gratification, perhaps no more than a feeling of pleasure, originally evoked by the *unconditioned stimulus* of some appreciative or flattering words uttered by one, could because one was contiguous in the stimulus field at the time it occurred, be automatically linked to one as a *conditioned stimulus*. This, it was pointed out, was similar to the instance in which the bell became linked as a conditioned stimulus to the drooling response of the dog, which was originally evoked only by the food or acid (i.e. unconditioned stimulus). Some students were delighted, but some appalled. Man often likes his mysteries. Take them away from him and he will protest much like the baby deprived of its candy. People often hate psychologists for it.

The cues in a face, a body, a gesture, the sound of a voice may, any of them, be conditioned ones born of some or many past pleasures experienced with persons who had equivalent or similar stimulus values. Now an occurrence of one or some combination of such cues or stimulus qualities automatically "turns us on," redintegrates fragments and scraps of the old responses. It all may occur without awareness on our part of what those cues are and with our total ignorance of a process like conditioning. The object can thus fascinate us, so that we linger, and maybe interact. If some of the hidden prophecy is fulfilled by rewards reexperienced, and new ones are added, we can easily be "in love."

A THEORY OF SEXUAL ATTRACTION

Sexual attraction need not be a mystery to all of us, and surely cannot be if we have some ability to note what is happening in us when we look at and cannot readily tear our eyes away from a lovely girl. Cannot one feel the kiss forming on his lips in anticipation, the caress tingling in incipience in his fingers, the pressure toward contact with that body vaguely forming, the beginnings of tumescence in his genitals? What we experience as sexual attraction, which has both conscious and unconscious components, is, it is believed, primarily a product of the exteroceptive, interoceptive and proprioceptive feedback from visceral, glandular and striate muscular responses aroused by responses of the sort just mentioned.* These commonly combine as a total response to the object person with more or less clearly conscious perceptual appraisals and appreciations of various attributes of his or her face and body, as well as with some fantasied consummatory actions involving him or her. The amount of the attraction feelings consciously experienced which are contributed by these latter, and more clearly conscious responses, is likely to be highly variable

---

*Poets and other laymen (nonpsychologists) have often spoken of the "chemistry" in intersexual attraction. Perhaps this is not a mere figure of speech, for Barclay (1971) reports that a specific chemical, urinary acid phosphatase, a prostatic enzyme, is a specific indicator of sexual arousal; that is, that it increases only under conditions of sexual arousal, and not under other arousal conditions. It is at least conceivable that this "chemical reaction" is also a feedback influence, and thus contributes to the total of such.

from individual to individual, depending largely upon the degree of his or her acceptance of his or her sexuality, in a moral sense. In some highly defensive people the conscious components of the attraction response may be quite minimal.

This formulation, let it be emphasized, conforms in all essential respects to the theory that we are attracted to those who are instrumental in the gratification of our needs. For in such instances we are already experiencing some gratification of our sexual need, even though merely vicariously, or through fantasy. It is, it is insisted, pleasurable for us to have such sensations and impulses and in our imagination to consummate their aim. Though the poignancy of our longing may never be reduced by actual fulfillment, such responses are actually pleasurable and gratifying in themselves, for the punification of their being thwarted in their goal of realistic enactment is outweighed by the play and replay of their desired enactment in our imagination.

Sexual (or physical) attraction has extraordinary power; so much, indeed, that it can continue to motivate desire for association and contact with its object in the face of what may be quite punifying indifference or rejection by the object. It is one of the extraordinary facts of life, long celebrated in our poetry and drama, that one enchanted by the charms of another will go to extraordinary lengths of behavior in his or her (more often his) attempts to have his love requited. Perhaps the persistence has its basis in the phenomenon of aperiodic or occasional reinforcement, as might be exemplified in the joke we have all heard. That is, the story about the young man being admired for his success with women, and having been asked for his secret of it, replied that whenever he encountered a girl with whom he wanted to have sex he simply said

"I sure would like to have sex with you."

"But," his audience asked, "don't they just slap your face?"

"Oh yes, I get my face slapped most of the time," he said, "but I also get a lot of sex partners!"

More to the point, is that sexual attractiveness, where it exists on the part of one person for another, is a special and exceptional instance of another's being a very powerful stimulus indeed; one reacted to as a resource or source of gratification for one of our most powerful needs, and a need limited by the supply of potential gratifiers. Not every person of the opposite sex has that same stimulus value for any given individual. To be sure, our cultural-social conditioning, building upon a probable biological bias to begin with, has stereotyped with massive emphasis the kind of face and physique in the other sex that people of a given sex find they respond to with desire and lust. Yet relatively few approximate the ideal constantly depicted in our film, television, magazines and other mass media, and hence have universal appeal. Even so, and fortunately for the most of us, each person, having a somewhat different need structure, also retains some idiosyncratic tastes in the matter. Since this is so, it commonly happens that relatively few people of a given sex have an extremely powerful stimulus value for arousing lust and longing for any particular one of us. That is, for each of us the supply is limited. Thus, when the person who does embody the requisite combination of cues is apprehended by us, even granting the unlikelihood of successful consummation of our motivation, it is aroused to such strength that only very adverse conditions, indeed, can counter the forces of attraction which have been generated. Although few might argue against such an intuitively plausible point, it becomes even more convincing when it is remembered what was stated earlier. *The attractive other has already begun to be a source of gratification for our need by means of our automatic conscious and unconscious hedonic appreciation of the sensory feedback from redintegrated somatic responses and our fantasied consummations.* He or she would have less power to attract us if the supply of persons of equal attractiveness value for us were greater or our demand less strong. The first condition might be met if physical, or, more specifically, sexual beauty were quite abundant, and the second if one were surfeited sexually, undersexed to begin with, or debilitated by malnutrition, fatigue, illness or the infirmity of age.

Although not guided by the sort of formulations embodied in the foregoing discussion, but rather by more strictly Freudian formulations concerning orality and the dependency need associated with it, Scodel (1957) presents evidence that at least renders a theory of sexual attraction based on need concepts a plausible hypothesis. Using, as stimulus materials, photographs of nude females, he found in a study of body features considered desirable by adult males a significant relationship between certain psychological characteristics of his subjects and their preferences as to size in female breasts. More specifically he sought to ascertain possible relationships between preference for either large breasted or small breasted females and the magnitude of the dependency needs of his male subjects. There was, he found, a quite significant difference between subjects in terms of the need variable as measured by the Thematic Apperception Test and the breast size preferred. Males found to prefer small breasts in females gave significantly more dependency themes in their TAT responses than males who indicated either a preference for large breasts or were lacking in any apparent breast bias. This result, which, it is noted by Scodel, is "contrary to a widely held Freudian hypothesis" (1957, p. 374), he interprets in terms of a reinforcement rather than a frustration theory of drive strength. In terms of this theory, large breast preference would be regarded as a consequence of continued satisfaction of dependency needs in earlier experience rather than their frustration at that time. Preference for small breasts, thus he implied, is a consequence of frustrated dependency needs.

In a more comprehensive study of heterosexual somatic preferences, Wiggins, Wiggins and Conger (1968) used silhouettes of nude female figures and requested their 95 male undergraduate subjects to make paired comparison ratings of these. Stimuli were varied systematically with regard to sizes of breasts, buttocks and legs. Personality variables of the subjects, including measures of their needs by the EPPS, were also obtained, and correlations were computed to ascertain what if any relationships obtained between these variables and their body parts preferences. The silhouette figures were constructed in such a manner that the dimensions of breasts, buttocks and legs varied independently from basic, standard, or ideal ones arbitrarily decided upon. Each of the body part dimensions could assume the value of the ideal (0) or could be moderately large ($+1$), large ($+2$), moderately small (-1) or small (-2).

Of most relevance here are their findings with regard to preferences in relation to needs. As might be expected, the average male highly preferred the ideal female figure, and preference for this body type was significantly correlated with only the sex drive as measured by the Edwards scale. Preference for moderately large breasts ($+1$), but not larger ones ($+2$) nor smaller than ideally dimensioned ones, was also positively and significantly correlated with n sex. The sex drive was not significantly related to any other preference, although certain other needs were. For example, n order was correlated positively with a preference for very large (+2) buttocks, while n endurance was positively associated with a liking for very small (—2) buttocks. Autonomy, a masculinity-linked need, was positively correlated with a liking for very large (+2) breasts, while n nurturance, a femininity-linked need, was significantly negatively correlated with +2 breast preference. Nurturance, further, was positively related to a strong degree (.38) with preference for the small (—1) breasted female. The authors make no attempt to interpret this latter finding, but to this writer it seems to be what would have been expected, on the basis of his own understanding of the nurturance need as it would function in a male with reference to females. The most appropriate object for the male's nurturance motivation would, of course, be a child, and who among women are more childlike in appearance than small breasted ones? For a nurturant male such a female represents the closest approximation to the child. At the same time, the large breasted female, which the nurturant male rejects (there is a negative correlation of .25), is the quintessence of the female representing the least appropriate object for a nurturance need; namely, a *mother figure*, or at least a *fully mature female*.

This interpretation, although it seems plausible in accounting for the Wiggins et al finding, does not, unfortunately, quite square with Scodel's finding that men preferring small breasted women gave significantly more "dependent" responses to TAT cards. Although Wiggins et al included the succorance items in their administration of the Edwards' Personal Preference Schedule, they did not find n suc to be significantly correlated with small breast preference. To be consistent with Scodel's finding there should have been a significant *r* it would seem. Since the two studies do not agree as to the reality of the phenomenon, the writer's hypothesis concerning the motivational dynamics underlying small breast preference requires additional research to be either supported or disconfirmed.

Those males who preferred the large breasted figure were, it would seem, unlike those who preferred small breasts, cathecting a *fully mature female figure*, unless one wishes to interpret preference for such a figure in Oedipal terms; to the effect that such males are seeking mother substitutes. This seems dubious of justification, however, and this preference is more simply and plausibly explainable in terms less psychopathological, for these big mammary men are strongly sex driven specimens and highly masculine in terms of needs related to liking for big breasts. They tend to be high in the masculine-type needs of autonomy (independence) and exhibition, to be nonnurturant, to have masculine interests and to read sports magazines. Asked to list those magazines they read regularly, large numbers of those preferring the very large (+2) breasts mentioned *Playboy*. A big breasted beauty for such males as these is no mother figure it seems clear, but rather, just a very female *female*. The most distinctive secondary sexual characteristic of the female figure is her breasts, and on the semantic differential rating scale these males rated breasts as both *strong and good*. To them, apparently, since the breast in general is good, then a lot of breast is better. Men are very logical creatures.

SOME RESEARCH ON PHYSICAL ATTRACTIVENESS

Sexual allure or sex appeal is not to be considered as wholly synonymous with what is referred to as *physical attractiveness*. The latter is a more general and inclusive term, containing the former, but incorporating as well, much that can be viewed as object cathexis based on ego enhancement needs or status needs rather than object cathexis arising from the more purely libidinal motivation of the sex drive *per se*.

Walster, Aronson, Abrahams and Rottman (1966) offer what appears to be a pioneer study of the importance of physical attractiveness in dating behavior. They did not, unfortunately, propose any relationship between this variable and the needs of their subjects, nor obtain any data with regard to needs, but instead, sought to test two hypotheses derived from level of aspiration concepts and a third one based upon other ideas. The first two (in effect) were:

1. individuals who are themselves very attractive physically will require that a romantic partner (date) possess more physical attractiveness than will a less physically attractive individual.

2. If potential partners varying in physical attractiveness encounter each other in a social situation those individuals who are similar in physical attractiveness will most often attempt to date one another.

In their third hypothesis they proposed that an individual would not only choose a date of his own degree of physical attractiveness, but also that after actual experience with potential dates of various degrees of attractiveness, he would express the most liking for a partner of approximately his own degree of attractiveness.

These hypotheses were tested in a field study conducted at the University of Minnesota with 752 freshman males and females who had been recruited by the inducement of a bargain price of one dollar each to attend a "Computer Dance" during preregistration orientation week. Participants filled out questionnaires under their assumption that the information would be processed by a computer so as to match them with a person of the opposite sex on the basis of personal qualities and traits. The questionnaires yielded information regarding the degree of self-acceptance and level of self-esteem of the subject, and the student personal files of the University were used to obtain information on other personality characteristics as well as the individual's high school grades and scholastic aptitude. They were queried as to their ages (nearly all were 18), height, race, religion, and asked to estimate their own popularity and physical attractiveness as well as their own 'personal attractiveness.' Finally, they were asked to state how physically attractive, how personally attractive and how considerate they expected their dates to be. As participants registered for the dance and filled out their questionnaires in what was set up as a quite elaborate processing routine, their physical attractiveness was, without their awareness of it, quickly rated (independently) by four judges who were assistants of the experimenters.

The dance took place two days after this procedure with the participants being paired, not by computer, as they had been told would be the case, but randomly, except that no male was paired with a female taller than himself. Subjects, during an intermission of the dance were required to fill out another short questionnaire which asked how much the individual liked his or her date, how physically attractive the date was, how much the date seemed to like the subject, whether or not the subject would like to date the partner again, etc. How often "couples" actually dated was determined by a follow-up enquiry four to six months later.

The results, as indicated in Table II, reproduced from the experimenters' own report, demonstrate that physical attractiveness is a very significant variable, indeed. It will be recalled that the experimenters had hypothesized that a subject who was himself (or herself) very

Sexual Attraction and Love

TABLE II

VARIOUS MEASURES OF THE SUBJECTS' LIKING FOR THEIR DATES
AND SUBJECTS' DESIRE TO DATE THEIR PARTNERS

(Walster, et al., 1956, p. 513)

	Date's Physical Attractiveness		
	Ugly	Average	Attractive
I. % Ss actually asking date out			
According to ugly male Ss	.16	.21	.40
According to average male Ss	.12	.25	.22
According to attractive male Ss	.00	.26	.29
II. How much S says he liked his date			
According to ugly male Ss	.06[a]	.57	.90
According to average male Ss	−.10	.58	1.56
According to attractive male Ss	−.62	.16	.82
According to ugly female Ss	.03	.71	.96
According to average female Ss	−.10	.61	1.50
According to attractive female Ss	−.13	.21	.89
III. % Ss saying they wanted to date partner again			
According to ugly male Ss	.41	.53	.80
According to average male Ss	.30	.50	.78
According to attractive male Ss	.04	.37	.58
According to ugly female Ss	.53	.56	.92
According to average female Ss	.35	.69	.71
According to attractive female Ss	.27	.27	.68
IV. How many subsequent dates couples had			
Ugly male Ss	.09	1.23	.73
Average male Ss	.30	.94	.17
Attractive male Ss	.00	2.08	.53
V. Amount S thinks date likes him			
Guesses by ugly male Ss	.47[b]	.52	.43
Guesses by average male Ss	.55	.64	.65
Guesses by attractive male Ss	.77	.53	.58
Guesses by ugly female SS	.41	.41	.35
Guesses by average female Ss	.38	.58	.55
Guesses by attractive female Ss	.63	.65	.61
VI. No. of Ss in each cell			
Ugly male Ss	(32)	(43)	(30)
Average male Ss	(43)	(36)	(41)
Atttractive male Ss	(26)	(38)	(38)

[a]The higher the number, the more the subject says he liked his date.
[b]The higher the number, the more the subject thinks his date liked him.

attractive would expect a date desirable to him (or her) to be more
physically attractive than would someone else who was less attractive.
Their data confirm this hypothesis. However, their second hypothesis

was not confirmed. The subject's attractiveness did not significantly interact with the date's attractiveness in determining his attempts to date her, his desire to date her, or his liking for her. Moreover, the analysis of variance revealed that the only important determinant of whether or not the date was asked out again was *how attractive the date was.* Their third hypothesis, that individuals would best like dates similar to themselves in physical attractiveness, also failed to be supported by the data. From Table II, Sections II and III, it can be seen that by far the strongest determinant of how much liking a subject felt for his partner was simply how attractive the partner was. The more attractive the male or female the better he or she was liked and the more desire for further dating there was.

Another significant finding of this research was that none of the other measures—those on self-acceptance and self-esteem, introversion-extroversion, intelligence (or scholastic aptitude), masculinity-femininity, and social skills and manners—proved to have any important relationship to liking or to desire for further dating.

Some Cautionary Comment

One should not jump to the conclusion, however, that such factors are of neglible importance in dyad formation, especially in the formation of more durable dyadic relationships. Nothing like this is demonstrated. The time span involved in the Walster, Aronson, Abrahams and Rottman research is much too short to allow these factors to exert their ultimate influence. Even where the time span is much longer their determinative strength commonly has to counteract the powerful influence of the sexual attractiveness of possible alternative potential partners who may in addition be not especially deficient of these assets in point. Sexual attraction, it should not require to be insisted, because it is so obvious, is the raison d'etre of intersexual dyad formation in the first place, and in the research in question it has artificially been given an unobstructed field in which to reveal its power. Further, these 18 year-old freshman males and females are probably more dominated by sexual motivation at this time than they will be, most of them at least, ever again in all their lives. They are also at this time probably far more motivated to establish their sexual identities and prove to themselves and others their social desirabilities than they are to find life-long partners. There is a definite danger that the impact of the

Walster et al. research may lead us to a distorted and oversimple conception if we are forgetful of certain other considerations. *It is important to recognize that intersexual dyad formation is dominated by different needs and interaction goals at different times.* And, further, that already established and institutionalized relationships such as marriage are subject to various stresses and strains relating to needs and goals. These are those devolving upon changing needs, balances among needs of the respective partners, and the emergence of new or different interaction goals and meta-personal goals as the inevitable events and circumstances of the partners' lives change and they undergo changes themselves.

The power of physical attractiveness in interpersonal attraction is probably a complex function of many variables, one of which is doubtlessly the sexual conditioning which persons in a given culture undergo, beginning at an early age. There may be innate, biological, determinants of what will be responded to as sexually desirable in the opposite sex. However, anthropologists have found such wide variations in what is considered attractive (for example, in one African society the men want their females to be *fat*) that the cultural shaping of preference seems indisputable. At any rate, if the sexual attractiveness of the object is high it alone may be sufficient to instigate the beginning of interaction and the establishment of a relationship. But there are additional gratifications that accrue to one who is able to affiliate with a partner whose physical attributes to a high degree embody the socially and culturally defined desirables. It is by such public association that he or she thus establishes his or her own attractiveness, not only in his or her own eyes, but also in the eyes of the world of other people. That is to say that being the associate of or being the possessor of a beautiful woman or a handsome man enhances one's own value, not only in one's own appraisal but in the evaluations of one's worth by others. The Walster, Aronson, Abrahams and Rottman research suggests that the gratifications on the basis of the physical attractiveness factor may, in fact, at certain times be so salient in intersexual attraction that they may greatly attenuate or even negate the influence of other need gratifications when the forces created by the latter run counter to them. A much longer period of observation, obviously, would be needed to determine the true nature of the relationships in question.

The hypothesis offered here is that, while initial physical attraction is the prime mover in intersexual dyadic relationships, for the formation of those enduring beyond some casual exploratory and exhibitory dating, the one night stand, or, at most, a few tosses in the hay, there must be gratifications of other needs not strictly sexual or status-enhancing in nature. Individuals, unhappily, often must compromise. Discovering that beauty is often only skin deep, they ultimately come to seek, and sometimes find, a relationship, which, while maximizing the gratifications obtainable by them for some or many of their most relevant needs, falls short of their ideal aspiration level in certain others. They must ultimately expect too, since they are competing in the love market with others of their own sex whose attractiveness value may be to varying degrees greater than their own, to accept what they can get for what they themselves have to offer in exchange, or suffer deprivations hardly tolerable for most people. This all should be remembered when, in a later part of this essay, the usually small magnitudes of correlations between partners on various need variables is treated; for, given all the conditions and compromising factors noted here, these could not be expected to be otherwise than they are. One, in fact, in reflecting upon all the difficulties which attend the working out of the reciprocal need gratification process in dyad formation, may come to share with the writer the feeling that finding any systematic patterning of need correlates at all is much more than slight testimony of its power.

A NOTE ON LOVE AT FIRST SIGHT, ETC.

Not easily distinguished from initial attraction is what appears to be merely another name for the same thing, the phenomenon popularly spoken of as "love at first sight." It probably is simply a way of referring to an extremely powerful initial feeling of attraction. Finally, there is the phenomenon referred to as a "crush," often a "secret love," on the part of one person for another, with the love object often being quite unaware of the other's feelings. The classical example is the instance of a young girl in love with a movie idol with whom she has had no personal contact. Here would seem to be a case, though the hypothesis cannot be tested in this study, of a person having fulfilled the instrumental role in being the stimulus for arousing responses in the loving one that are in themselves gratifying to his needs in an autistic vicarious way.

CHAPTER FOUR

THE BASIC THESIS OF THE INSTRUMENTAL THEORY AND A THEORY OF THE ORDER OF PRIMACY OF PARTICULAR NEEDS IN INTERSEXUAL ATTRACTION AND LOVE

THE PROBLEM of accounting for the creation of a condition of mutual love between male and female, is at the same time one of accounting for their choosing each other and committing themselves to each other as mates. All of it is seen to be a phenomenon born of an interpersonal interaction process which we have already, in effect, characterized as one of *reciprocal instrumentality*. The concept is not wholly new, but neither is it so familiar that a few sentences describing it will not be useful, for it is in terms of it that the formulations constituting the entire theoretical framework are cast.

It is proposed that reciprocal loving and conjugal pairing is a function, primarily, of a process of *reciprocally gratifying behavioral interchange*. It is said, "primarily," because it is recognized that an individual's transactions with others, external to the relationship, may be instrumental to the need gratification of the other and, hence, contribute to the individual's attractiveness. Reciprocally gratifying behavioral interchange refers to an interaction wherein both the interacting parties engage in behaviors that are either satisfying in themselves to one or both parties, or are reciprocally gratified by the behavior of the other, or the products of it or the consequences of the behavior, or all of these. This assumes that some behaviors are gratified in the execution of them *per se*. For example, caressing a sex object could be pleasurable to the caressor without the caressee behaving in any way at all—he or she could be utterly passive or even dead. Such instances are not the rule, of course, but rather, the rare exception. The gratification is more often some particular response by the other. For instance, the caressor is rewarded by the expressions of pleasure and appreciation made by the caressee or gets caressed himself in return. The latter responses are themselves gratifying to both persons in the interchange.

The central thesis of the instrumental theory of interpersonal relations as it applies to intersexual dyad formation may be formally stated as follows:

In intersexual dyad formation each person seeks, among his circle of acquaintances, within the compass of his self-acknowledged compeers, to form a relationship with that person or those persons whose behavioral and other resources provide (or are perceived to provide) maximum gratification and minimum punification for his needs.

Perhaps the phrase "self-acknowledged compeers" is needful of some explication. It means, simply, all those included as acceptable associates in an intimate sex-love relationship, but it is variable with the goal of the association as the person himself defines it. He or she may be quite willing or even eager to date, go steady with, carry on an affair with, or even live with, someone he or she would not consider eligible for marriage because of racial or religious or other grounds for exclusion. It is common today on campuses of universities with a liberal climate of attitude and opinion for White and Black to engage in intimate social and sexual intercourse, but few of these liaisons will result in marriage. One or both partners will usually have reservations which effectively exclude the other from equal status, such as to preclude a marital union.

The thesis as stated above is meant to apply, not to marital choice or mate selection alone, but to the formation of any and all intersexual relationships. Hence needs must be expected to vary somewhat in salience with the interaction goal, whether it be merely dating, going steady, living together or marriage. It does not require to be restated in its entirety for each of these kinds of relationships, but only to have inserted in it some words or a phrase to indicate the kind of dyadic relationship under scrutiny in a given case. Thus, "In intersexual dyad formation, such as mate selection or marital choice, each person—."

THEORY OF THE HIERARCHY OF DETERMINING NEEDS

Sex

If intersexual attraction and love and the establishment of intersexual dyads in a love relationship are all to be accounted for as a function of the reciprocal gratifications exchanged between males and females, then for what *needs?* Surely the gratification values of all and sundry of the individual's manifold needs are not equipotential as determinants of intersexual attraction. Some would be far more important than others; having the status, in some cases, at least, of necessary, even if not sufficient, conditions for the phenomenon of intersexual erotic love to exist at all.

Actually, it is believed that only one need, *that for sexual gratification,* meets the requirement of being not only necessary as a condition, but in some cases, even a sufficient one. The ancient idea of intersexual complementarity was, of course, founded on man's experience that the two different sexes of human kind, were obviously expressly "made for each other" as far as sexual gratification was concerned. A person of the opposite sex represented in actuality, for all but a few deviants, the most satisfying beings with whom to interchange such gratifications, and for the vast majority, the only acceptable and appropriate objects. The sex drive is obviously so well established as an extremely powerful motivational force as to require no argument to that effect. But not as fully emphasized as it should be is the fact that the gratification experiencable from this need has a power which, for most people at least in the youth of their lives, so exceeds that resulting from other kinds of motivational reduction that it represents the most excruciatingly rewarding experience one of them can derive in interaction with another. Experiencing directly, or vicariously via fantasy, such gratifications from one of the opposite sex is, by the very theory of the nature of *intersexual love* in instrumental formulations, a necessary condition for its existence; and, hence, in this theory, it is conceived of as the major determinant of such an affect. Also, for some people at least some of the time, it may be *sufficient* to excite that response, that is, to be able to by itself alone, engender some *feeling of love* for the sex partner.

But it is not being argued that this occurs typically or even often.

Love, as it is conceived of in instrumental theory is not an *all-or-none* affective response. It varies in its magnitude or intensity on a continuum from a just barely noticeable thing we may call a positive affectional evaluation of the object, to a response occasionally so intense as to amount to what some people describe as an ecstatic experience. Some people who have written about love, of course, have employed an entirely qualitative concept of it and have tended to describe it as a feeling akin to ecstacy, admitting little of degree. Such a concept is not scientifically very useful, even if true, whatever that may mean. It is being contended here, in keeping with a more quantitative conception, that sometimes, at least, responses of positive affect, or *love responses*, of comparatively great intensity may arise purely from erotic gratification. Love is, however, truly "a many splendored thing," and typically it is intensified in magnitude by the accompaniment of receipt of other gratifications of other motives from the object (i.e. partner).

Unfortunately, while the research to be reported in this volume does tend to support such a position, the data that would be required to settle the issue are not available in it; for, at the time the investigation was carried out, no adequate or valid measure of *degrees of love* had been developed. The samples of subjects employed in the studies reported here consisted of *engaged* individuals, and the state of being engaged was interpreted as an indication that the person *was* in love, and to a degree which is conventionally regarded as a maximum one. At least for people in our society, wherein marriages and commitments to marriage are expected to be practically always founded on love, and to represent the most tangible evidence to its maximum degree in the persons mutually so committing themselves, use of the behavioral criterion seems quite justifiable.

What has been said in the foregoing with regard to the power of sexual gratification in the evocation of love feelings should by no means be interpreted to imply that one is prone to experience such feelings with sufficient intensity with every person of the opposite sex to either want to repeat the encounter, establish an enduring relationship, or to marry him. Recall that the central thesis of the instrumental framework stated earlier in the chapter says ". . . *with that person or those persons whose behavioral and other resources provide, or are perceived to provide, maximum gratification and min-*

imum punification for his needs."

Now, not every female is for a given male one who has the physical and psychological attributes to maximally arouse, nor the erotic abilities to maximally gratify, his sexual needs. She may lack either the one or the other or both. Nor will just any male serve to gratify this motive for a given female. The demand and supply factors being what they are, a given individual of either sex is likely to experience strong feelings of attraction to one of the other whom he perceives, imagines to be or actually experiences as being more gratifying a sexual partner than others might be. It is to this person, other conditions being equal, that love feelings are likely to be experienced and with this person that a love relationship is likely to be established. Thus, in consideration of all of the foregoing, it is the sex need to which is assigned the greatest determinative value in intersexual attraction and love.

The Need for Affectionate Intimacy—Affiliation

One can have sexual gratification alone, but most people enjoy it more in interaction with someone else. So it is with all interpersonal needs. They require association with others to be gratified, all of them. As noted in the preceding chapter most of our needs, except the biologically originating survival needs *are* interpersonal ones. With uncommon exceptions man survives, but only with unhappiness, when alone. Short of physical or psychological torture, solitary confinement has always and everywhere been the most excruciating punishment that could be meted out to those thought deserving of such.

At the very least people want and need to associate with *other people*, with the degree and closeness of association desired varying, it appears, with the strength of need, or needs, established in the early and formative infantile and childhood experiences of the person. The needs underlying associative behaviors are seemingly, too, an interdigitating complex of specifics, such as a need for interpersonal security (Sullivan, 1947, etc.), a need for intimacy, a need for companionship, a need for inclusion (Schutz, 1958) a need for affection and possibly others. Murray (1938) termed this last mentioned one *the need for affiliation*, and, as he defined it, it impelled a person to form a highly intimate, affectionate and synergistic relationship with another person. His conception of it corresponds quite closely with what the writer conceives of as *a need for affectionate intimacy of association*, but the name Murray gave it, *affiliation*, inadequately reflects either his own or the writer's conception. In the word itself, no truly high degree of affectionate intimacy of association is necessarily implied, at least, it is thought, to most people. *Affinity* would seem somewhat more appropriate for capturing this flavor. But since affiliation is so well ensconced, its usage will be conformed to here.

The object of the affiliation drive, need not, of course, be a person of the opposite sex, for male can have affectionate intimacy with male and female with female. However, it is observed that the culture of our society and that of many others incorporates norms of behavior which operate to discourage and restrict in various ways the degree of intimacy, and hence the degree of gratification obtainable for the need, with members of one's own sex. At the same time most societies glorify and maximize the opportunities for achieving such gratification with members of the other sex. Great degrees of intimacy between persons of the same sex, when observed or suspected by others, are quite typically accompanied by suspicions of homosexual urges or homosexual actions on the part of the target persons.* To be so regarded is so punifying to all but a minority of people as to instigate powerful avoidance patterns of behavior in them. But one can go as far as one likes, and maximally gratify his needs, with one of the opposite sex with general approbation and even laudation. The social structure is so arranged that marriage represents a relationship permitting and promoting so great an intimacy and affectional interdependence that it is characterized poetically and religiously as a bonding that makes the parties to the contract "as one."

So impelling is the need for affiliation, and so contrived the circumstances of its maximum gratification, that it is in instrumental theory postulated as the second most important need in the hierarchy of determinants of intersexual attraction and love. It is toward one who promises to, or who is experienced as, gratifying the need

*It is interesting, and also has some relevance to what will be said later, that women, in seeming societal recognition of the existence of somewhat stronger needs for affiliation in them, are permitted considerably greater displays of intimacy and affection with members of their own sex than men are and without nearly as much of the consequential disapprobation and suspicion with regard to homosexual inclinations.

most completely that the strongest degree of attraction should be felt, provided, of course, that such a person is also sufficiently gratifying sexually.

The Need for Maintenance and Enhancement of Sexual Identity and Role

A great importance has been emphasized in depicting the role the cultural order plays in the shaping of our needs and of the conditions of their satisfaction. But to complicate matters still further, man, having contrived a cultural system and social order calculated to insure the survival of himself and his progeny, has built into its structure not only the institution of marriage and devised rules for regulating the expression of the sexual urge, but has also assigned a differing social role for each sex. Simultaneously, he has set up a socialization process designed to construct the personality that individuals of each of the respective sexes require to fill that role as well. This involves the conditioning of those of the respective sexes to strive toward rather distinctive goals in each case and to develop behavioral resources in themselves which will be necessary for reaching them. This is accompanied by the teaching of them in one way or another to cherish their natural and socially created sexual identities and roles; to defend them against depreciation, loss, or excessive compromise. A powerful drive for sexual identity and role maintenance is thus established in all normal individuals. Moreover, ideals are established by society, or arise spontaneously in the social process that are either calculated to, or simply effectively operate to additionally incite the individual to *enhance* that sexual identity and role. Since the roles in respective cases are designed or developed in relation to the other sex in each instance and defined in terms of comparisons with and in relations with and to the other sex, their maintenance and enhancement can in some important respects only be achieved in interrelationship and interaction with that other sex.

The postulate of a sexual identity and sex role maintenance and enhancement drive: Individuals of the respective sexes are strongly motivated in ways congruent with the cultural definitions of their sexual identities and roles as these, together with the needs which are generative of behaviors expressive of them, have been embodied in their personalities. And ceteris paribus, in intersexual dyad formation each will seek a relationship with that person whose own needs in-stigate behaviors most facilitative of and promotive to the gratifica-tion of this motive.

Now, not every female is for a given male an ideal or efficient interaction partner for this maintenance and enhancement of sexual identity and role; nor for a given female will relating to just any male accomplish this aim for her. Each must, to gratify his need, then, find someone of the opposite sex whose own motivational and be-havioral system (whose need and resources structure) is compatible to and promotive of this goal. Hence a powerful drive toward find-ing and attaching to oneself such a partner becomes for most people a very impelling force, and experiencing gratification of the drive with a particular member of the opposite sex creates strong bonds of attraction and love for him or her.

For a female to accomplish sexual identity and role maintenance and enhancement, requires that the man be one having the motiva-tional structure and behavioral system that will allow her to func-tion in her particular variant of the actually highly standardized and idealized female role. This is one in which, with respect to the male, she, the female, is submissive, dependent, affectionate, but in addi-tion very sympathetic, understanding and nurturant, as well as at the same time sexy, and, within safe limits, playfully venturesome. It is a complex package of not entirely harmonious elements, being, in reference to what is expected of the male, markedly *weak and dependent* in important respects but tempered with certain kinds of strength as well. The male required must be one who can evoke and gratify submissiveness and dependency needs and behaviors in her, allow her to feel protected and cherished and provide her with the material requirements necessary for her economic security and well being, as well as bring her the respect, esteem and status she craves. At the same time he must gratify her needs for affection, understand-ing, sympathy and emotional support, as well as be able to respond to and share her playfulness and sexiness. In short he must be, above all, *strong in many ways;* independent, decisive and controlling, at times very aggressive and, of course, achieving. Seemingly too, he will ideally be weak enough in certain not so importantly identity compromising ways to make her feel needed in an emotionally sup-portive and nurturant sort of way. Clearly the male identity and role and that of the female were culturally designed to be complementary to each other in patterning, even as their sex organs are by biological agents.

For members of each sex to have the identities they ideally have and to enact the roles they ideally do, they have each been equipped with patterns of motives that ideally operate to sustain them. The motivations in point have at least a commonality of names in respect to both sexes, but receive different emphasis in the personality make-ups in the respective cases. For example, both have what we can call a need for independence in some degree, but it is typically much more strongly developed in the male. Both have dependency needs too, but in this case they are typically distinctly more strongly developed in the female.

For each to seek and find a partner who maximizes opportunities for sexual identity maintenance and enhancement, means, of course, that such a partner must gratify sufficient of the needs constituent to the identity in sufficient degrees for the grander, or, in a sense, more all-inclusive and derivative higher order need which includes them to be gratified. But, what is more, gratifications of certain particular needs will be of considerably greater importance in the contribution they make to this end than others will, and what these gratifications consist of will differ for each sex in accordance with what has already been noted about the make up of the need systems and behavioral patterns of each. That is, for the male the need or needs that must be importantly gratified for his sex role maintenance and enhancement will be different from those required for this purpose for the female.

The Sexual Indentity Drive and the Postulate of Generic Congruency

As to what these relevant needs might be for the respective sexes, suggestions have already been given in the brief characterizations noted in the foregoing with regard to the behaviors expected of persons of differing sexual identities in respect to their relation to each other. These suggestions concerning the relevant needs in the case of the respective sexes as well as the theory of the sexual identity drive itself were derived partly, but not mainly, from some close study of both the previously published work on intersexual attraction as well as that on need theory and measurement.

In scrutinizing Winch's work on complementarity of needs, attention, it was found, was repeatedly focused upon the dominance-deference and the nurturance-succorance pairs as examples par excellence of the complementarity phenomenon. In reflecting upon these examples the fact that one of these, dominance, is strongly linked to masculinity in our society and in most others, while another, nurturance, is equally strongly associated with femininity became salient. Winch and other students have not, apparently, been as impressed by this as the writer. Winch implicitly ignores it, presenting the essential data with which he supported the complementarity theory without differentiation of his predictions and their outcomes in terms of gender. Yet all of the nine variables involved in his nuclear predictions, as can be seen in Table VI (Chapter 5), are strongly sex linked needs. The behavioral traits devolving on these are, in our culture as well as in most others, the chief distinguishing aspects of the masculine and feminine personalities. Achievement, aggression, autonomy, dominance, and exhibition are all distinctly male needs, while affiliation, deference, nurturance and succorance are, with comparable eminence, female. The point should scarcely require documentation, but it is well borne out in the data presented in the EPPS manual with regard to difference of scores on all of these variables for the different sexes. This is reproduced here in Table III. In either or both the collegiate and general adult samples male-female differences in means for these variables are significant—at the .01 level or higher (Edwards, 1959, p. 10). Smaller local samples will, to be sure, differ occasionally from this pattern in their results, but, it is suggested from existing research data, only to slight and unimportant degrees.

Barbara Day, in commenting upon her own findings pertinently remarks, "These findings on differences between the males and females of courtship couples on the personality variables used in this study are consistent with the different role expectations and cultural training of males and females in the United States. Men are generally expected to be independent, aggressive, and dominant, to place emphasis on achievement and occupational success, and to show the more obvious interest in the opposite sex. Women, on the other hand, are expected to be more deferent and look up to others, more socially inclined (affiliative), more helpful and motherly (nurturant) yet

Sexual Attraction and Love

TABLE III

DIFFERENCES IN MEAN SCORES ON THE EPPS VARIABLES FOR THE
NORMATIVE SAMPLES

(Adopted from Edwards, 1959, p. 10)

| | College Sample | | General Adult Sample | |
| | Means | | Means | |
Variable	Men	Women	Men	Women
Achievement	15.66*	13.08	14.79*	13.58
Deference	11.21	12.40*	14.19	14.72*
Order	10.23	10.24	14.69	15.59*
Exhibition	14.40	14.28	12.75*	11.48
Autonomy	14.34*	12.29	14.02*	12.10
Affiliation	15.00	17.40*	14.51	17.76*
Intraception	16.12	17.32*	14.18	15.28*
Succorance	10.74	12.53*	10.78	12.86*
Dominance	17.44*	14.18	14.50*	10.24
Abasement	12.24	15.11*	14.59	16.89*
Nurturance	14.04	16.42*	15.67	18.48*
Change	15.51	17.20*	13.87	15.99*
Endurance	12.66	12.63	16.97*	16.50
Sex	17.65*	14.34	11.21*	8.12
Aggression	12.79*	10.59	13.06*	10.16
N	760	749	4031	4932

*This mean is significantly larger (at the 1 percent level) than the corresponding
mean for the opposite sex.

needing to be helped and protected by the male, intuitive in understanding oneself and others (intraceptive) and more accepting of
guilt or blame (abasive)" (Day, 1961, p. 436).

There is certainly nothing novel here for any of us, for we are all
either male or female (transexualism being ignored) and all know it.
The patterning of sexual identities and traits is ancient in our culture,
and even if the present trend toward blurring or abolishing the distinctions continue at the rapid pace with which change is occurring,
they will still take a long time to obliterate. An important point is
that the socialization we all undergo orients us each to look for some
qualities in the opposite sex which we ourselves are supposed to lack,
so that an aura almost of the magical attends our interest in and fascination with persons of the other sex. Beyond the physical, for a
male the beauty that the male does not possess and so poignantly longs
to possess in possessing the female *does begin at the skin.* But beyond

it he seeks the warmth, the tenderness, the care, the paradoxically coexisting feminine helplessness and feminine *strength* of nurturance, and the intuitive understanding she is supposed by him to possess within as well. For her, the magic is in his *strength*, which is the very essence of his maleness to her, besides which his beauty pales in importance. Beauty in a female fuses with a quality of weakness, it-self an appealing and protective impulse-arousing vulnerability and irresistible affectionateness, the strength of nurturance and caring, while permeating the whole with a sexiness and implicit promise of mysteries yet to be revealed. Nature, at the same time, makes her physical self an embodiment of it all that transcends in its natural art any other beauty man has known. In more prosaic vein it is her *femaleness* that the male finds so compellingly attractive. *He* is, *ideally*, no less a masterpiece in the eyes of the feminine beholder, for his beauty or, rather, we are accustomed to say, his handsomeness, is ideally the living embodiment of strength, and if his physical attri-butes do not attest it, but have instead the prettiness of weakness in them he is not, *for her*, a MAN.

The complementarity that Winch discovered among his nine nuclear variables was masculinity-femininity. Doubtless, if he found it in both directions it was there because each sex does possess all the nine need-born traits, but in different degree and always subtly trans-formed in a male or female in such a manner as to be congruent with his or her essential and basic maleness or femaleness. Is male nurtur-ance the equivalent of female nurturance? It is not. Nurturance is expressed in such different ways by males and females that here as in other instances it is meaningful to speak of *sexual style*. Males ex-press the behavior that gratifies their nurturant need through a gentle and often directive *dominance*, teaching, showing, gently pointing the way, but with a firmness and assuredness few females are likely to be able to convey. Nurturant need in the female is expressed in a style more suggestive than directive, less dominating than merely *helping*, with more affection attendant on it. It carries, too, an aura of sympathy and tenderness few males are capable of communicat-ing—if, indeed, they have these feelings in quite the same sense as a female does, which latter is doubted.

The same polarity of sex linked traits could, of course, be described as a strong-weak one. This, indeed, is appropriate, except for the value laden characteristics of these terms. In many cultures strength is almost worshipped and weakness despised. No male, however, is likely to despise *female* weakness, for it is part of her charm for him. Strength, while almost universally *admired in the male*, is only sometimes and in some ways admired in the female. It is incongruous with our popular conception of femininity for her to be considered *strong*. When she does have strength she is likely to be damned as too masculine. There is such a strong association between the terms strength and masculinity and weakness and femininity that to mention one brings the other to mind. Assertive-receptive is another alternative; but again a polarity strongly associated with masculinity-femininity, so that, no matter which pair of terms may be used, the same associations are made, and properly so.

In pursuing this line of feeling and thought, the observation that much of complementarity as well as many other phenomena of need mechanics and dynamics, are in intersexual need relations functions of the masculine and feminine identities of the respective members of the attracted pair compelled reflection. Was this ubiquitous and ever prominent factor to be treated simply as a more or less static condition obstructing the nice and orderly operation of forces of attraction or repulsion generated by the hitherto recognized need systems of the partners to the dyadic relation? Or was it not so insistently intrusive because behind it was a force which, although unmeasured on any scale, was in itself a need, with possibly a power in intersexual attraction and repulsion almost as great and all pervading as n sex itself? It was the latter that was concluded and which was embodied in the postulation of a sexual identity and sex role maintenance and enhancement drive that was presented earlier. Because so very much is to be made of it is what follows it is repeated here so that it be close at hand.

"Individuals of the respective sexes are strongly motivated to behave in ways congruent with the cultural definitions of their sexual identities and roles as these, together with the needs which are generative of behaviors expressive of them, have been embodied in their personalities. And, ceteris paribus, in intersexual dyad formation each will seek a relationship with that person whose own needs instigate behaviors most facilitative of and promotive to the gratification of this motive."

This is a highly general proposition, and, to bring its implications to focus more specifically and directly upon the present task, a corollary is deduced. This has more utility in generating predictions of the nature of the specific correlations between the needs of affianced persons which are intended here and which will be presented subsequently.

The postulate of genderic congruency; or of intersexual attraction arising from genderic congruency of needs and resources: In intersexual interaction the behaviors instigated by those most distinctively sex-linked needs will have high attraction value if found in a person of the sex they are associated with most strongly in the social-cultural definition of sex type. They will have low attraction value if found in a person of the sex with which they are popularly regarded as less congruent or incongruent. In more concrete terms, male dominance has high *attractiveness value* for females, but female dominance has *less* attractiveness value for males. Again, *female nurturance* has high attractiveness value for males, but male's nurturance has less attractiveness value for females.

Closer examination of Winch's own findings are entirely in keeping with this principle in many particular respects. For example, he found "significant positive correlations between husbands' need for succorance and wives' need nurturance *but not the reverse*. That is, h nur was not significantly correlated with w suc" (Winch 1954, 19, 241-249).

What the concept of genderic congruency is intended mainly to signify is that males become attractive to females to the extent that they as males possess the behavioral resources typical of males, while females become attractive to males to the extent that they display the behavioral resources typical of females.

It is the impression of the writer that large numbers of people assume that individuals in selecting a spouse or lover look for someone under the implicit assumption that such a one can or should be the principal gratifier of all of their needs. Yet, there appears to be no data that would warrant such a view, and it must be made clear that it is not an assumption of the instrumental theory. Rather, the point of the theoretical development in progress is that certain needs are distinctly more important than others in this process of mate selection. Further, it is assumed that individuals vary in the extent to which they seek and expect to find in a lover the behavioral resources which would gratify their whole array of needs.

A female with high n succorance might thus be expected to look for nurturance *strictly as such* not in a husband or lover, so much as in a mother figure, an actual mother or a female friend. These latter might be expected to possess this resource to a much more salient degree than a male. To be sure, as will be seen later, males have various kinds of relevant strength that can at least serve as partial substitutes for any lack of nurturance per se which they may have, and hence may exercise a certain degree of attractiveness to females with strong succorance needs because of that. Males high in n deference, to take another example, may well be attracted to particular females not because such females have the resources of dominant behavior which a strong deference need requires for its gratification, and which they could more easily and readily find in another male, but rather, on the basis of some other behavioral resource such as deference itself, affiliation or nurturance which females possess. These latter, it will be explained more fully in a later context, are each of them, themselves in some ways gratifying to the deference need.

Types of Genderic Congruencies and Incongruencies

It is useful to utilize the concept of genderic congruency as a way of characterizing and describing correlational directionality in reference to particular juxtapositions of needs of the respective sexes. To indicate just what is meant by this it is necessary to describe the several types of genderic congruency and incongruency that may be found. Table IV has been prepared to chart this territory. As can be seen, there are three varieties, all of which occur in the data having to do with correlations of pairs or disparate needs and in that with respect to same needs as well.

1. *Bidirectional congruency*, where the correlation is between a gendericly congruent need for the male and a gendericly congruent need for the female (e.g., m dom-f def),

2. *Unidirectional incongruency*, where a gendericly congruent need for either male or female is correlated with a gendericly incongruent need for either male or female (e.g., m suc-f nur).

3. *Bidirectional incongruency*, wherein a gendericly incongruent need for one sex is correlated with another need which is incongruent for the other sex (e.g., m def-f dom).

TABLE IV

TYPES OF GENDERIC CONGRUENCES AND INCONGRUENCES
USING CERTAIN GENDERICLY ASSOCIATED NEEDS
AS EXAMPLES

Bi-directional Congruency	Unidirectional Congruency (or Unidirectional Incongruency)	Bi-directional Incongruency
Male Dom-Female Def	Male Suc-Female Nur	Male Def-Female Dom
Male Agg-Female Aba	Male Dom-Female Agg	Male Suc-Female Agg
Male Exh-Female Suc	Male Dom-Female Dom	Male Aba-Female Aut
Male Aut-Female Aff	Male Nur-Female Nur	Male Aff-Female Exh
etc.	etc.	etc.

To complicate the situation, both congruency and incongruency, it should be recognized, are matters of degree; judgments about which, in the absence of data strictly to the point, are more or less fallible. Since the degree to which any given need is conceived to be congruent for a particular sex is defined by the magnitude of the needs' association or linkage to members of that sex, some means of establishing such degree values is, of course, needed.

It is meaningful and possibly helpful to look for criterial values in the magnitudes of the mean scores for various needs with respect to which the two sexes are found to differ significantly. These are presented in Table III. As can be seen from the nationwide collegiate sample mean scores, if one uses the magnitude of the mean as the index of relative degree of congruency, for the males it is sex, dominance, achievement, autonomy, aggression and exhibition in that rank order. Exhibition is included in the list despite its not being significant, because it does reach a difference value of statistical significance in the general adult sample and is popularly supposed (at least as it is defined in the Edwards test) to be more characteristic of males than females. In terms of the magnitude of mean criterion for females the most congruent need is affiliation, followed in rank by intraception, change, nurturance, abasement, succorance and deference.

Another and somewhat more sophisticated index of degree of congruency, and hence the preferred one, is the rank order of size of differences between sexes in mean scores for these variables. Employing this with Edwards' data, the ranking is sex, dominance, achievement, aggression, autonomy, and exhibition, with the only difference in this and the first ordering being a one rank transportation for aut and agg.

But when this same kind of comparison is made for the female sample, the only one of the seven sex linked items occupying the same position in both rankings is deference; last in both. The others, in order, are abasement, affiliation, nurturance, succorance, change and intraception.

Although no empirical index or objective measure of it is at present available, thus having more of the status of a postulate than of a fact, there is still another dimension to the genderic congruency factor that must be mentioned. This dimension resides in the relative magnitudes of the *threat property* which the behaviors devolving upon the various motivations which have just been considered possess. The male-linked needs such as aggression, dominance, achievement, exhibition and autonomy are all self-assertive drives, highly invested with threat property, and, hence, in interpersonal interaction, with members of either sex they are likely to produce punification and conflict. This markedly reduces the attractiveness value of behaviors activated by these drives when males encounter them in females, and to a distinctly greater degree than will the gendericly congruent female behaviors be reduced in attractiveness value when encountered by females in males. Affiliation, nurturance, abasement, succorance, deference and intraception not only have no *threat value,* punify no one and produce no conflict by the behaviors they activate; but, rather, other things being equal, beget affection and kindness. This important qualitative difference in gendericly congruent behaviors has consequences which will be repeatedly seen in what follows. A major one which can be noted as an hypothesis now is that *correlations between love partners' scores on measures of these sex linked needs will show marked differences in magnitude; being low for the male linked needs with high threat property and relatively higher for the female linked needs.*

A Test for the Sexual Identity Drive

Accepting the criterion employed in identifying them as the best available indicator of the needs measured by the EPPS which are most highly involved with sexual identities in our culture, then it is in gratifications of these specifically noted ones in particular that gratification of the drive for sexual identity and sex role maintenance itself would be found. If this is true, then it follows that individuals who are strongly driven by the needs characteristic of their given sex group are most likely to be most attracted to those of the other sex who are likewise strongly driven by the needs characteristic of their sex group. This implies that in a sample of love partners (engaged couples) the correlations between their need scores on the respective sets of most closely sex-linked needs would, other things being equal, be higher than the correlations between them on need scores less closely linked to sexual identities. Should this be demonstrated to be true it is believed that it would constitute strong evidence for the existence of the postulated sexual identity and sex role maintenance drive.

Two hypotheses with reference to the consequences of the foregoing reasoning may now be set forth. These are cast in terms of the expectation that the most suitable measure to be used in a future investigation to test these propositions would be a modified version of the EPPS. This, with its large sampling of needs, is seemingly the most adequate instrument involving interpersonal needs available, although far from exhaustive of the universe of such.

With the exception of the higher magnitudes of the correlations on the sexual and affectional (Murray's n affiliation) needs between males and females, the following should be found.

1. The *need strengths of partners in a love relationship should be higher between individual pairings of members of these needs linked most strongly in the respective sexes to sexual identity than the correlations between those less closely associated with sexual identity.* These pairings would involve, it should be understood, not *same* needs, such as male autonomy-female autonomy or male succorance-female succorance, but rather conjugations of different needs, linked, each of them respectively to identity of male or female, such as: male achievement-female deference, male exhibition-female intraception, etc.

2. Moreover, for all to be as it logically should be in terms of this reasoning, *the most importantly sex linked need of the male, dominance, should be more highly correlated with the most importantly sex linked need of the female, affiliation, than either of these variables is with any other different need.*

Those who recall the quite recent discussion of the normative data presented by Edwards (1958) regarding mean scores of college students on the various need measures comprising the EPPS may well take issue with the writer in his assigning first places to dominance and affiliation respectively, for in terms of that data, these places are actually occupied by n sex and n abasement. The writer has what he believes are excellent reasons for disregarding the placements as determined by Edwards' data, but this is, regrettably, an awkward circumstance for disputation and advancement of those reasons. Hence it can only be stated immediately that the assumptions that dominance *is* the most importantly male-linked need and that affiliation *is* the most importantly sex-linked need in the female are believed to be clearly indicated on both theoretical and empirical grounds. However, an adequate rationale for them devolves upon such technical considerations that it is better prorogated to a later context. Therein it is expected that the reader will have had the necessary familiarity with sufficient data and discussion re the position taken to find it justified in terms of the rationale. It will be explicated in Chapter 7.

Later, other specific hypotheses are to be developed from the theoretical position so far disclosed, but not until it will have been augmented and elaborated by a number of additional postulates in the effort to specify the nature of the *mechanics and dynamics of need relatedness in intersexual attraction.* These two problems are separate from, but closely bound up to and intricately involved with that as to which needs are of greatest determinative significance in the establishment of love relationships. These postulates will be presented in the discussions comprising later chapters. Before going on to them, however, there is more to be proposed as to the relative determinative values of certain, as yet unnamed, other needs. These are ones which, like the sexual identity drive, are not measured by the EPPS, nor, it seems with any other scale in actual use as yet. Although measures of variables of a nature somewhat similar to them exist, considerable additional research and development appears to be needed before mensurative operationalization will be achieved for the specific ones in point.

The Need for Interpersonal Security

Sullivan (1947, 1953, etc.) in his theory of interpersonal relations has stressed the need of the individual to feel secure and accepted and positively valued by others. He has characterized much of man's social behavior as "security operations"; that is as responses designed to ward off and protect the individual from the anxiety that would be experienced as a consequence of the dreaded rejection of himself by others and by their denial of his self worth. Not only is there a great deal of attention and discussion in the writings of Sullivan himself addressed to this point, but it has also been stressed by Maslow (1942b, 1943, 1945, etc.) and by various other personality theorists. Severally their discussions of motivational dynamics of personality have centered upon a poignantly felt need on the part of the person to be secure in his feeling that he is loved, liked, accepted, and appreciated as a person of worth by others with whom he associates.

There is seen in this discussion and theorizing a good deal of overlapping of meaning in the case of the motivation referred to and the conceptualization of Murray's n affiliation. There is also no clear separation conceptually between a need for security, as such, and a need for self esteem. There again seems to be some overlap. Yet there does seem to be enough difference in the several cases to distinguish as a separate motivational variable a *need for interpersonal security.*

Maslow, who has been the most explicit commentator on and most searching student of this variable uses, however, not this term for it, but defining it much more broadly, and characterizing it variously as a feeling or syndrome as well as a motive, refers to it as psychological security-insecurity (1942, 1945). Conceived of as a need, he includes it in his well known hierarchy of motives under the term "safety." He has proposed (1943) a theory of the specific order of the sequential development of needs, in terms of the history of the person's need satisfactions. This is as follows: 1. physiological needs, e.g. hunger, thirst; 2. safety needs, e.g. security, order; 3. belongingness and love needs, e.g. affection, identification; 4. esteem needs, e.g. prestige, success, self respect; 5. need for self-actualization, i.e. the desire for self fulfillment.

Maslow argues that the more basic (i.e. earlier developed) need must be adequately satisfied before the next "higher" need can emerge in the development of the individual. This adequate satisfaction does not, however, mean that the more basic need does not continue to function throughout the individual's life in some strength, for only in rare instances and for only brief intervals of time would a given need be gratified so completely as to vanish from the psychological scene. Some individuals' needs for security, moreover, might continue to function at relatively high levels of intensity throughout life. The same could be said for any later developed need.

Maslow and his associates (1945) developed a test for the general security need, but because of its considerably great length (75 items) as well as the inappropriate breadth of the concept underlying it, it was impractical for use in the investigations involving the EPPS, at least at this time. However, the writer believes there is highly credible clinical evidence for a need for *interpersonal security* and that it is a greatly important need for almost everyone. Had a specific measure of it been included along with the fifteen Murrayan needs it would have proven, it is thought, to be *next in importance in the hierarchy that is being proposed with regard to the determinants of intersexual attraction*: that is, *fourth*, following the need for maintenance and enhancement of sexual identity and role.

The Need for Self Esteem

Skipping Maslow's next need in the hierarchy proposed by him, belongingness and love, for it seems already placed in the writer's own scheme under the name of affiliation, his esteem need, or at any rate, one to be called a *need for self esteem*, is postulated to be fifth in importance in determinance of intersexual attraction.

Unfortunately since no measure of a *need for self esteem*, as such, is included in the sampling of the Murray list of needs, the measures of which comprise the data to be reported upon in this book, the hypothesis stated above is not expressly tested in this work. However, the role *feelings of self-esteem* is highlighted in a later chapter. It would impose too great a digression were it to be further discussed here.

Role of the Agreement Effect

In the review of leading theories of interpersonal attraction in chapter two it was noted that Newcomb's pioneer investigation on males' friendship formation revealed agreement in or similarity in beliefs and attitudes to play an important role in the process. It was also pointed out that later work by Byrne and his associates had confirmed and extended the generality of this relationship, finding that attitude similarity was a factor determinative of liking for a fictitious stranger of either sex. In the typical study, in what Byrne calls "paradigmatic research," experimenters have, after having measured their subjects' attitudes, manipulated the "reinforcer" (agreement) by systematically varying the proportion of answers to opinion-attitude items in contrived protocols revealed to the subject. These have been represented to him as being those of another subject who has responded to the same attitude-opinion questionnaire he has himself taken. The subject, after studying the stranger's responses, then evaluates him and indicates his degree of liking feelings for him. The greater the proportion of agreeing responses the subject perceives, the stronger the feelings of liking for or attraction to the fictitious other tend to be. The *agreement effect* has been revealed to also obtain where it has been paired with other attributes of the fictitious other, such as race, occupational status and military rank, as well as the physical attractiveness of the person.

Byrne, as noted previously, has interpreted the *agreement effect* in terms of need gratification; the discovery of or experience of similar responses in the fictitious other person being presumed to gratify a need for consensual validation. More recently Byrne has plausibly amplified his conception of the motivation processes underlying the *agreement effect* in such a manner as to reduce the need for consensual validation to a mediating role in connection with an underlying need for a feeling of effectancy in coping with the environment. Such a need can be gratified by finding that another agrees with one's views on things, for these views on things do, after all, represent coping responses.

Although future research may reveal the *agreement effect* to be a complex function of several motivational forces, it seems to this writer to be more or less simply a consequence of an aspect of his posited *need for self esteem.* The ability to cope effectively with the world of both people and things not only insures the individual's own survival, but is the instrument for obtaining most of the social and interpersonal gratifications he receives. Hence, it being so much of himself that it represents, the effectance when it is perceived to be high by him begets self love or high self esteem, but when low, the opposite—self hatred, or low self esteem. Sullivan (1947) and Festinger (1954) have both emphasized the dependence of the individual's own appraisal of the correctness and value of his attitudes and beliefs upon social processes; feedback in the form of the "reflected appraisals" of others in the case of Sullivan, feedback in terms of "social comparison processes" for Festinger. In Sullivan's terminology the effect of agreement is called consensual validation; in Festinger's self validation. Sullivan says, but Festinger does not explicitly, that such validation affects self esteem. The writer's theory, similar to Sullivan's and to Byrne's, holds that it does.

The theory, in brief, may be stated as follows: Since many of the individual's attitudes and beliefs about the world represent his solutions to the problems arising in his confrontation with it, and in his attempts to understand it, they are important aspects of his effectancy. When agreement with another is discovered or experienced and thus confirms the individual in his effectancy—concerning which he is presumably forever in some doubt—his evaluation of his effectancy, and hence of himself is raised. To those who provide such an important kind of gratification, a gain in self esteem, he is hence measurably attracted. The degree of attraction experienced would be a function of the following.

1. The person's existing level of self esteem.
2. The importance of the belief or attitude to his sense of effectancy.
3. The magnitude of the confirmation provided to the belief or attitude.
4. The comparative strength of his then existing need for self-esteem and that of other needs in the hierarchy of determinants of intersexual attraction and love proposed in the foregoing (sex, affectional intimacy, sexual identity, and interpersonal security).
5. The comparative values of whatever gratifications for these last mentioned needs are experienced in the interactional relationship with the person providing the consensual validation.
6. The degree of availability of gratifications of the consensual validation sort from other persons in comparison with the degree of availability of gratifications for needs of higher priority in the aforementioned hierarchy.

The research reported in the present series of studies, regrettably, does not include a thorough and exhaustive test of this particular theoretical formulation. Investigations planned for the future will have to decide as to whether or not the place of the *agreement effect* in intersexual attraction has been correctly assigned. Fifth place, as a kind of gratification for the need for self-esteem, may be either too high or too low. However, what data have so far been acquired in reference to the place of the *agreement effect* in intersexual attraction and love suggest that it is of comparatively minor importance in the overall scheme of determinants of these phenomena. Regrettably, the detailed analysis of these data which would be required to adequately document this point could not be included in the present work.

The Need for Self-Esteem and the Sexual Identity Drive

The discerning reader, recalling the postulation of a sexual identity and role maintenance and enhancement drive, as well as the rationale for the postulate, may wonder if the postulated need for self-esteem is not also intimately associated with such a drive. It is the writer's thesis that it is, and in the following sense. The sexual identity of the individual, being that most precious aspect of his selfhood, is striven to be maintained and enhanced in part, at least, because the individual's sense of effectancy is very much bound up with his being effective *as a male*, in the one case, or *as a female* in the other. Beyond this, however, is the need for a sense of effectancy in a general and non-sex linked sense, of course; and it is this more general need for sense of effectancy that is primarily linked up with the general need for self-esteem which has been postulated. It should be understood that in assigning only fifth rather than third place to the postulated need for self-esteem that this was done out of the consideration of the latter need apart from the former. It such a conceptual distinction is not observed, and if the two needs are to be considered a unit, then the writer, with the need for self-esteem so conceived, would shift it to third place, the place now occupied in his theory by the sexual identity drive. Given the present circumstances, however, this does not seem either advantageous or required. Future research may well be directed to determining whether the postion taken is warranted.

Actually, at present the conceptual fusions and imbrications in this domain of motivation are such as to make it difficult if not impossible to clearly separate the components in what seems to be an interdependent nexus of needs, wherein a need for sexual identity and effectancy, a need for interpersonal security, and a need for self-esteem in the more general sense are interlocked. That does not mean that one cannot, of course, objectively operationalize and separately measure the components or their presumed effects in interpersonal processes, but it does make it difficult to do so.

Criteria of Relative Priority of Determinance and Some Practical Limitations

Although it has been clearly implied in the foregoing, no explicit mention has been made as to the specific criterion to be employed in validation of the relative rankings of the determinants discussed above. This is to be simply the relative magnitude of the coefficients of correlation revealed between engaged partners on indices of strength of the sex, affiliation and sexual identity needs. Given the kind of data we can reasonably expect to acquire from engaged couples, which is that constituted of their responses to psychological tests, obvious alternatives seem wanting.

In employing correlational magnitudes to assess the relative importance of these three determinants it must be clearly understood that they are, each of them, expected to be revealed to have such high potency that truly large differences would not be found. This means that there is no expectation that the difference magnitudes of correlational values between partners on indices of sex drive, indices of the need for affectionate intimacy and indices of the sexual identity drive would, in terms of magnitudes as a criterion of difference in importance between them, be large enough to reach conventional significance levels. That is, they would not be expected to achieve such significance with samples of the small size that it is practical to obtain under the limiting circumstances of time and finances obtaining at present. Since all of these variables are believed to be determinants of relatively great power, it is expected that there are not such great differences in determinative importance among them as to produce *large* correlational differences. And, since with small samples these are *required* in order for difference values to meet the consensually acceptable significance criteria, one could not realistically expect to confirm or disconfirm one's theory in virtue of them. It is believed that only with large samples would the magnitudes of correlational differences among the three postulated determinants reach such levels of confidence. And this would be expected only in virtue of the difference in *sample size*, and not because the magnitudes of the differences themselves. These would be expected to be roughly the same in the larger samples as in a smaller one. Hence, in the projected study, only a confirmation or disconfirmation in terms of rank order could be anticipated, less certain and satisfying though that may be.

SUMMARY

The following postulate was stated as the central thesis of the instrumental theory of intersexual attraction. In intersexual dyad formation each person seeks, among his circle of acquaintances, within the compass of his self acknowledged compeers, to form a relationship with that person or those persons whose behavioral and other resources provide, or are perceived or expected to provide, maximum gratification and minimum punification for his needs.

A hierarchical ordering for the five most important needs as determinants of intersexual love was proposed as follows: 1. sex, 2. affiliation, 3. sexual identity and role maintenance and enhancement, 4. interpersonal security, and 5. need for self-esteem.

A NOTE CONCERNING DATA RELATING TO THE THEORY

Data with which to test the accuracy of the theory with respect to the placement of the first three of these hierarchically ordered needs is at present available and is to be fully reported in a later chapter. However, because two important additional aspects of the instrumental theory which have yet to be developed are to be tested with this same data, it is both convenient and necessary to defer presentation of it until at least the less complex of the two will have been delineated, as it will be in the next chapter. The reader who is impatient to know the details of the outcome with respect to this particular aspect of the theory may wish to postpone the reading of the intervening material until he has looked ahead to relevant data and the interpretation of it in chapter seven, thus ascertaining whether and to what extent the theory presented in the foregoing discussion is supported. For the less exacting reader, the outcome may be summarized here in a few sentences.

The data are interpreted as clearly and unequivocally supporting the theory in that the predicted relationships are found. The correlation between fiancés on n sex was the highest correlation on any *same* need as well as the highest in the entire 225 item correlation matrix dealt with in this research. Affiliation was the second most highly correlated *same* need in the matrix. Further, almost all of the *same* needs having higher affectional property were more highly correlated across gender than those lower in this property. The pair of *different* needs most highly correlated across gender was male dominance-female affiliation. In addition, practically all of the most highly correlated *different* needs, those at .01 levels of significance or higher, were strongly sex linked ones, as they were predicted to be in relation to the postulated sexual identity and role maintenance and enhancement drive. Moreover, the patterning of correlational values for the entire matrix fully supported the theory that such a drive was operative.

MECHANISMS OF INTERPERSONAL NEED GRATIFICATION: THE THEORY OF INTERMOTIVATIONAL MECHANICS

PROBLEMS

ONE OF THE PROBLEMS posed in chapter three, it will be recalled, was: "How can we account for the fact that samples of partners in a love relationship are revealed to be similar in certain needs but different in others?" In the attempt to answer this question a theory of the nature of the mechanics, or coinstrumentalities, of reciprocal need gratification was developed. It attempts to explain the means by which the behaviors instigated by either the *same* need in both male and female or by a *different* need in the respective cases could result in either reciprocal gratification or punification in an interaction episode or in an enduring relationship between them.

Need gratification, our mediating variable, which is presumed to be the causal agent of attraction, is not, in a correlational study such as this, observable, nor would it be to anyone anywhere else except the gratified one. In theorizing concerning it as an agent in the attraction effect, which we suppose to be a function of the sorts of behavior that are activated by particular needs, we have to assume that we know either from our own experience or, much better, from scientifically demonstrated effects produced by the need engendered behavior, how much of a gratifier that behavior is. The accuracy of our theory will be compromised in its efficacy in accounting for or predicting attraction-repulsion outcomes to the extent that our assumptions about gratifiers are inaccurate. Clues to important gratifying behaviors as well as important punifying ones can be found in a variety of ways, but a relevant and available one lies in studying tables or correlations between the needs of known interattracted persons, and if possible comparing the magnitudes of these r's with

89

those found for the same variables in a sample of randomly contrived couples. If the correlation in a given case is high (and positive) we are likely to infer that the gratification values of the behaviors instigated by the respective needs were high. If the correlation is low we are likely to infer that the gratification values are low. If the correlation is negative our inference is that there was punification rather than gratification with respect to the behaviors activated by the needs in point, so that persons both having high strengths of the respective needs did not tend to be attracted to each other, fall in love with each other or get engaged to be married.

But gratification and punification are also functions of *need strength*. If one likes coffee only a little, one will not derive as much gratification from drinking it as one will who really loves it. Hence, on this reasoning, when the observed correlations between partners on any pair of needs is high, we also infer that the strengths of need were also high and that this circumstance, resulting in high reciprocal gratification, functioned to bring the two persons to get engaged. If the correlations are low we assume that the strengths of need were also low, or that one might be high with the other low in a random sort of way. In either case we infer that the attracted partners' need strengths on this variable or pair of variables was not a very important causal condition in bringing them to form a love relationship with each other.

Although this line of reasoning seems plausible enough, it is contradicted by Winch's theory, which holds that the need strengths of interattracted partners should be different rather than similar, and that correlations on *same* needs would thus be negative rather than positive. The data collected in several studies, as was pointed out earlier, failed to support this notion, with there being, instead, more often than not, more evidence of similarity in need strength on *same* needs between interattracted persons of opposite sex. As yet, so far as the writer has been able to learn, no one has offered an explanation for this, and seemingly most people have simply accepted the fact of similarity as of some causal significance in itself. This, as the writer has pointed out previously, is not so.

Winch employed a *mechanism*, that of complementarity to account for and to predict relationship characteristics between pairs of same and different needs, which most people have thought made good sense, although it appears that they did not examine sufficiently either the conception of it he employed nor its implications. It is partly to do both of these things that is the purpose of the thinking reported in the present chapter. But further, it is to present newly conceived *mechanisms* useful in accounting for and predicting the relationship character that exists or should exist between interattracted partners with respect to pairs of same or different needs. And, finally, it is addressed toward explaining, using these newly developed mechanisms or coinstrumentalities, why there should or should not be similarity between partners in measured strengths of *same* needs.

THE BASIS OF ANALYSIS

Since data of the writer's own accumulation was not available as a basis for inferences necessary to theory construction, resort was had to that which had been acquired by other researchers who had attempted to replicate Winch's findings and wherein they had all employed as a measure of the needs the Edwards Personal Preference Schedule. This provides indices to the need strengths of fifteen of the Murrayan variables.

The aim was to attempt to construct mechanisms and principles that would have wider significance and utility than simply that of explaining the need dynamics characteristic of the Murray schema. Yet, analysis of this schema was believed to be the most appropriate starting point for the purpose, and for a variety of reasons.

1. Some information on interpartner correlations is already available regarding the Murrayan variables, whereas it is lacking for others.

2. The Murrayan need schema has been for some thirty and more years of the past and is currently still the most prominent and widely familiar one.

3. Because of its familiarity and wide employment in previous research a reemployment permits the theory both as it is being developed and later when it is tested to be related to and contrasted with previous findings and existing theoretical formulations, giving it meaning and evaluation, partially at least, in terms of the frame of reference provided by them.

4. Finally, because serious students of intersexual attraction are likely to have a more thorough understanding of the Murrayan

needs than of any other set, they will be more able with these, presumably most familiar to them, to accept or reject or otherwise deal with the characterizations that will be given of them by the writer in the pages to follow. It will be obvious to them that only by the correctly assigning of consequences, gratifying or punifying to an interacting other, to the behaviors devolving upon a given need, can its role as an attractor or repulsor be accurately assessed. And also that without such accurate assessment no insight may be had as to how it functions in intersexual attraction.

This last point merits additional emphasis.

Every need is by definition a distinctively different motivational variable, and hence produces a kind of behavior peculiar to itself. *Such a condition precludes any likelihood of successfully describing how behavioral interactions between two people motivated, as they may be, by two given same or different needs can result in mutual gratification or in reciprocal punification by stating some single general principle or even three or four of such.* Only to the extent that motivational variables have shared or common properties can they be dealt with in terms of large generalities, and, unfortunately, these large generalities are in every case compromised and qualified by the specific properties of the motivational variables involved. These points should be kept prominently in mind in pursuing the course soon to be embarked upon.

WHY A THEORY OF INTERMOTIVATIONAL MECHANICS IS NEEDED

What was seen as necessary to explain the raison d'etre of similarities in need strengths of lovers was, first of all, some theory as to the mechanics of reciprocal instrumentality of pairings of particular needs. That is, what was required was an understanding of the mechanisms by means of which gratifications stemming from the behaviors activated by the motive of one person are exchanged for the gratifications stemming from the behaviors activated by the motive of the other. Complementarity is one such mechanism or circumstance effecting the exchange of gratifications between persons, but, as classically conceived of and defined, it has reference to *difference*: supplying what is lacking for completion of some state of affairs. It was Winch's idea that for mutual gratification to obtain between lovers their needs would have to be different, rather than similar in order to fit this conception. But since Winch seems clearly to have been wrong, and there is more similarity than difference in the need strengths of interattracted partners on *same* needs, it is obvious that some other mechanism or set of circumstances must have produced this result. Hence it was seen that an explanation of similarity hinged on the discovery of such a mechanism or set of circumstances; and later, when one was discovered and found not to work for all cases, it was seen that there might be several of them that operated to produce the effect with which we are concerned.

To discover these required a more thorough look at the conditions which must be fulfilled in order for reciprocal gratifications to be experienced in an interaction episode or in recurring and continuing interactive relationships between members of a dyad.

The most obvious necessary condition seen is that, in order for the behavior stemming from the motive of one person to be gratifying to the other, the other must have some motive himself, which, in order to be gratified, requires, in a sense, the sort of behavior produced by the first person. And, what is more, that this motive be one actuating behaviors in the second person that simultaneously could gratify the first person's motive.

When the list of fifteen needs measured by the EPPS, for which correlations found in various investigations of needs among dyadic partners was examined with an eye to determining whether or not the above condition was fulfilled, it was quickly obvious that it was not. Several of the needs in the list could not be seen in the way required above to be related to any of the others in the list. It was realized that this was a serious obstacle to overcome, and might not be successfully surmounted, but it was nevertheless decided to pursue the analysis further in the hope of being able to develop an understanding of intermotivational mechanics, or, at least, what might be called a theory of it.

The component principles of such a theory are best revealed by following the writer's analysis of the data from which they were derived.

GUIDELINES FOR THE ANALYSIS OF NEED GRATIFICATION MECHANISMS

It will be helpful for the reader at this point to recall the several questions posed as guidelines for understanding need relatedness in the earlier part of this work. Because of their great importance, by virtue of the guiding principles implicit in them, they are repeated here in a slightly condensed form for the reader's convenience.

1. To what degree does need x function in interpersonal interchange? This varies considerably among the need variables which are relevant to intersexual attraction.

2. What sorts of behaviors are likely to be motivated in the respective sexes by need x?

3. What stimulus values does behavior instigated by need x in a person of one sex have for a person of the other?

4. Are the behaviors elicited by need x and which are gratifying to it in a person of one sex of such a character as to gratify or punify some need or needs in the others, and if so what need or needs might be so involved?

5. What is or are the goal or goals sought, or the conditions to be brought into being for accomplishing the gratification of need x?

6. If these aforementioned differ with gender, then in what ways?

7. Is the behavior instigated by need x related to some need or needs for which no data were obtained in the present study and, if so, what need or needs might be involved?

8. In an interaction episode between the persons, apart from the direct gratification of the reciprocally instigating needs, what are some indirectly resulting or mediated gratifications which could result for one or both persons in the process, and what needs, if this occurred, would be thus gratified?

9. What are the possible effects on a person of a given sex of his witnessing behaviors generated by a given need in the other in the other's interaction with third parties, groups of people, and animals, and what are the effects of observing the other's manipulation of physical objects, his execution of various tasks, etc.?

The analytical procedure which was initially pursued involved using the sort of questions listed in the foregoing in a kind of *need instigated behavioral interaction process analysis*. This took the form of setting up hypothetical interactive situations between a male and a female, imaging each to be motivated at the time by a given need, and then attempting to perceive the consequences. It was required, because of the incompleteness of the need system in terms of which the analysis had perforce to be conducted, to occasionally supply a missing need with an hypothetical one. These usually if not always were needs people are known to have, ones which have been measured, inferred to exist by many psychologists, or simply rationally necessary in terms of the assumptions and conceptions of need theory. Once a meaningful and plausible pattern of actions and reactions in a given such instance of confronting need with need was seen, it was tried out mentally to ascertain whether it would apply in other need confrontations with a different "cast of characters." When and if it could be seen to have application to such other cases it was formulated as a postulate and incorporated into the framework of the emerging theory of intermotivational mechanics.

The method lacks elegance, and may be even considered crude and naive, for in reality people do not encounter one another as segments constituted of disembodied needs, but rather as total personalities with their entire equipage of needs, abilities, interests, traits, values, attitudes and beliefs all assembled. Always then, the analysis had of necessity to proceed on a ceteris paribus basis. But, this after all, is also the case for almost any other kind of analysis as well.

The procedure was also hampered from the outset by the inability to anlyze motivated interactions simply in terms of the abstract conceptualizations of the needs as indicated by such terms as nurturance, intraception, succorance, dominance, etc. Whole conglomerates of particular behaviors are subsumed under each of such rubrics, and the name given may reflect only the most global and general of the behavioral qualities incorporated in the conceptual entity. Nurturance and succorance, for example, embody the giving and receiving of affection as well as of various kinds of emotional and cognitive support, borrowing and lending of physical objects such as books or tools, and many other interactions, not all of which could be simultaneously juxtaposed. Analysis could and did proceed by usually simply selecting a typical instance from the behavioral indices of a given need and tracing its effects in interaction episodes. That some oversimplification could result from such a practice is a hazard which must be frankly acknowledged.

THE FACT OF SIMILARITY OF NEED STRENGTH

Attention in analysis was first directed to the correlations found between partners for the same need, using the most recent and readily available data; that from the study of Banta and Hetherington (1963). Their research was undertaken to investigate complementarity and similarity of needs in both mate and friendship selection and involved 29 clusters of six Ss each. The University of Wisconsin students constituting these clusters, consisted of an engaged couple and a male and female friend of each fiance. All Ss were administered the Edwards Personal Preference Schedule to obtain measures of their needs. The Banta and Hetherington data are reproduced here, in part, in Table V.

The evidence in Table V to the effect that similarity in strength of any given need in the list is systematically and not just coincidentally related to intersexual choice is quite impressive. Not only are practically all of the needs positively correlated for fiances, but most of them are of substantial magnitude and a majority are either significant at or above the .05 level or fall only slightly below it. Moreover, the similarity in strength on a given need is systematically related to the degree of intimacy of the several relationships shown, generally being greatest in the case of the engaged couple. It decreases for relationships with lesser degrees of intimacy, until for the very least intimate relationship, that between the male fiance's male friend and his fiancée's female friend, it disappears altogether or approximates what one might expect on a more or less chance basis.* All of this is powerfully suggestive to the effect that M and F have been caused to choose each other because of the dynamic effects of similarity in the strengths of these various needs having resulted in reciprocal gratifications.

As indicated earlier, after closely examining and attempting to understand what might be occurring in the interactions motivated by each of these fifteen needs, certain hypotheses were derived. They are presented here as postulates descriptive of the mechanism by means of

*These pairings; the ones between the male fiance's male friend and his fiancée's female friend, are not quite the equivalent of random matching of strangers or unacquainted males and females, but they do approximate that condition. It thus seems meaningful to contrast the need correlations of these presumably non-interpersonally attracted pairs with those of the maximally interattracted, the engaged; thus giving some idea of the extent to which similarity in need strength is important in intersexual dyad formation.

TABLE V

CORRELATIONS IN NEEDS MEASURED BY THE EPPS FOR MALES AND
FEMALES IN RELATIONSHIPS OF VARYING DEGREES
OF INTIMACY

(Adapted from Banta and Hetherington, 1963)

(N = 29)

Need Measured	A Engaged Couple	B Male Fiancé X his female friend	C Male Fiancé X his fiancée's female friend	D Male Fiancé's male friend X fiancée's female friend	E Difference in Fisher Z Values of A & D
Achievement	−.01	−.13	−.09	−.23	−.22
Deference	.52*	.42*	.35	−.04	.64b
Order	.48*	.34	.28	.13	.65b
Exhibition	.39*	.28	.02	.20	.21
Autonomy	.39*	.49*	.11	−.07	48.a
Affiliation	.24	.25	.03	.09	.15
Intraception	.38*	.04	.29	.04	.36
Succorance	.36	.13	.38*	.11	.27
Dominance	.25	−.13	−.37*	.09	.16
Abasement	.44*	.33	.17	.13	.34
Nurturance	.16	.24	.06	−.12	.28
Change	.29	−.06	−.01	.24	.05
Endurance	.51*	.20	.15	−.21	.87c
Sex	.79*	.74*	.26	−.12	1.19c
Aggression	.16	−.04	−.22	−.35	−.52a
Average r	.36	.21	.09	−.01	.55a
Number of r's significant at .05 level	8	3	2	0	

*Significant at the .05 level
a. p < 05, one-tailed
b. p < 01, one-tailed
c. p < 001, one-tailed

which need instigated behavior of interacting persons results in mutual gratifications or punifications and to attraction or repulsion in the respective cases.

As the analysis progresses specific predictions in keeping with the various postulates as to the directions and magnitudes of correlation for particular needs will be stated, there being the intention to test for their accuracy in a later investigation.

THE MECHANISM OF RECIPROCALITY

Some needs seem to function in a simple reciprocating way. The affectional needs are most often of this type, but the characteristic is not limited to them, as will be seen later.

The postulate of reciprocality (or of reciprocally gratifying needs): Some needs instigate behaviors that are simultaneously gratifying to the person instigated by the need and to the interacting other whose behavior is instigated by the *same* need. That is, needs exist that actuate both parties aroused by them in an interaction episode to make responses gratifying both to themselves and to the other; so that both are practically simultaneously producing gratification for the other as well as consuming the gratifications the other is himself producing.

When individuals encounter and interact with each other, and are both actuated by such a need, a strong mutual attraction between persons having similar strengths of such a need would be expected to develop as a result of their interactions.

This would be so because each might be expected to produce behaviors of fairly high gratification value in larger quantities than others with disparate strengths of the need.

EXAMPLES OF RECIPROCALITY
Sex

The most obvious example of the reciprocal mechanism in intersexual relations would be the sex need itself, which is at the same time the most important need in such relations. This need, referred to as heterosexuality in the EPPS manual (Edwards, 1959) is there defined as follows: "To go out with members of the opposite sex, to engage in social activities with the opposite sex, to be in love with someone of the opposite sex, to kiss those of the opposite sex, to be regarded as physically attractive by those of the opposite sex, to read books and plays involving sex, to listen to or to tell jokes involving sex, to become sexually excited."

In the Banta and Hetherington sample of fiances, n sex has the highest correlation of all, .79. This is certainly as it should be in a relationship based upon its motivating forces. There would seem to be only punification for at least one partner in a case wherein they were ill matched in terms of this need. For, if one were high in sex drive whereas the other were low in it, the high one would receive, almost certainly, less gratification than he desired. The low one would at the same time almost certainly be punified in one way or another because his or her more sexually demanding partner would be likely to be more or less continually complaining of his or her coldness and lack of interest.

Prediction 1: On any appropriate measure of n sex in affianced partners the correlation should be positive in direction and moderate to high in magnitude.

Affiliation

Another excellent example of a need with high reciprocative property is found in the case of the need for Affiliation. This need was defined by Murray in terms of the implied desires and effects as follows: *"to draw near and enjoyably cooperate with an allied O, an O who resembles the S or likes the S. To please and win affection of a cathected O. To adhere and remain loyal to a friend"* (Murray, 1938). The motive is defined, by the sort of items which are used to measure it, in the EPPS manual by the following description. "To be loyal to friends, to participate in friendly groups, to do things for friends, to form new friendships, to make as many friends as possible, to share things with friends, to do things with friends rather than alone, to form strong attachments, to write letters to friends."

As an example of how the reciprocal mechanism functions the following episode has been devised. M, motivated by a strong n aff and probably always on the lookout for new friends, but especially females, espies F at a fraternity party, and, responding to cues indicative in some way to him of her being someone he might like, asks her to dance. F, also being activated by affiliative impulses (part of the reason she came to the party in the first place), accepts the invitation with obvious pleasure, thus immediately reinforcing M, gratifying his n aff, as his having asked her to dance gratified hers. Each, eager to make a new friend, shows in his or her verbal and non-verbal behavior a pleasurable appreciation of the other, exchanging compliments on each other's dancing skill and style. Sitting the next one out, they engage in exchanging impressions and opinions about the party, other persons present or absent, and a host of other matters. Assuming each capable of pleasing the other by what is said or implied in such an interaction, each finds gratification for his affiliative need and hence will experience feelings of attraction. M is highly likely under such circumstances to ask F for a date and F to accept his invitation, whereupon in that and in possibly many subsequent interaction episodes further reciprocal gratifications of their respective needs for affiliation may be enjoyed. A progressive intensification process is often seen in reciprocally gratifying exchanges of this sort, particularly in instances wherein the strengths of the respective needs for affectionate intimacy of association are high and the gratifications exchanged are great. Persons seem to behave in such a way under such circumstances as to try, in effect, to influence an increase in their own gratifications *received*, by *tendering* in *return response* slightly greater magnitudes of gratification to the other. If this *interpersonal response strategy* succeeds in its apparent aim, and if both persons are employing it, the progressive increments of gratification can with surprising speed greatly intensify the closeness and intimacy between them. It is observable, too, that in instances where the desire or need for intimacy of affectionate association is quite unequal on the part of the respective parties in the encounter, the result is likely to be quite different. With only one of them tendering increments of gratification in his return responses, while the other continues to offer none, intimacy will not increase in intensity, but remain at a relatively low level.

Since both parties to an interaction mediated by the affiliative need are motivated toward the same goals and employ similar behaviors in the process of reaching it, each has maximum likelihood of gratifying the other as he gratifies his own need. The postulate of reciprocality accounts for this case with maximum effectiveness. In view of this, the relatively small correlation (.24) for affianced partners reported in the Banta and Hetherington study is not what would be expected, but the writer cannot account for it, and can only reassert his own position.

The n aff is the need variable in the EPPS scheme which most clearly embodies the more specific needs to give and receive *affection* (Murray, 1938, p. 175). It was stated earlier in this book that it was expected to actuate behaviors of such prime salience in intersexual attraction, as to result in a correlation coefficient between the affiliative needs of partners exceeded only by that for Sex itself. Murray's own conception of the affiliation need is that "The aim of the n Affiliation is to form a synergy: A mutually enjoyed, enduring, harmoniously cooperating and reciprocating relation with another person. The S must like and be liked by the O before synergy is possible. A synergy should result in the reinforcement of emotions and needs . . ." (Murray, 1938, p. 175).

If one looks at the items, previously noted in an abbreviated form, that supposedly operationalize Murray's conception, they seem to fall quite short of the mark, if the intent was to reflect this. The closeness of intimacy and the synergy of feeling that he characterized it as having seems missing, with the representation of this supposedly most affectionate need attentuated to the point of perhaps reflecting only a rather generalized friendliness. This is a manifestation of affectionateness of need, to be sure, but one not adequate to indicate its more intense aspects. It is the latter, of course, which has the higher relevance in an intersexual love relationship, and one might wish that a measure of them more satisfactory on that score had been available. In speculating on what might have happened in the B and H study that would result in the low and nonsignificant correlation, it is perhaps not too much of a reach to suspect that in responding to these items many of the S's in that investigation were not thinking of persons of opposite sex in doing so, but of friends mainly of their own gender. A response set such as that, if existing with any substantial number of the sample of Ss, could well have depressed the magnitude of the obtained correlation, so as to inaccurately reflect the 'true' relationship.

Prediction 2: The correlation coefficient between the scores of affianced partners on n aff should be positive in direction and moderate in magnitude.

A PROCEDURAL NOTE

Because of the very large number of specific predictions made in this chapter (31 in all) no one could be expected to remember them all until the data from the study evaluating them as well as the method of its acquisition is presented. This it is not practical to do until the theory of intermotivational mechanics has itself been delineated more or less completely. Since this enterprise requires extended discussion it is recognized that some impatience on the reader's part may be experienced with regard to knowledge of results. It is, hence, strategic to embody brief and non-discursive reports of outcomes at appropriate points in the progress of the present analysis, reserving what little discussion of them is warranted until the later context. Such discussion, actually, will be quite minimal even there, since the nature of the outcomes, where incongruent with what is predicted, are not to this writer readily amenable to alternate explanations, although they may, of course, be so to the reader.

Both predictions one and two stated above were confirmed at or above the .01 significance level. The highest correlation of the entire 225 item matrix was for n sex, being .64. The second highest, .56, was for n affiliation.

Of the fifteen needs in the EPPS only the correlations between partners in the cases of n aff and n sex seem to be simply, straightforwardly, and sufficiently accounted for as examples of the operation of the principle of reciprocality. Each of the remaining thirteen needs offers one or more peculiar problems in its relatedness, sometimes necessitating the positing of additional forces and a careful weighing of their respective strengths in calculating the net resultant, as to whether it be attraction or repulsion. Discussion of those needs whose interpartner correlation *seems* interpretable as an instance of reciprocality, but is somewhat problematical, are best deferred until additional mechanisms of interpersonal need gratification are presented.

THE PRINCIPLE OF PUNIFICATION AVOIDANCE

It is difficult to see how two people of opposite sexes would ever be likely to experience repulsion to each other out of the operation of their respective needs for affiliation, presuming that they each had the need in some strength. That is not to suggest that it would be sufficient in itself to insure attraction, for even if such a need were maximally gratified in an interchange between them their levels of gratification in alternative relationships available to them might be so much greater that the one in question would be relatively low in comparative attractiveness. But it is easy to see how the operation of certain other needs, because the behaviors they motivate may be in one way or another punifying to the other person, may produce strong forces of repulsion.

Repulsion will be reciprocal if the behaviors of both are punifying, but even if only the punified one is repelled while the punifying one is attracted, the net outcome will be repulsion. Thus, in situations wherein one or both needs of potential partners beget behaviors of a punifying nature, a relationship of *need conflict* may be said to exist. For example, where both partners have substantial scores on a need for aggression, one might well expect, not attraction at all, but repulsion. This is, of course, based on the assumption that aggressive behaviors are directed toward the partner in the respective cases, which may not be necessarily the case at all. It is at least possible that although each were highly aggressive, the aggression might not be in either case directed toward the partner, but toward others outside their dyad. It seems more likely, however, that such behavior would not be so nicely distributed.

The postulate of punification avoidance: When needs are of such a nature as to instigate behaviors which are punifying to others a strong force of repulsion would be expected to be generated in cases where two interacting persons each possessed the need in considerable strength. Hence, to minimize or avoid conflict or punification, persons with high strengths of such needs would not be expected to choose each other as partners.

A male and female respectively so equipped would tend not to form a dyadic relationship with each other, but to have selected others whose motivational strength with regard to the given need or needs was dissimilar to their own. Hence, the operation of this dynamic, ceteris paribus, should result in negative correlations between the relevant need scores of those who have already actually become partners in a relationship. This, of course, describes the simple, clear and extreme case. Where the conditions are such that the dynamism operates less strongly, as it would where the consequential punifications were milder or where counteracting dynamisms were also in operation, the correlations might be expected to be less negative; that is, to be small or negligibly positive ones, or, of course, of zero magnitude.

THE POSTULATE OF IRRELEVANCE

Negligibly positive, negative or zero correlations can also result when neither gratification nor punification of the other is a consequence of the possession of a particular pair of same or different motives on the part of the respective partners. Where the operation of the need of each neither contributes to the other's satisfaction nor results in his punification neither high positive nor high negative correlations would be expected, since the needs in question would be more or less irrelevant to either attraction or repulsion on the part of either person. This, for the sake of future reference will be known as *the postulate of irrelevance*. To state it more formally:

The postulate of irrelevance (or of irrelevant need relationships). When in interaction episodes the interacting parties are instigated by either same or different needs which produce behaviors neither par-

ticularly gratifying nor punifying to the other person nor to the one
instigated by the need in question neither appreciable attraction nor
repulsion would result.

An example of this can be seen in the instance of innumerable transactions carried out in everyday life wherein whatever needs are operating are neither very strong nor very personal, as in the case of those
involved when exchanging greetings with an acquaintance, clerk, etc.
The need to be proper and show good manners is all that may be involved, and the gratification for either party is practically inconse-
quential.

There exist, of course, many situations and circumstances in life
where in encounters and interactions one person's need is measurably
gratified whereas those of the interacting other are not. Any attraction developing here would be expected to be only in one direction
rather than mutual. The same, or a similar, expectation would apply
to the case where in interaction one is gratified and other punified.
Here, however, there would be expected to be one-way attraction
and one-way repulsion. Such cases, although interesting, are not ones
seen as applicable to any appreciable degree to the kind of interpersonal relationships we are concerned with here, hence there seems little point in exploring their implications further.

THE MECHANISM OF COADJUVANCE
Aggression and Dominance

In the Banta and Hetherington sample the correlation for n agg be-
between partners is small; only .16. It is the smallest positive correlation, tied for this distinction with n nurturance and far below the .05
significance level. On the basis of the foregoing analysis this is entirely appropriate, and even a zero or negative correlation would be as
well, at least in some samples. But the positivity of the correlation in
the B and H sample should not be dismissed, it is thought, as merely
the artifact of chance factors. This seems unwarranted in consideration of the trend shown for it to become increasingly negative with
increasingly less intimate relationships. It is negative for the relationship between male financés and the girls they maintain a friendship
with but did not become engaged to, which suggests that they didn't
choose these girls because they were too *unaggressive*. The dominance
need is another which might be expected to constitute a conflicting

need relationship, yet the correlation between fiancés is again a positive one; .25. In terms of the data reproduced in Table V, exactly the same statements made with regard to n agg could be made in the case of n dom. Finally, in the cases of the needs for achievement, and autonomy, both less clearly conflicting ones, the same analysis applies, although the trends are less perfect ones. Attention will be given to this later, but let us first look at what is happening in the case of needs like agg and dom. These needs, have much in common, being correlated to the magnitude of .21 in Edwards' sample of 1509 subjects (Edwards, 1959). The following descriptions indicate the samples of preferences for behaviors which are used in the EPPS as indices of these needs. "*Aggression*: To attack contrary points of view, to tell others what one thinks about them, to criticize others publicly, to make fun of others, to tell others off when disagreeing with them, to get revenge for insults, to become angry, to blame others when things go wrong, to read newspaper accounts of violence. *Dominance*: To argue for one's point of view, to be a leader in groups to which one belongs, to be regarded by others as a leader, to be elected or appointed chairman of committees, to make group decisions, to settle arguments and disputes between others, to persuade and influence others to do what one wants, to supervise and direct the actions of others, to tell others how to do their jobs." The needs as Murray himself conceived of them are intimately related and instigate such similar behavior that they can be dealt with almost as a unit. "The Aggression drive—operates to supplement Dominance when the latter is insufficient" (Murray, 1938, p. 151).

As an illustration of the interaction effects of dominance, let us suppose that M and F are discussing the quality of law enforcement in contemporary American society, and find themselves in disagreement. M, motivated by n dom, emits dominating behaviors in regard to F in the form of a statement intended to show her to be ill-informed, and show his superior knowledge. The goal of the need and the effect desired is domination of F, who may either accept being dominated without resistance, put up some resistance, or engage in counter dominating behavior. The latter would be expected of an F high in n dom herself. If M's dominating efforts are not totally frustrated by F's counter-action, he wins this round, makes his point, and is gratified by the feeling of being dominant. F, losing, is punified but she is thus instigated to fight back (n agg) and does so, tellingly; so that now she is dominant, and gratified, whereas M is punified. In the interaction both gratifications and punifications have occurred to both, and might seem to cancel each other, but there are additional rewards to each party which gratify needs existing in them both. Examples are needs for excitement, expression of feelings and displays of abilities to each other and to others who may be present. These are some of the pleasures of competing which people in our society in large numbers have been socialized to value. It must be admitted that they cannot be experienced in interactions with people who won't compete, because they lack needs which promote it, nor enjoyed with people whose relevant needs do not instigate them strongly enough to make them good sparring partners.

Thus, we can account for the positive correlations in the cases of apparently conflicting needs. The correlations are low and would be expected to be so, because if M and F are both extremely strongly motivated by n dom (or n agg) they might escalate an enjoyable competitive contest into an over-kill reciprocal assault, making the outcomes for each other so punifying that alternative relations would be sought.

From the foregoing analysis a third postulate of need mechanics is educed: *the postulate of adjuvance* and coadjuvance. When in interaction episodes the behaviors which arise from the instigation of two *given needs*, either the same or different, in the respective actors are capable of simultaneously arousing and gratifying one or more *secondary or associated needs* in each of them, then persons possessing the *given needs* in appriciable strength are likely to be to some extent attracted to each other. The strength of the attraction generated would be contingent upon the strengths of the *given needs* and upon whether the behaviors produced through the action of the *given needs* is gratifying or punifying to the other person in the interaction. Even if the *given needs* promote behaviors that are punifying to the other,

---

*Adjuvant is defined in Webster's Collegiate Dictionary (1940) as "helping" or "helpful," as "an assistant," but also as "That which aids or modifies something, as a subsidiary ingredient in a medicine." The term, especially in the latter definition, comes closer than any other of which the writer is aware to aptly characterizing the mechanism he is postulating here, and for which some name is needed. The term facilitatory is a possible alternative, but it is devoid of that "subsidiary ingredient" asset and is less common in use as well as hard to say. Helpful, regrettably, is not sufficiently specific.

the gratifications arising from the actions carried out in terms of the *secondary or associated needs* involved may so exceed the magnitude of the punifications as to result in a *profit* for each of the interacting parties. The net result is attraction rather than repulsion. In cases where the given needs are themselves ones promotive of reciprocal gratification, the attraction engendered by them would be enhanced by the additional gratification stemming from the actions promoted by the *secondary or associated needs. Coadjuvance* is essentially a mutually facilitatory condition, arising from the behavioral interplay between persons in such a manner as to result in reciprocal need gratification of motives the arousal of which was mediated by the behavioral interaction arising originally, or principally, from the instigation of *other* motives. Thus even when needs have properties which promote conflicts between persons, the forces of repulsion generated by them may be thus partially or entirely cancelled out or overcome by forces of attraction also generated by them. These latter arise by virtue of these needs instigating behaviors mutually facilitatory to gratification of one or more other needs which have become aroused in the interplay of behaviors.

Coadjuvance, although it has been invoked here as a principle applicable to accounting for the fact that people attracted to each other are found to have a certain degree of similarity in drive strength in respect to need variables promotive of conflict between them, should not be thought of as a phenomenon limited to such circumstances. It is applicable to circumstances arising from the interplays of behaviors motivated by compatible or congruent needs as well. This can occur in possibly numerous ways. An obvious one of which is that of providing agreement with, and thus affording consensual validation to the other for particular attitudes, beliefs, and values pertaining to a given motive. As noted earlier in this work, Byrne (1961, 1969), Festinger (1950, 1954), Newcomb (1956, 1961), and Sullivan (1947, 1953) have all conceived of consensual validation as a motive in itself, and Newcomb and Byrne have both documented its importance as a factor in interpersonal attraction. Further, if two persons have similar or congruent goals, each can provide the other with the kinds of acceptance, understanding, sympathy, helpful knowledge, encouragement, emotional support, recognition and praise for achievement which psychologically facilitate his goal striving and attainment. So general and multiform is the mechanism of coadjuvance that it must be regarded as one of the most important means of mutual need gratification in interpersonal attraction. This point will be returned to in a later context of this development. But first it is necessary to state certain other principles which have been implied or illustrated in the preceding discussion of conflict and competition.

THE MECHANISM OF COPROCREANCE

It not uncommonly happens in discussion and argument, perhaps originally provoked by virtue of the respective assertive needs of two persons, that not merely is there emergent the excitement which is so gratifying to the competitive drive; but other gratifications as well. Especially when the competition is carried on primarily at a high level of intellectual interchange, new perspectives, insights, understandings, all of which are experiences gratifying to the n cognizance of one or both partners, may be engendered. If this is simply a unilateral phenomenon then the mechanism is that of procreance. If it were bilateral then it would be proper to describe the process as a coprocreant one. It can be seen as a special case of the general phenomenon of coadjuvance, but its distinctive character and importance, even granted its rarity, are such as to give it more prominence than it would have otherwise by denoting it by a separate postulate.

The postulate of procreance* and coprocreance. Needs promotive of conflict and competition between persons may instigate cognitive interactions between them that are generative of new ideas, insights, and understandings in one or both parties. Hence, among intellectual persons, at least, the mutual repulsion engendered by conflict producing drives is partially countered or negated by positive forces of attraction which are also engendered.

THE MECHANISM OF VICARIOUSNESS

The behavioral effects and consequences which have been thus far discussed are strictly interpersonal, but there are other possibilities of gratifications accruing to M and F via parapersonal interactions which they are both highly likely to observe. For example, F, high in n dom or

---

*Procreant, meaning procreative, generative, productive (Webster's Collegiate, 1940), is chosen as a designation for this newly identified mechanism in preference to the possible alternatives because it carries the suggestion of a *creative process* somewhat better than they do, and it is thus closer to capturing the writer's intended meaning for this mechanism.

n agg, seeing M in action with others, wherein his high n dom or n agg instigates effective dominating behavior, can both vicariously enjoy his dominance gratifications and at the same time experience the kind of ego-enhancement born of pride in possessing or associating with a highly effective and masterful person. The effects for M, witnessing F in this way could be quite the same, but are more likely than in her case to give rise to such punifications as feelings of jealousy and threat. This point will be returned to later in another context, for it has important implications which must be considered.

Winch saw this vicarious factor as so important, but also as so variable among people, that he conceived of it as a trait of personality, named it *vicariousness*, and sought to assess its magnitude in the "need interviews" with his subjects. He reports positive correlations between his young spouses on vicariousness and n dom and for n exh and n achievement as well. He also found positive correlations for vicariousness and status striving, another need not measured with the EPPS, but one assessed by him in "need interviews." Vicariousness he defines as "the gratification of a need derived from the perception that another person is deriving gratification" (Winch, 1958, p. 90). The mechanism of identification is involved in vicariousness, of course, and Winch drew heavily on psychoanalytic thought in giving it a highly salient role in his complementarity theory. It has no equivalent such prominence in the set of formulations which constitute the instrumental theory, but vicarious gratification via identification is entirely tenable as a postulated mechanism of need gratification. Like coadjuvance, it is seen as useful, especially, in resolving the apparent paradox of obvious positive attraction between persons in the face of their each possessing drives that are conflict and punification producing. Hence:

Postulate 5: The postulate of vicariousness and covicariousness. Needs which motivate behaviors productive of effects and consequences which are perceptible or cognizable to others, such that gratifications may be supplied vicariously to others via these psychological processes, engender forces of attraction. These may counter or negate any forces of repulsion generated by the needs in behavioral interaction. Inasmuch as both partners may be engaged in such a process in their interactions, a mechanism of covicariousness is also posited.

Vicariousness would perhaps not be seen as a force of any great strength in interpersonal attraction if there were only the one way gratification involved, for A (the actor) would experience no gratification specifically coming from W (the witness) and hence could not be attracted to W on this basis. However, if he also were to, as seems plausible, identify to some extent with and vicariously enjoy the other's joys, triumphs and successes, there would be a distinctly reciprocal condition obtaining, one of *covicariousness*. It is believed that this is in fact a common feature in sexual intercourse between lovers. Of course, there are many other gratifications being reciprocally exchanged there, such as a partner's effectance motivation being gratified by obvious and tangible evidence of his being able to gratify the other's erotic needs. This is not what is meant by vicariousness here, for there is no identification involved in its case.

Prediction 3: In any appropriately representative sample of fiances the correlation between partners with regard to any appropriate measure of n aggression will be positive in direction, but small in magnitude.

Prediction 4: For n dominance a small positive correlation should also be found.

Outcomes: Both predictions were confirmed as to direction and magnitude. M agg-f agg ($r = .06$, $p < .30$); m dom-f dom ($r = .16$, $p < .10$).

THE MECHANISM OF COAGENTIALITY
Achievement

Brief reference was made before to elements of similarity between the need for achievement and the ns dom and agg. From the definition given in the manual of the EPPS, and reproduced below, it can be seen that n ach is not, as represented there, an interpersonal need, but essentially an intrapersonal one. None of the items have reference to other persons with the exceptions of "to be a recognized authority," and "to be able to do things better than others."

"*Achievement*: To do one's best, to be successful, to accomplish tasks requiring skill and effort, to be a recognized authority, to accomplish something of great significance, to do a difficult job well, to solve difficult problems and puzzles, to be able to do things better than others, to write a great novel or play."

One might criticize the test items as inadequately sampling this variable, for a broader conception and one more in keeping with

Murray's original formulation, might well include *the successful manipulation of people* in the roles of manager, teacher, psychotherapist, etc. That all might be implied and is quite possibly so perceived by the respondent. The gratifications for achieving the goal, might seem to give a sense of effectancy, increased self esteem, etc., but its rewards are basically interpersonal; the recognition, esteem, fame, etc. won by it from others. It would seem most likely to enter the interpersonal behavioral arena via conversation about ambitions and personal goals and a recounting, not necessarily boastfully, of one's past successes and present status positions indicative of it, actual or potential. M and F are highly likely to acquire this sort of information both from each other and from other persons early in their acquaintance. The exchanges of recognition, praise, appreciation, in themselves direct gratification for the need, though not its only kind, qualify it for placement in the reciprocative category of need relations. Moreover, it can be vicariously gratifying in reciprocal ways, all of which should make it a strong force in interpersonal attraction. It has the peculiarities of being all at once a highly intrapersonal need, being metapersonal in its direct operation, and interpersonal with respect to its gratifications. It also has the property of *agentiality*.

Needs do not have to be directly interpersonal to result in the reciprocal gratifications that beget interpersonal attraction. Their instigations may in many cases lead to mutual satisfaction though their motivating of behaviors articulated to aspects of the socio-economic environment rather than to the other person in an ongoing relationship such as the mixed sex dyad. Achievement is perhaps the best example of this in the EPPS list. Its motivation may result in making lots of money and in higher socio-economic status, fame, esteem, etc. To the extent that a person, usually a female, perceives a potential mate as having the motivation and ability to achieve such goals and is herself desirous of them, she might be expected to be attracted to such a man because of his potential for mediating such gratifications for herself. He would be her instrument, in effect, because of his needs instigating behaviors which served as agents for her own need gratifications.

The Postulate of Agentiality and Coagentiality. Needs which generate behaviors which are instrumental to the gratification of others engender considerable forces of attraction toward the person in whom such a need is operative, even when the attracted person has little of the same need himself. But, ceteris paribus, when similar strengths of the same need exist in prospective mates, attraction may be mutual on this basis, each being agential to the satisfaction of the other.

In other words, when the effects produced by the operation of a need in one person are instrumental to the receipt of gratifications by another in a relationship, the latter person will be attracted to the former. The former may receive his rewards both outside the relationship, in the form of wealth, status, recognition, etc., but also within it, in the form of praise and appreciation from the latter. Thus can the attraction be mutual.

However, agentiality, quite possibly, can work both ways, for each partner's efforts may result in the benefit of both himself and the other. For example, spouses who both are high achievers are common in American Society, even if not greatly numerous.

The postulate of coagentiality contains the condition of other things being equal, it should be remembered. For a need conflict relationship is a property of this situation of n ach vis à vis n ach, just as in the cases of various other assertive drives such as n dom and n agg. Repulsive forces are set up that may nullify the forces of attraction for n ach. Males often indicate their distaste for, aversion of and repulsion from, ambitious and achieving females who might be otherwise highly attractive to them. Who has not often heard this verbalized by a male as "I don't want any competition" in disclaiming any romantic interest in some girl whose need for achievement has been observed by him? The same attitude of aversion to a competitive circumstance vis à vis males seems not to exist in females, but rather the reverse, if indeed they perceive it as such. It is suggested by the —.01 r in the Banta and Hetherington data that there the forces of attraction and repulsion have in effect cancelled each other out, relegating n ach to an impotent role in the effectuation of mate selection. This is contradicted, however, when notice is taken of the increasing dissimilarity of the need strengths for n ach in the more remote relationships. What is suspected, is that the true relationship of n ach X n ach is quite complex, with most females strongly attracted to males with high n ach, but with males on the other hand, being in some cases attracted strongly, in others mildly and in a goodly number of cases repelled. The correlation coefficient obscures such details, so other techniques would have to be used to reveal them. In any case, it seems reasonable to expect something like what is found in the Banta and Hetherington data to be found in other cases with comparable samples. It would be expected that a higher correlation would be found in a sample containing males whose n ach had already resulted in relatively high actual achievement. The reason for this is that such males might be expected to be more self-confident and less threatened by the prospect of a relationship with a female high achiever than would males whose claims to achievement were less secure. Thus the relationship obtaining with regard to n ach between members of a dyad will be likely to vary with the level of actual achievement obtaining, especially in the male part of the sample.

A similar hypothesis is that males whose n ach scores are high will select females whose scores on n ach are also high if the former are high in self esteem. Although the EPPS does not contain a measure of self esteem as such, it does have a measure of n abasement. Low scores on n aba would at least indicate a relative absence of inferiority feelings, hence,

Prediction 5: Males scoring low on n aba will tend to choose females with higher scores on n ach than those chosen by males who are high in n aba. More specifically, males scoring low on n aba will correlate higher with females on n ach than males scoring high on n aba.

Prediction 6: In a sample of college student engaged couples drawn from a population in which both n achievement and actual achievement are very high (as at UCLA, where only the top 12% of high school graduates qualify to even enter), the correlation for n ach will positive but quite low.

Outcomes: Both 5 and 6 confirmed. The low scoring males on n aba had an r with f ach of .44, $p<.005$. The high scoring males on n aba correlated $-.01$ with f ach ($p<.50$). The difference in r's was highly significant: $p<.025$. For m ach-f ach the r was .13, $p<.15$.

THE MECHANISM OF COMPLEMENTARITY
Succorance and Nurturance

How is it that males and females both with similar strengths of need for succorance, the prime example of a dependency need, can be attracted to each other? On whom is each to depend? In the Banta and Hetherington samples the r of .36 just misses the .05 criterion. Here is a case, it seems clear, where persons who both are apparently oriented toward receiving emotional support are attracted to each other. The succorance need definition is as follows. "*Succorance*: To have others provide help when in trouble, to seek encouragement from others, to have others be kindly, to have others be sympathetic and understanding about personal problems, to receive a great deal of affection from others, to have others do favors cheerfully, to be helped by others when depressed, to have others feel sorry when one is sick, to have a fuss made over one when hurt."

The behaviors that would be instigated by n suc in M would apparently be of the kind that would arouse sympathy and concern, tenderness, helpfulness, etc. in F. These responses of F, if made, would be gratifying to M. But it would seem to require that F in order to respond in these ways would have to be motivated by some need herself. It would require a different need than that activating M's behavior, that is clear. A need to give sympathy, help, etc. is called *nurturance*, which, even though F herself has a strong need for succorance, she may possess in sufficient strength for its activation by the powerful stimulus M's behavior provides. If this were so, the gratifications sought by M could be provided, and simultaneously F would gain gratification for her nurturance need. It is also reasonable to suppose that F, also having a strong n suc herself, is more able to quickly and readily understand what M needs; perhaps more ably than anyone else, for to truly understand the feelings of another requires having had the same or similar feelings oneself. Assuming that F has a nurturance need of some strength she is thus more likely than other, non-succorant, persons to know the kinds of responses sought by M and easily make them. But, even assuming no n nur itself to be aroused in F, she probably has a need for affiliation (i.e., to give and receive affection), and for intraception, a need for giving and receiving sympathetic and empathetic understanding, and these needs, if activated, could result in the kinds of responses that would be gratifying to M. Here, where different needs are each being mutually gratified in the respective interactors, we have an instance of what is known as the mechanism of *complementarity*. Now if M, when F was driven by a succorance need, was motivated by *his nurturance need* (or an allied one) to gratify her *in turn*, complementarity would again be exemplified. Taking into account the bidirectional total interchange involved in these events, there is represented an instance of what will be called *reciprocal complementarity or cocomplementarity*.

The mechanism of complementarity is of such importance as to make appropriate a more complete discussion of its nature and implications. There has been manifest a gross misunderstanding and confusion in the literature on interpersonal attraction. Murray, one of the first psychologists to note in a systematic way the relation between n suc and n nur, also stressed their complementarity, and so clear is his description of this mechanism that we can profit by following his discussion of it in relation to nurturance and succorance. "The n succorance is the tendency to cry, plead or ask for nourishment, love, protection or aid; whereas the n nurturance is the tendency to satisfy such needs in a succorant O. Thus the two needs are complements. The succorance drive seeks a nurturant O and the nurturant drive seeks a succorant O" (Murray, 1938, p. 181).* Component item content description of nurturance in the EPPS conforms very closely to his conception of it. "*Nurturance*: To help friends when they are in trouble, to assist others less fortunate, to treat others with kindness and sympathy, to forgive others, to do small favors for others, to be generous with others, to sympathize with others who are hurt or sick, to show a great deal of affection toward others, to have others confide in one about per-

*Apparently some of the same forces of attraction are operating in the case of highly succorant persons as those present in the subject of the anxiety arousing experiments of Schacter and others (Schacter, 1959). In these it was found that girls made highly anxious by the prospect of being shocked in an experiment to which they had reported to participate showed a stronger desire to affiliate with other girls while waiting for the experiment to begin than did subjects who were low in anxiety. Most relevant here is the fact that they showed a desire to affiliate not with some unanxious girls made available, but *only* with girls in the same situation as their own. What is strongly suggested is that their penchant for girls in the "same boat" with them, is their, probably unconscious, feeling that only someone undergoing the same experience as they were could possibly know how they felt and give them the understanding, support, security, reassurance, etc., which they felt in need of. Emotional understanding of another's feelings requires, as intellectual understanding does not, that one have had or have now those same feelings oneself.

sonal problems."

The principle of need complementarity is that upon which Winch based his own theory of interpersonal attraction, and, since it is involved in the instrumental theory in a significant role as well, certain important differences in conceptualization between himself and the writer must be noted. Before these can be made clear it is necessary that a careful examination of Winch's formulation be made.

Need complementarity, according to Winch's formulations, exists *"when A's behavior in acting out A's need X is gratifying to B's need Y and B's behavior in acting out B's need Y is gratifying to A's need X,"* (Winch 1958, p. 93). Further, he says, "Now it is not necesary that A's need X be a different need from B's need Y. For example, if A is high on the dominant need (call this +X, then we should hypothesize that A would be attracted to a person low on dominance (call it −X), and we should hypothesize that if B's is −X, B would be attracted to A (because of A's +X). I have used the phrase type I complementariness to the state of affairs wherein one person is high on any need and the other is low on the same need. The hypothesis that if one spouse is high on some specified need then the other spouse will be low on that same need is equivalent to saying that with respect to type I complementariness the interspousal correlations are hypothesized to be negative.

Where A's need is different (say, nurturance) from B's (say succorance), we will call this state of affairs type II complemtariness. And since +X may be hypothesized to call for +Y in some cases and −Y in others, type II complementariness may be hypothesized to call for positive interspousal correlations in some instances and negative in others." (Winch 1958, p. 94). He goes on to state, "With this backdrop on the meaning of 'complementary' . . . we are now ready to present the central hypothesis: *In Mate selection the need pattern of each spouse will be complementary rather than similar to the need pattern of the other spouse."* (Winch 1958, p. 96).

Ten of the Murray conceived needs were employed in his study, namely, abasement, achievement, approach (his name for affiliation), autonomy, deference, dominance, hostility (his name for aggression), nurturance, recognition (his name for exhibition), and succorance. For all of these he hypothesized negative interspousal correlations on

TABLE VI

PAIRS OF VARIABLES HYPOTHESIZED TO BE COMPLEMENTARY
BY WINCH

(Original Names Given by Murray, 1938, are used)

(Winch 1958, p. 96)

Abasement–Autonomy	Autonomy–Deference
Abasement–Dominance	Autonomy–Aggression
Abasement–Aggression	Deference–Dominance
*Abasement–Nurturance	Deference–Aggression
*Abasement–Exhibition	*Deference–Nurturance
Achievement–Deference	*Deference–Exhibition
*Achievement–Dominance	Dominance–Succorance
Achievement–Exhibition	Nurturance–Succorance

*Indicates a hypothesized relationship not supported by Winch's data.
(Winch 1958, pp. 113-114).

the basis of his concept of type I complementariness. On the basis of his "need interview" data he thought he had supported his hypotheses, for he found negative correlations. He does not report magnitudes, but only direction as support for the hypotheses. For type II complementarity the relationships between the pairs of needs in Table VI were hypothesized to be positive. He gives no pairs for which negative correlations were hypothesized. Again he offers in support of these "hypotheses" indicated in Table VI, only the direction, not the magnitude of the correlations.

An important proposition in the instrumental theory, not until now made explicit, because until now not revelant to any particular point at issue, is that for a mutually gratifying relationship, complementary or otherwise, to obtain between any two given needs of two persons it is required that they both be gratifyable either directly or indirectly in at least some of the interactions of the respective persons.

Winch's 'type I complementarity' as a mechanism of reciprocal need gratification is quite unacceptable in the theory being developed here, not primarily because no data other than Winch's own support it (and even his only weakly at that), but because it is erroneously conceived. If the conditions it assumes were to actually obtain it could not mediate the mutual gratification in interactions of the respective parties that is presumed to be necessary in order for mutual attraction to result.

To show why this would be so let us take his own favorite example. Say A is high in dominance and B is low, and there is interaction between them. A, activated by n dom behaves in a dominating way. B, having a weak n dom, is instigated only weakly to counteractive effort to dominate A, or, in other words, puts up little or no struggle for the position of dominance, which is the goal or gratifying state of affairs for both his and A's need. A is able to dominate, and is gratified in doing so. But what about B? What's he getting out of it? In order to be gratified in this interchange he would have to be motivated by *some* need, and if it is assumed, as implied in the concept of type I complementarity that his need was also n dom, that need is not gratified, for he doesn't accomplish the dominance he is motivated, however weakly, to seek. Since his n dom was weak in the first place, he is not punified too much by losing to A the prize of dominance, but how is he gratified? The mechanism for his gratification is absent. To supply it requires positing a need to be dominated, or a need for submission, but that forthwith changes so-called type I complementarity into type II. The type I concept will simply not work. There is no complementarity in it. That serious students of intersexual attraction could have apparently accepted such fallacious reasoning for nearly two decades is, to say the least, puzzling. It is impossible for this writer to see how Winch himself, could have supposed any mutual gratification to occur in such a relationship, but he expressly did so, saying explicitly of "type I" complementariness: "the same need is gratified in both A and B but at very different levels of intensity." (1958, p. 94).

The condition of one-way gratification of need which type I "complementarity" describes is not in and of itself unacceptable. It is, on the contrary, acceptable to the theory being developed here that one-way gratification of a given need does contribute something to the attraction, for, in the foregoing example, where A was gratified by dominating B, it would result, ceteris paribus, in his being attracted to B. B would not be attracted to A, on this basis, however, even though his punifications are minor.

There seems every likelihood that in almost any relationship between individuals numerous instances of such unilateral gratification would be found. Such relationships would not endure on a voluntary basis, however, unless the non-gratified one in an interaction such as that described above were able to achieve a gratification level in other interchanges with the partner which was high enough to offset his punifications and result in his being attracted to the partner on the basis of the "profit."

In the above example, where A dominated B without B wanting him to do so, B's punification would vary with the amount of n dom he himself had, being minimal at very low values of need strength on n dom, but being greater in magnitude if he had, for example, a moderate strength of n dom. Even so, if off-setting gratifications were to be present in the interchange he might experience feelings of attraction to A. Suppose, for example, that B has a strong need for approval, and A gratifies this need in his interactions with B by bestowing approval in return for relatively unchallenged dominance. B receives gratifications of high value to him. If his options for other relations are few (or his "comparison level for alternatives" is low), he may well be attracted to A, because his gratifications exceed his punifications. He does experience a profit, and if he feels he couldn't do better in another or any other relationship available to him he will tend to remain in this one, which is, it should be recognized, a complementary one. If, however, B's punifications exceed his gratifications in magnitude, and are not counteracted in their effect by the anticipated punification of loneliness, he will be repulsed and will abandon the relationship, even if no other is available to him or even in prospect. No person will remain in a relationship of a *voluntary* kind if the person's *limit of tolerance for punifications* is exceeded in it. More formally put, in the instrumental theory each person is conceived to have a *limit of tolerance for punifications*, which represents that point at which, for him, his punifications in a relationship exceed his gratifications in it. When that occurs in a voluntary relationship, repulsion from and abandonment of the relationship will result even if optional relationships are not available nor in prospect for him.

Need complementarity, itself, can take several forms, but the basic and essential principle relative to complementarity to be embodied in the instrumental theory is that *only different needs which instigate behaviors gratifying to each other can be complementary.* More specifically, for needs to be complementary they must *be different in quality or kind* and productive of *different kinds of behavior.*

This does not necessarily require that the needs be measured on a unipolar scale, where there is a range from zero magnitude or strength of the need to some apogee value imposed by the limitation of the scale itself, which is the case for those needs measured by the technique employed in the EPPS. The need could quite permissibly be measured on a bipolar scale designed for opposites, such that one end of the scale represented one need and the other an opposite need, as for example, dominance—submission, nurturance—succorance, exhibition—modesty, etc. At some point in the scale, decided upon either by some rational or empirical criterion, the values might presumably reach zero strength for either need, and as they increased in the direction of either pole, would come to represent degrees of strengths for the need located there. But, on a unipolar scale measuring any given need, the low values on the scale simply mean low values for that need, not high values, or any values at all, for some other need. A zero need strength on n nur does not mean n suc.

Another difficulty with the conception of need complementarity as employed by Winch is that, although he seemingly clearly enough defines it by saying that it exists "when A's behavior in acting out A's need X is gratifying to B's need Y and B's behavior in acting out B's need Y is gratifying to A's need X," he leaves it quite vague and obscure as to how one is to identify such complementary pairs. Just *what* needs under *what* circumstances can so function? The examples that are given by him beguile us into thinking we understand the process and that it is a meaningful and useful concept when he uses the obvious ones of dominance—submission and nurturance—succorance. However, if one will examine Table VI again, it will be noted that posited as complementaries are achievement—dominance, achievement—exhibition and autonomy—aggression. It is difficult to see how these pairs of assertive needs could function in a complementary way. Indeed, they have more the aura of conflict about them than any obvious coinstrumentality, especially in the case of the autonomy—aggression pairing. Perhaps Winch supposed a vicariousness mechanism to be operating. Conceivably, in a marriage, one's spouse's achievement or his effective exhibitionist behaviors could be a source of vicarious gratification to the other spouse's motive in that brace of needs, and this same mechanism might have been what he had in mind in the other two pairings as well. But he does not say so, and one is left quite mystified as to any principle other than that of vicarious gratification which would have led him to predict a complementary relationship for these pairings. Even the hypothetical vicarious gratification, it must be admitted, is not really plausible when invoked for explaining these latter.

DIFFUSE COMPLEMENTARITY

The other thirteen pairings in Table VI seem more plausible, even though a single one of the needs; e.g. abasement, is posited as complementary to not just one other need, but to five different ones, namely autonomy, dominance, aggression, nurturance and exhibition. Deference, similarly, enters into another six of the sixteen pairings; specifically, with achievement, autonomy, dominace, aggression, nurturance and exhibition. These seem to make sense in terms to the effect that a given need, like deference, does not have to be tied to any single assertive need, like dominance for instance, but can be operative and evocative of deferential sorts of behaviors that can be gratifying to these other assertive needs as well. What is implied is that the concept of need complementarity may include both specific complementarity and generalized (or diffuse) complementarity. This appears quite meaningful and also a quite useful enlargement of the concept.

The hypothesized relation of complementarity to interpersonal attraction which is to become part of the theory being developed may be stated in the form of a postulate as follows.

The Postulate of Complementarity: Need complementarity obtains whenever a given need having a more or less distinctive goal exists in one person and requires for its gratification the kinds of behavior motivated by a different need in another person, which need in turn requires for its gratification the kinds of behavior instigated by the first person's need. Whenever persons thus equipped encounter each other forces of attraction would be generated in interactions of these individuals.

For needs to be complementary, to put it still another way, it is required in the instrumental conception of complementarity that they be different in quality and have different goals. Also the behavior or behaviors instigated by both of the needs must be capable of being mutually gratifying in themselves or in their effects to both the person in whom the need was activated and to the other person with whom interaction is occurring. For example, if A is activated by a need to be amusing and B is activated by a need to be amused, and A emits amusing behavior, both are reciprocally gratified.

The foregoing formulation is intended to be sufficiently precise to differentiate complementary need relationships from all others. But also the intent in phrasing it has been to permit the inclusion of the phenomenon which has been previously referred to as *diffuse complementarity*. Thus there is encompassed the possibility that any of several needs with somewhat similar properties in common may function as complementaries for any given need. More specific detail will be addressed to this point later on.

COMPLEMENTARITY AND RECIPROCALITY

In instrumental theory the main stress is not upon complementarity, important though that is, but, rather, on the more basic concept, that of *reciprocality*.

It is instructive at this juncture, since reciprocality has been sufficiently discussed, to return for a moment to Winch's statement, quoted earlier, to the effect that *complementarity* exists "when A's behavior in acting out A's need X is gratifying to B's need Y and B's behavior in acting out B's need Y is gratifying to A's need X." This is followed by his statement "Now it is not necessary that A's need X be a different need from B's Y." He then describes his concept of "type I" complementarity, which it has already been argued, fails to meet the requirements of need gratification theory. But ignore that for a moment, and suppose that needs X in A and Y in B are both sex. Then it follows from Winch's formulation that A's behavior in acting out A's sex need (X) is gratifying to B's sex need (Y) and vice versa. This has been seen as a *reciprocally gratifying need relationship* in terms of the conceptions of instrumental theory. *Yet it fits very nicely the definition Winch gave for complementary need relationships.* The formulation offered by him enables us to make no distinction between these two, for they are in terms of it identical. To have a distinctive meaning and to be a truly useful concept in accounting for interpersonal attraction the term complementarity, it is again insisted, must be limited in its definition and reference to the description of a state of affairs that can only exist between pairs of *different* needs.

NATURE OF AND VARIETIES OF RECIPROCAL COMPLEMENTARITY OR COCOMPLEMENTARITY

As has been indicated in the foregoing discussion there are several forms or varieties of complementarity; namely direct or simple complementarity as compared with diffuse complementarity, and a type which was called *reciprocal complementarity* or *cocomplementarity*. It was this latter form that was exemplified in the discussion of the relationship among m nur-f nur, m nur-f suc and m suc-f nur and invoked to explain why the correlations in each of these should be positive. Although it was strongly implied in that discussion it is perhaps wise to forestall any misunderstanding by making quite explicit the following point.

In order for reciprocal complementarity to obtain, as opposed to merely a unidirectional complementarity (the only kind which appears to have been previously recognized), both persons must have both of the needs (e.g., n suc and n nur respectively), in some effective strength; that is, in a strength capable of instigating the behaviors of both sorts. In the case of nurturance and succorance this implies that positive correlations between M and F on both needs would obtain.

The exemplification of cocomplementarity given previously did not particularize it as one of *intraepisodic cocomplementarity*, but such a distinction has some utility, for there is also *transepisodic cocomplementarity*. Intraepisodic cocomplementarity refers to the circumstance wherein the reciprocation of kinds of gratification, like a temporary alternation of roles, occurs within a single interaction occasion or episode. In transepisodic cocomplementarity, in contrast, the reciprocation and alternation of complementary roles involves two or many separate interaction episodes, and it is probably more characteristic of, and more of a binding force in, long enduring relationships than is intraepisodic cocomplementarity.

Let us close this discussion of complementarity phenomena with a return to our target variables, nurturance and succorance, in the respective sexes, and indicate what the expected correlations among them are.

Prediction 7: In any appropriately representative sample of fiancé's the correlation between them with regard to n suc will be positive in direction and moderate in magnitude. The *magnitude* prediction in this case is made on purely empirical grounds, that is, on what has been found to be true before, rather than on the basis of principle.

Prediction 8: There will be a positive correlation between fiancé's of this same sample on any appropriate measure of nurturance. Again, the correlation magnitude, based on previous empirical findings, will be moderate.

Prediction 9: There will be a small positive correlation between female nurturance and male succorance, and

Prediction 10: There will be a small positive correlation for male nurturance and female succorance.

Prediction 11: The correlation between m nur and f suc will be smaller than that between f nur and m suc.

The latter prediction, that of smaller magnitude for the correlation between m nur and f suc is made on the basis of the principle of genderic congruency, the nature of which was discussed in the preceding chapter.

Outcomes: All predictions confirmed as to direction, but with less consistency as to magnitude: r for n suc = .23, p < .05; r for n nur = .36, p < .01; f nur-m suc, r = .33, p < .01; m nur-f suc, r = .07, p < .25. Prediction 11 was also supported.

EXHIBITION

Perhaps the best example of *intraepisodic reciprocal complementarity* is found in the case of n Exhibition. This need is described by Edwards, in terms of the items used in the EPPS as indicators as follows. "*Exhibition*: To say witty and clever things, to tell amusing jokes and stories, to talk about personal adventures and experiences, to have others notice and comment upon one's appearance, to say things just to see what effect it will have on others, to talk about personal achievements, to be the center of attention, to use words that others do not know the meaning of, to ask questions others cannot answer."

Let us take just one such behavior, "to tell amusing jokes and stories," and pursue its consequences. M, motivated by n exh tells F a joke which gratifies M's need if F responds with laughter and appreciation, like, "Wow, that's a good one!" F, we can reasonably assume, has *a need to be amused and entertained*, and M's product has thus high exchange value and is consumed with gratification by F. Out of her own n exh, and presumably as an additional show of appreciation, F tells M a joke in return. M consumes the product with enjoyment (having also a need to be amused and entertained), and so the interchange of gratifications results in feelings of liking of M and F for each other. If M is interacting with F2, who, let us say, has a low need for exhibition, F2 may reward M with the appropriate laughter, etc., but having little n exh herself, she is less likely than F was to tell jokes in return, so M's payoff is less high with F2 than it was with F. He is less likely to continue or repeat interaction with F2 in terms of this need, and especially unlikely to do so if his comparison level for available alternative interaction is high. He will not be as strongly attracted to F2 as he will be to F.

Reciprocal exchange need relationships of this complementary sort, ceteris paribus, may be expected to be among the strongest to be found, since high degrees of gratification are made possible through their operation. However, some reciprocal exchange relationships contain the possibility of punifications being produced, which, when present, may be expected to reduce the strength of attraction in terms of such needs as are involved. Examine, again, the consequence in interaction which may occur between two persons both high in n exh. One may have more talent or skill in telling jokes than the other, and hence may suffer some loss in self-esteem because of the inescapable contrast of his talents with those of the other. His gratifications are thus reduced, and he may find his payoffs better in a relation with someone else, who, not so high in need exh, does not punify him as much. Since n exh is an assertive need and instigates assertive behavior, of which the telling of jokes is perhaps of the most innocuous variety, it, even in that case, conflicts with the assertive need of the other person to some degree. Hence, an element of contest and conflict is likewise present in this interaction context, so that each person in his productions may find himself trying to outdo the other. Losses in a game like this are punifying; hence, to the extent to which these risks are a characteristic of interactions in terms of this need, we should expect its efficacy in providing mutual gratification to be compromised. It seems probable that a more satisfying combination would be one wherein one or both persons are moderately high in this need or else one is high and the other moderate, for here, although there might be some reduction in the gratifications of one or both, the likelihood of punification and conflict is lessened. We should not expect persons high in n exh to be attracted to those low in n exh because the latter are not likely to engage in the kinds of behavior that are reciprocally gratifying. The one-way output, if not punifying, is at least too insufficiently gratifying to be expected to result in mutual attraction. For all of these foregoing reasons we should expect a substantial, but not high correlation between persons on n exh. In the Banta and Hetherington data it is .39, just above the .37 needed for significance at the .05 level.

Prediction 12: In any appropriately representative sample of engaged couples the correlation between partners with regard to any appropriate measure for n exhibition will be positive in direction and small to moderate in magnitude.

Outcome: $r = .19$, $p < .10$.

What has been said about the reciprocally complementary characteristics of n exh could perhaps also be seen to apply with regard to n dom and n agg, but not with nearly the same assurance, in terms of the analysis previously presented. In the behavioral interactions devolving upon these particular assertive drives, the mechanisms and dynamisms of coadjuvance and coprocreance seem to have the larger role.

Even in the case of n ach the reciprocal complementarity principle might account for some considerable part of the need's operation, for in the exchanges of information designed to win recognition and approval from one another, and in the exchanges of such recognition and approval, the reciprocal mechanism is involved. At this point of theoretical development the inclination is not to attempt to set up any rigid and mutually exclusive categories of need mechanisms and dynamics for given needs. But rather, to identify only as many mechanisms and dynamic principles as are needed to account for the many phenomena of need relatedness in interpersonal attraction and repulsion. The interactions arising from any specific pair of needs may simultaneously involve, it should be clear, several of the mechanisms so far identified.

DEFERENCE

This is probably the case with need deference, which will be considered now. A definition follows: "Deference: To get suggestions from others, to find out what others think, to follow instructions and do what is expected, to praise others, to tell others that they have done a good job, to accept the leadership of others, to read about great men, to conform to custom and avoid the unconventional, to let others make decisions."

The deference need has consensually been seen by students of need dynamics as complementary to n dominance, with them apparently assuming the complementarity to be a unilateral one between any two individuals under consideration. Such a conception would not help us to explain any appreciable correlation obtaining between partners on n def itself. However, if both partners could be assumed to have at least moderate strength of n dominance (and thus be positively correlated on it), then the correlation between them on n deference could be accounted for in terms of the mechanism of cocomplementarity. This might be all that is needed to account for the significant positive correlation of .52 found in the Banta and Hetherington sample. But it is observed to be the second largest correlation coefficient, exceeded only by that for n sex, in the whole array. That suggests that it may have direct reciprocal properties (which applies to needs which are the same for both persons), or be affected by need dynamics and mechanisms not yet identified. Examination of the items defining n def make the operation of the need on the basis of simple direct reciprocality seem quite plausible. The sort of behaviors involved in 'conforming to custom' and 'avoiding the unconventional' suggest that people making these kinds of responses, may be drawn together in part at least on the basis of the mutual ease of interacting with each other. It would be at least trying to each of them, if not utterly impossible, to relate to and interact with nonconforming and unconventional people. For example, in their conversations and interactions each will be instigated, perhaps much of the time by n def, to praise the other, tell the other pleasant things and generally reciprocally exchange gratifications of that nature with him. Everyone, of course, except the complete boor, does a lot of this sort of thing—we all have some n def—even though we may not be highly aware of the gratifications of it. It is quite conceivable that two persons with *strong* needs for deference might, because each produces gratifications for the other at the same time that he himself is being gratified, be strongly attracted to each other. Finally, and less importantly, with respect to the conformity to custom and convention, it should be noted that people are gratified in finding consensual validation of their opinions and attitudes. M and F, both high in n def, will in the voicing of feelings and opinions to each other and to third persons, exchange many such gratifications (an example of coadjuvance). As Newcomb and Byrne have shown, these are powerful forces of attraction.

Prediction 13: On any appropriate measure of n def the scores of a sample of fiancés drawn from a typical collegiate population will be found to be positively correlated to a small to moderate degree, but for a UCLA sample it is predicted to be small.

Prediction 14: The correlation magnitudes on n def will be found to be higher in communities which are conservative, traditional and conventional in behavioral 'climate' than they will be in more unconventional and avant garde behavioral atmospheres. The Banta and Hetherington sample was drawn from a midwestern university population, which may be presumed to reflect the conventional and conservative midwestern middle class values, attitudes and behavioral style. It may be expected to differ in the importance of the deference need for its members, as contrasted with the emphasis this need is likely to have in a sample of couples at UCLA, drawn as it is from a community with distinctively nonconventional and perhaps even avant garde characteristics. Such a difference in correlational magnitude, if found, would also lend credence to the contention that n def functions, not just as a reciprocally complementary need with n dominance (and possibly others), but in a simple reciprocal way as well.

Prediction 15: There will be a small positive correlation between males' n dom and females' n def, indicative of a complementary relationship.

Prediction 16: There will be a small positive correlation between females' n dom and males' n def.

Prediction 17: The correlation between f dom and m def will be smaller in magnitude than that for m dom-f def.

This prediction is based on the principle of genderic congruency.

Outcomes: All of the foregoing predictions were confirmed as to direction as well as to magnitude. The magnitude of the correlation for m def-f def (.29, p < .01) was smaller than that found in the Wisconsin sample (.52), as predicted; but the difference was not great enough to reach the conventional .05 level. It had p value of .10. Males' n dom and Females' n def had an r of .19, p < .10, while the reverse relationship, m def-f dom, was smaller, as predicted: r = .15, p < .15.

The larger correlation for the partners' n def as a *same* need, i.e. m def-f def as compared to the two correlations m dom-f def and m def-f dom is interpreted as indicating that Deference has more gratifying function in the reciprocal sense, as suggested in the foregoing, than as a reciprocally complementary gratifier for the partners' respective dominance needs.

AUTONOMY

In a previous context, where properties of certain of the assertive drives were being discussed, it was pointed out that in the cases of n dom, n agg and n ach there was an increasingly positive relation between males and females with respect to these needs in keeping with the intimacy of the relationship. The more remote the relationship, the less positive the correlation was found to be. The trend is similar, but less regular in the case of another assertive need, that of autonomy, which shows a correlation coefficient of .39 between the scores of the fiancés. Autonomy is defined as follows in the EPPS manual. "*Autonomy*: To be able to come and go as desired, to say what one thinks about things, to be independent of others in making decisions, to feel free to do what one wants, to do things that are unconventional, to avoid situations where one is expected to conform, to do things without regard to what others may think, to criticize those in positions of authority, to avoid responsibilities and obligations."

Although the goal of autonomy motivation is neither domination or victory over others and it is essentially nonaggressive in its aim, it is self assertive. Self assertive behavior has for many, if not most people, it appears, a stimulus value invested with challenge, and this perhaps in proportion to a given person's own drive toward self assertion. Hence, it seems likely that two strongly autonomy driven people, unless their views on things and their tastes and preferences closely coincided, would often find themselves in conflict productive of punifications for each other and, hence, would be mutually repelled rather than attracted. This would lead us to expect a negative correlation on n aut between actually attracted persons. But we have seen, from the B and H data cited above, that the r for engaged couples is a positive .39.

It is suggested that this result may be accounted for by recognition that two persons with somewhat disparate as well as mild or moderate strengths of autonomy motivation, and thus presumably less self assertive, could gratify each other's "need to be uninterfered with" by each of them letting the other alone, so to speak.*

Implied here, of course, is a motive on the part of these mildly autonomous individuals to behaviorally respect the other's perceived need for noninterference. If we can assume such a duality of motives in the moderately autonomous respective individuals, which might be summed up as a sort of "live and let live" way of behaving on their part, then we have the basis for a reciprocally complementary gratification mechanism. Hence, we would expect some force of attraction to be generated in encounters between individuals motivated in these ways.

Prediction 18: The correlation between fiancés on n aut will be positive in direction and small to moderate in magnitude.

Outcome: The r was, indeed, small: .13, p < .15.

AN HYPOTHESIS CONCERNING
SELF ESTEEM AND THE ASSERTIVE DRIVES

In the course of the foregoing presentation each of the several important assertive and male sex linked drives, namely achievement, aggression, autonomy, dominance, exhibition and sex, have been discussed. Although it occasions a minor digression, it is, nevertheless, with the familiarity thus gained, convenient at this point to state an

---

*Proposed here as an hypothesis to be tested in later research is that one reason for the findings of Byrne, Newcomb and others that people are attracted to and like others whose attitudes and beliefs are similar to or in agreement with their own is that such a state of affairs is mutually gratifying to their respective needs for autonomy. Such a circumstance allows one to go one's way, believe what one wishes, so to speak, without the constraints associated with affiliation with others of contrary ways or conflicting views.

important hypothesis concerning the magnitude of interfiancé correlations on each of the latter five and the level of self esteem of the male partner. In brief, the correlational magnitudes in the respective cases are expected to vary with this latter; to be found greater when it is higher except in the case of m-f exhibition. In the latter case the correlation is expected to be lower. The hypothesis with respect to agg, aut, dom and sex is similar to that made earlier for achievement when the relation between that need and level of self esteem in the male was discussed. It will be recalled that in that case it was hypothesized that males scoring high on the n ach who were not high in inferiority feelings, i.e., did not score high on the n aba scale, would select mates whose scores on n ach were more similar to their own than males who were high in n aba scores, with this being manifested by a higher positive coefficient of correlation.

The rationale for the n ach-n aba interaction was that the male with higher self esteem would find himself less threatened by feminine "competition" than someone less secure in his feeling of self worth. Hence, instead of the high n ach female being made less attractive to him out of his fears of being outdone in achievement by her, she would be distinctly more attractive to him than a girl whose n ach was low. Several forces contributing to the attraction, suggested in the preceding discussion, but not brought to bear explicitly on this point are the following.

1. The gratification of a self-enhancing or ego-enhancing sort to be gained by affiliation with an achieving person.

2. The consensual validation of one's attitudes and values (*re* achieving).

3. The possible vicarious gratifications.

4. The gratifications accruing from the possible coagential operation of their common drive.

5. The particular feeling of gratification resulting from the belief that the most perceptive and most complete appreciation and esteem for one's achievements are likely to be found in persons who have also tried to achieve significant goals.

The other assertive drives mentioned are in each case, it has been shown in the preceding chapter, also linked to masculinity and male social role. Fear of competition with the female on the basis of them motivates the less secure, i.e. more inferiority ridden male, or male high on n abasement, to select females with lower scores on n agg, n aut, n dom, and n sex than those that will be chosen by the more self confident, or less inferiority plagued male. Hence:

Prediction 19: Males who are low scorers on n aba will tend to select females whose scores on n agg are more similar to their own than those chosen by males who score high on n aba.

Prediction 20: Males who are low scorers on n aba will tend to select females whose scores on n aut are more similar to their own than those chosen by males who are high scorers on n aba.

Prediction 21: Males who are low scorers on n aba will tend to select females whose scores on n dom are more similar to their own than those who will be chosen by males who score high on n aba.

Prediction 22: Males who are low scorers on n aba will tend to select females whose scores on n sex are more similar to their own than those who will be chosen by males who score high on n aba.

Prediction 23: Males who are low scorers on n aba will tend to select females whose scores on n exh are less similar to their own than those who will be chosen by males who score high on n aba.

More specifically, and perhaps less confusingly, males scoring high on n aba will correlate higher with females on n exh than males scoring low on n aba.

Exhibition, it is true, is an assertive drive and is perceived and responded to as such by other individuals. But, as will be argued more cogently in a later context where it does not, as here, incur a distracting digression, Exhibition is a compensatory drive, motivated at a deeper level by feelings of inferiority and inadequacy. These feelings the asserting oneself in exhibitory manner conceal, in effect or by design, both from others and from oneself.

Predictions 5, 19, 20, 21 and 23 it should be understood are not ones drawn from postulates concerning need gratification mechanisms per se, but rather from an hypothesis pertaining to intrapsychic motivational dynamics. The interesting implications of this latter will be explored more freely in a later chapter.

Outcomes: All of the five differences in the correlations were in the direction predicted, but all except the one for achievement failed to reach the .05 significance level.

INTRACEPTION

The correlation between fiancés of the B and H sample on n intraception is both substantial and significant; .38. The definition of this need in terms of the items on the EPPS is as follows. *"Intraception*: To analyze one's motives and feelings, to observe others, to understand how others feel about problems, to put one's self in another's place, to judge people by why they do things rather than by what they do, to analyze the behavior of others, to analyze the motives of others, to predict how others will act."

This need is, in terms of the items which are employed to measure it, both an intrapersonal need and an interpersonal one. It is a need to understand other's behavior and to see their side of things. It carries the implication in at least some of the items of a tolerant and forgiving or accepting set of orientations. Hence it is also an aspect of the need to give affection.

In interpersonal interchanges of behaviors, those behaviors which might be minimally expected to devolve upon it would be manifestations of understanding via words, gestures, facial expressions, expressions of feelings, etc. By positing a need to receive understanding from others and by assuming that intraception implies a need to express it, we can easily see that the reciprocal complementarity mechanism is involved in its operation in such a way as to produce forces of attraction between people.

Prediction 24: There will be a positive correlation between the needs of partners on an appropriate measure of n int. The magnitude expected is small to moderate.

Outcome: Supported: $r = .17$, $p < .10$.

ABASEMENT

Abasement, it is evident from the B and H data, is increasingly associated with the closeness of relationship between males and females, being increasingly larger in magnitude of positive correlation in keeping with degree of intimacy. It has been conceived of as a need and is measured as such on the EPPS. Yet this is difficult to accept on the part of the writer. The definition in terms of items on the EPPS is as follows: *"Abasement*: To feel guilty when one does something wrong, to accept blame when things do not go right, to feel that personal pain and misery suffered does more good than harm, to feel the need for punishment for wrong doing, to feel better when giving in and avoiding a fight than when having one's own way, to feel the need for confession of errors, to feel depressed by inability to handle situations, to feel timid in the presence of superiors, to feel inferior to others in most respects."

Essentially it is a feeling, rather than a need that is involved in this concept. It is a sense of little worth, of inferiority to others, of guilt and self blame, of depression over one's inadequacy to cope effectively with the environment (personal as well as impersonal) and a fear of stronger, more adequate people who are seen as too powerful to struggle against. If a need is involved here, surely it had better be conceived of as a need to avoid having such feelings, or a need for safety in a world of threatening others. It is reassuring to find that the formulator himself was not of a dissimilar mind. "One questions whether n abasement should be considered a drive in its own right. Except for the phenomenon of masochism, abasement seems always to be an attitude serving some other end: the avoidance of further pain or anticipated punishment, or the desire for passivity, or the desire to show extreme deference" (Murray, 1938, p. 82).

Given this vantage, one can readily interpret the positive correlation between engaged persons as based upon each providing acceptance and safety for the other. Because each has inferiority feelings, each can easily understand the other and be comfortable and unthreatened in associating with him. Assuming few or no out and out masochists in the typical collegiate sample of engaged partners, one would surely expect that one fearful, timid, guilt ridden person would find another attractive rather than some assertive, adequate, dominant, aggressive individual, for the latter would only make him feel worse than he already does.

Described in a more concrete way, M, impelled by n safety and n acceptance actuates behavior toward F that is indicative to her of his feelings of low self regard. F, herself motivated by n safety or n acceptance or both, responds in an accepting and understanding way, thus satisfying M's need. She gratifies herself while doing so by her feeling that her behavior toward M is insuring of safety or acceptance in return. This is validated by his behavior toward her in an immediate response having the same significance to her as hers was intended to have for him.

The need mechanism here is essentially a reciprocating one, but the posited needs for safety and acceptance can also be readily hypothesized to be reciprocally complementary with the ns nur of the respective interacting parties. Both dynamisms combine in their effects to produce forces conducive to attraction for persons high in feelings of inferiority (or low in feelings of self esteem).

Prediction 25: The correlation of scores on n aba will be positive and small in magnitude.

Prediction 26: The correlation of scores on n aba for males and n nur for females will be positive in direction and small in magnitude.

Prediction 27: The correlation of scores on n aba for females and n nur for males will be positive in direction but small.

Prediction 28: The correlation between f aba-m nur will be smaller in magnitude than that between m aba-f nur.

This prediction follows from the postulate of genderic congruency.

Outcomes: Confirmed as to both direction and magnitude. The interfiancé r for abasement was .23, p < .05. M aba-f-nur: r = .24, p < .05. The r for f aba-m nur was, as predicted, smaller: r = .18, p < .10.

CHANGE

The need for change is positively, but not significantly correlated in the B and H sample. This, it is hypothesized here, is no mere chance coincidence, but rather, is based upon a definite force toward liking set up by reciprocal gratifications experienced in interaction. The definition of n change is appendant. "*Change*: To do new and different things, to travel, to meet new people, to experience novelty and change in daily routine, to experiment and try new things, to eat in new and different places, to try new and different jobs, to move about the country and live in different places, to participate in new fads and fashions."

The mechanism by which two people provide reciprocal gratifications when each is driven by this motive seems clear. M and F, both so motivated, provide the occasions for each other's gratification by making responses having novelty value for each other. The need is conceived of as one to both produce and consume novelty, hence there is no requirement for a complementary need, and thus the mechanism is a simple reciprocal one as so construed.

A less ambiguous measurement could easily separate the production and consumption components into two separate needs, which would not, necessarily, be of identical strengths. If this were done, the positive correlation between partners could be accounted for as an instance of reciprocal complementarity.

Prediction 29: The correlation between affianced persons should be positive and small to moderate in magnitude on n chg.

The prediction about range of magnitude is based on the assumption that populations may differ in the demand for this gratification as well as in the supply. In a more conventional collegiate sample (Wisconsin), as contrasted with one characterized by more avant garde norms—which include a high value on new experience and novelty (UCLA)—the correlation between members of a dyad with regard to n change should be smaller.

Outcomes: Confirmed: m chg-f chg: $r=.30$, $p<.01$. Not confirmed was the prediction to the effect that the UCLA correlation would be larger. It is practically identical in magnitude with the Wisconsin r, which was .29.

ORDER

Order is not quite the opposite of change, for that in the Murray system would be Sameness (Murray 1938, pp. 200-205). In the B and H midwestern sample the correlation coefficient of .48 suggests that people are strongly influenced by it in selecting each other. It is also suggested that it is endemic in the collegiate population from which the sample was drawn, since even the most remote and more or less fortuitous couplings still exhibit a positive correlation in terms of it. "*Order*: To have written work neat and organized, to make plans before starting on a difficult task, to have things organized, to keep things neat and orderly, to make advance plans when taking a trip, to organize details of work, to keep letters and files according to some system, to have meals organized and a definite time for eating, to have things arranged so that they run smoothly without change."

Order is primarily measured in terms making it an essentially intrapersonal need, but it might be expected to prompt behaviors with interpersonal exchange value as well. In the circumstance of considering one as a life companion one might well be sensitized to notice the other's behavior and form impressions of his or her orderliness or disorderliness, for, for the orderly person to live with disorder is punifying and vice versa. Orderliness might be expected to be revealed in social interactions in the instance of promptness in keeping dates and rendezvous, and in many other ways. For example, to make plans in advance of taking a contemplated trip together, a kind of behavior generated by this motive, would seem not only highly sensible, but also likely to result in an enjoyable experience for both partners in contrast to what might well happen (or ill happen) if either or both neglected to do any planning. The mechanics of this need's operating could be various. That is, sometimes coadjuvant, sometimes coagential, and at others perhaps simply reciprocating.

Prediction 30: The correlation on n order for a typical collegiate sample of engaged couples will be positive, and small to moderate in magnitude, the latter depending somewhat upon the particular characteristics of the population from which the sample is taken. In the relatively avant guarde and unconventional population at UCLA both the demand for and supply of this behavioral commodity are quite different from those obtaining at the University of Wisconsin nearly ten years ago. The correlation to be expected on n ord in a UCLA sample would almost certainly be smaller, as it would also at U.C. Berkeley, or San Francisco State.

Outcomes: Confirmed for m ord-f ord: $r=.27$, $p<.05$. The UCLA r of .27, while much smaller than the Wisconsin .48 was not sufficiently smaller for the z value difference to reach the conventional .05 level of significance.

ENDURANCE

What has been said about n order could almost be repeated for the last need in the EPPS list. "*Endurance*: To keep at a job until it is finished, to complete any job undertaken, to work hard at a task, to keep at a puzzle or problem until it is solved, to work at a single job before taking on others, to stay up late working in order to get a job done, to put in long hours of work without distraction, to stick at a problem even though it may seem as if no progress is being made, to avoid being interrupted while at work."

Again we have a basically intrapersonal need, and one even more distinctly so than order. Yet it too probably has some interpersonal attraction value. One can imagine it operating in a context where M and F are engaged in some project wherein each has agreed to carry out certain portions of the work by himself, but where the project is doomed to failure if either partner doesn't complete his assignment. If both do so, and the project is carried through to completion, both are gratified by the result. More so, of course, if the project is successful in outcome, but some even if it is not. Each has gratified his own need, but at the same time acted in such a way as to gratify the other's need.

As another example, let us suppose that M and F have agreed to go on a hiking trip together over a system of mountain trails in some wilderness country that both have heard about and wanted to see, and that they have enthusiastically started out upon their trek. M has high n end, but, F, though quite capable of making the trip, physically speaking, has low strength on this need. On the second day of what was to have been a four day trip they come to a small mountain hamlet serviced by a bus on a road leading to town, and F decides she has "had it" and insists that she and M abandon their intended goal and go home. She has satisfied her own n end, but poor M is frustrated in the realization of his goal and hence punified. It is not likely that mutual gratification of n end will contribute any positive force to their attraction, but rather the opposite, since a gratification level sufficient for F's strength of n end was inadequately gratifying for M's stronger endurance drive.

The result of the first example, to revert to it, was a happier outcome, that of mutual gratification of each partner's n end, and hence makes a positive contribution to their mutual attraction. The mechanism is a coagential one.

Prediction 31: There will be a small positive correlation between affianced partners on n end.

Outcome: Confirmed at a non-significant level: $r = .16$, $p < .10$.

SUMMARY OF PRINCIPLES OF INTERMOTIVATIONAL MECHANICS

The principles of coinstrumentality of need mechanics in reciprocal need gratification which have been adduced are not nearly as numerous as the predictions which have been derived from them, and which, it has been seen are largely confirmed. Yet, they are sufficiently abundant to justify a recapitulation of them at this point. Additional formulations having to do more with the *dynamics* of intersexual attraction than with the *mechanics* as these do, will be presented in later chapters.

1. *The Postulate of Reciprocality (or of reciprocally gratifying needs)*: Some needs instigate behaviors that are simultaneously gratifying to the person instigated by the need *and* to the interacting other whose behavior is instigated by the *same* need. That is, needs exist that actuate both parties aroused by them in an interaction episode to make responses gratifying both to themselves and to the other; so that both are practically simultaneously both 'producing' gratification for the other as well as 'consuming' the gratifications the other is himself producing.

When individuals encounter and interact with each other and are both actuated by a need of this sort, a strong mutual attraction between persons having similar strengths of such a need would be expected to develop as a result of their interactions. This would be so because each might be expected to produce behaviors of fairly high gratification value to himself and the other in larger quantities than others with disparate strengths of the need.

2. *The Postulate of Conflict and/or Punification Avoidance*: When needs are of such a nature as to instigate behaviors which are punifying to others, a strong force of repulsion would be expected to be generated in cases where two persons each possessed the need in considerable strength. Hence, to minimize or avoid conflict or punification, persons with high strengths of such needs would not be expected to choose each other as partners.

3. *The Postulate of Irrelevance (or of irrelevant need relationships)*: When, in interacting episodes, the interacting parties are instigated by either same or different needs which produce behaviors neither particularly gratifying nor punifying to the other person nor to the one instigated by the need in question, neither appreciable attraction nor repulsion would result.

4. *The Postulate of Adjuvance and Coadjuvance*: When in interaction episodes the behaviors which arise from the instigations of two *given needs*, either the same or different, in the respective actors are capable of simultaneously arousing and gratifying one or more *secondary or associated needs* in each of them, then per-

sons possessing the *given needs* in appreciable strength are likely to be to some extent attracted to each other. The strength of the attraction would be contingent upon the strengths of the given needs and upon whether the behaviors produced through the action of the *given needs* were gratifying or punifying to the other person in the interaction. Even if the *given needs* promote behaviors that are punifying to the other, the gratifications arising from the actions carried out in terms of the secondary or associated needs involved may so exceed the magnitude of the punifications as to result in a *profit* for each of the interacting parties. The net result is attraction rather than repulsion. In cases where the *given needs* are themselves ones promotive of reciprocal gratification, the attraction engendered by them would be enhanced by the additional gratifications stemming from the actions promoted by the *secondary or associated needs.*

Coadjuvance is essentially a mutually facilitative condition, arising from the behavioral interplay between persons in such a manner as to result in reciprocal need gratification of motives the arousal of which was mediated by the behavioral interaction arising originally or principally from the instigation of *other* motives.

5. *The Postulate of Procreance and Coprocreance*: Needs promotive of conflict and competition between persons may instigate cognitive interactions between them that are generative of new ideas, insights, and understandings in one or both parties. Hence, among intellectual persons at least, the mutual repulsion engendered by conflict producing drives is partially countered or negated by positive forces of attraction which are also engendered. This is regarded as essentially a special case of coadjuvance.

6. *The Postulate of Vicariousness and Covicariousness*: Needs which motivate behaviors productive of effects and consequences which are perceptible or cognizable to others, such that gratification may be supplied vicariously via these psychological processes, engender forces of attraction. The forces of attraction thus produced may counter or negate any forces of repulsion generated by the needs in behavioral interaction. Inasmuch as both partners may be engaged in such a process in their interactions, a mechanism of covicariousness is posited.

7. *The Postulate of Agentiality and Coagentiality*: Needs which

generate behaviors which are instrumental to the gratification of others may engender considerable forces of attraction toward the person in whom such a need is operative even when the attracted person has little of the same need himself. But, ceteris paribus, when similar strengths of the same need exist in prospective mates, attraction may be mutual on this basis, each being agential to the satisfaction of the other.

8. *The Postulate of Complementarity*: Need complementarity obtains whenever a given need having a more or less distinctive goal exists in one person and requires for its gratification the kinds of behavior motivated by a different need in another person, which need in turn requires for its gratification the kinds of behavior instigated by the first person's need. Whenever persons thus equipped encounter each other powerful forces of attraction would be generated in interactions of these individuals.

Various forms of complementarity such as reciprocal complementarity or cocomplementarity and diffuse complementarity, besides the direct complementarity described above, are posited.

UNITY IN THE DIVERSITY: RECIPROCALITY

Now that each of the coinstrumentalities or mechanisms that have been educed from the preceding analysis stand listed before us it can be seen that there are both similarities and differences among them. While each is sufficiently different from each of the others to make the distinctive identification of it of value from the point of view of its contributing to our understanding, there are basically only two main mechanisms of *reciprocal* need gratification; namely reciprocality and complementarity. The first obtaining when the needs are the same or similar; the second when the needs of the respective interactors are different. Mutual exchanges of gratifications via these, moreover, are the ones most commonly found. Each of the other mechanisms identified are ones that to produce mutual gratification must function reciprocally, **and are** thus essentially merely special cases of reciprocality. Agentiality and adjuvance are, in each case, one way mechanisms in themselves, but do operate reciprocally. Thus what has been termed coagentiality is merely reciprocal agentiality, and what is called coadjuvance is merely reciprocal adjuvance. Procreance, of course, is merely a special case of adjuvance, which, since it can also be reciprocal, is called coprocreance when the reciprocality obtains. Vicariousness, another one-way mechanism, is essentially only a special case of agentiality. Since it can be reciprocal it is, when so, termed covicariousness. Finally since reciprocality of complementarity also commonly obtains we recognize its reciprocal status by the term cocomplementarity. Even simple unidirectional complementarity can be seen, readily enough, to be a kind of reciprocality.

LIMITATIONS TO THE EMPLOYMENT
OF THE MECHANISMS

While the mechanisms of coinstrumentality presented in this chapter, namely; reciprocality, coadjuvance, coagentiality, covicariousness, and complementarity, are proposed as means of understanding and accounting for the phenomenon of similarity of the need strengths of dyadic partners in a love relationship, their limitations must not go unremarked. Not only do they require to be supplemented by additional and more dynamic propositions concerning need relations later to be presented, but no one of them can be automatically and indiscriminately applied to forecasting the direction and magnitude of correlations of any and all needs of interattracted persons. Before any one or more of them is useful, the specific and general properties of the needs one is concerned with must first be identified and understood. Only to the extent that one is successful in doing this will he be able to discern which of the mechanisms applies. An indiscriminate employment of any one mechanism of reciprocal need gratification, be it reciprocality, coagentiality, complementarity or some other, can only result in predictive failures, as the research work which in the past has addressed itself to the issue of similarity vs. complementarity of needs seems clearly to attest.

We are dealing here with phenomena of an extraordinary complexity. Those who expect a theory able to account for intersexual attraction in terms of some single simple formulation such as that of complementarity or symbioticism or what not to be presented here will find themselves unrewarded. Elegant simplicity is usually desired, but can usually be had only for a heavy price, it being possible only for very limited universes of response processes. Even then it is likely to have its simplicity only in virtue of restricting its utility to that of accounting for only the most gross and obvious relationships between or among the variables which it subtends.

One can, of course, err on the side of overelaborateness, too. What is being referred to as instrumental theory is intended to apply to and account for the operation of many variables and forces in intersexual attraction, and for doing so, is expected, when "completed," to consist of a framework of theoretical formulations from which hypotheses can be derived and specific predictions made. Only if these latter are confirmed or measurably supported, of course, will such a framework find acceptance as a valid and useful intellectual resource.

In later chapters, which deal with another problem in the understanding of the attraction phenomenon, most of the additional principles constituent to the instrumental framework will be supplied. However, before the presentation of that material, the theoretical developments and hypotheses already delineated need to be fully evaluated in terms of the research data which was specifically acquired for that purpose. After a brief description of the research method in the following chapter effort will be addressed to that purpose.

CHAPTER SIX

SUBJECTS AND METHOD

IN ORDER TO TEST the predictive efficacy of the instrumental theory, data were cumulatively acquired over a three-year period from a fairly large sample of male and female subjects intimately associated with each other in a dyadic relationship. The principal data, as has been indicated previously, were derived from a modified version of the Edwards Personal Preference Schedule.

SAMPLE

The sample chosen for the present analysis consisted of 71 engaged college student couples; individuals who had made a choice of each other and a commitment to getting married; to being each other's mate. Although the main focus of the theory for the evaluation of which the data collection was intended is with regard to the basis of intersexual attraction and love, rather than simply with mate selection, that choice is here regarded as an equivalent expression of the phenomenon. Persons in the sample chosen, engaged persons, are regarded as having selected a marital partner. That is, in short, saying that what we have here is data considered appropriate for revealing the basis of mate selection, as well as that for attraction and love. Not all researchers would agree that this is the most appropriate kind of sample for an investigation into factors involved in mate selection. Winch (1958, 1968), for example, has argued that couples already married are *the* appropriate sample for such a study, and his own inquiry was based on a sample of 25 already married pairs. Although his couples were married less than two years, such persons must have already experienced the most intensive period of adjustment that occurs in the typical marriage. This has consequences for the need relatedness between them that are totally unknown to us and which might well have been productive of precisely the need relationship found by Winch. If one argues that engaged couples in a substantial percentage of cases (estimates vary from 30-50 percent) will not follow through with marriage and that their mate selection is thus to be considered only tentative, let him remember that the existing divorce rate in our society indicates that marriage is an almost equally tentative choice. College student engaged pairs were employed not only because Winch and others have based their research on college students and there is thus permitted comparisons with this. But also because Murray's need system was derived from the study of them and Edwards' test for measuring the needs was developed by use of and for use with them. They were also more readily available as subjects than representatives of other populations. The latter are neither typically highly motivated to participate in scientific studies nor readily approachable. When they are induced to participate they are even more likely than college students to become subjects because of factors of intelligence and motivation. This may make them more unrepresentative of the population from which they were recruited than college students are of their segment of the population.

Subjects were recruited to the present project variously. In large part this was simply by it being offered as a study in which they could participate for an hour's laboratory credit in any of several psychology courses at UCLA requiring several hours of such participation on the part of any student taking them. In other instances they responded to posted signs on campus bulletin boards which offered them the magnificent sum of $1 per couple for taking part. In still other instances the motivating force exploited was that of cooperating with a highly attractive sorority sister in a project wherein the appeal was made on the latter's part that she needed their cooperation for its expedition. The subjects were a cross-section, more or less, of the heterogeneous UCLA undergraduate population, with every race, creed and color having some representation but none so much so as to markedly represent any minority group except WASPS. Jews were possibly more numerous in the sample than they have been in any previous one used in this type of study, constituting approximately ten percent of the total. This was almost inevitable without deliberate effort being made to exclude them, for their representation in the student body at UCLA has been estimated to be in excess of one-third. All subjects were less than 25 years old, with almost all being under 22. The median age was 20. The rationale for the openness of the sample was simple. There are no data which would indicate that acculturated minority group members, as any of such included were, would deviate sufficiently from the majority as to require being excluded. Once we have the general and global understanding of the phenomena of intersexual dyad formation and mate selection, particular attention to the diverse groups may have more point. Then we can look for exceptions and complications which may be intrinsic in any special characteristics and circumstances of their minority group membership. There was, it should be made clear, no requirement that *both* members of the engaged pair be attending either UCLA or any other college or university. However, a majority of the couples were constituted of fiancés who were both attending UCLA.

THE NEED INDICATOR

Because it seemed possible that some of the conflicting previous findings might have been an artifact of response to the ipsative form of the EPPS, a change to a normative or single stimulus format was devised. Each item of the several need scales was arranged to be responded to independently by the subject by having him indicate on a five-point scale his degree of agreement or disagreement with it. This intensity of response device is not only a logical one, but corresponds to something individuals normally do in real life. It was expected, by thus permitting more latitude of response, that the variability of the resulting scores would be somewhat increased. This was not, however, considered nearly as important a change as the aforementioned one.

A number of analysts (Levonian, Comrey, Levy and Proctor, 1959; Feldman and Corah, 1958; Bendig and Martin, 1962; Scott, 1963) have been highly critical of the properties of the EPPS in its original form. Feldman and Corah concluded that carefully matched items in a forced choice format do not readily minimize the influence of the social desirability factor which this format was devised to control and that the forced-choice method may actually heighten the S's ability to make discriminations on the basis of this factor. Bendig and Martin point out that the ipsative scoring of the EPPS results in indices which are relative rather than absolute measures. It is argued by them that the question concerning correlations among the needs is confounded by the point that ipsative scores must tend to have negative intercorrelations, since a high score on one scale tends to depress scores on the other scales. They also note, as do Levonian, Comrey, Levy, and Proctor, that the application of factor analytic procedures to all 15 ipsative scores is not legitimate because of the lack of experimental independence among the items scored on each scale. This last point was especially important in the decision on format for the present research for it was intended in one aspect of it to make use of factor analytic techniques. Levonian et al also point out that the forced-choice item encourages low reliability of response by presenting to the individual what in some cases appear to be equally applicable statements and in other cases equally inapplicable ones. Difficult choices such as these not only tend thus to maximize the number of unreliable choices for the S, but may create hostility, annoyance, and other negative attitudes promotive of carelessness of response. Besides consideration of these various points, the writer also reflected on the great difference in the forced-choice test and the essentially single stimulus type of question usual in methods like Winch's "need interview." Hence the revision to a normative type of test seemed a quite justified tactic toward making conditions of data collection more uniform between the present investigation and that upon which the complementarity theory was based. The so-called "need interview" employed as the major technique in Winch's research was a relatively "structured" procedure which involved asking questions such as, "how do you feel when someone steps in front of you in a queue in a crowded restaurant?" and "how do you feel when you see your name in print?" (Winch, 1958). The 135 unique items incorporated in the EPPS were ordered in such a fashion that no two indicative of a given need were in consecutive sequence. More specifically, beginning with an item indicative of need for achievement, there followed single items indicative of the needs for deference, order, sex, autonomy, dominance, aggression, exhibition, affiliation, succorance, abasement, nurturance, change, endurance and intraception. There then followed another item for achievement, and the occurrence of items indicative of each of the other fourteen needs in accordance with the order described above. It, itself, had been determined on a random basis. With the subject indicating his degree of agreement or disagreement on a five-point scale and nine items for each need, scores for each could range from 0 to 36.

It was reassuring to find that test-retest reliabilities of the need measures based on an independently run sample of 56 subjects, with an interval of three weeks between testings, turned out to be quite satisfactory, ranging from .72 to .91.

Subjects were not required to report to the testing place together for taking the test. They could report independently if they found this more convenient, and this was more often the case than not. When they did report together seating was arranged in such a way as to prevent there being any opportunity for them to communicate with each other during the test.

METHOD OF DATA ANALYSIS

The traditional and customary technique for analysis of the sort of data generated by test instruments and obtained without constraints of laboratory design is correlational analysis and interpretation, and it was the method followed in the present investigation also. Although at one time a factor analytic procedure had been planned, this was abandoned when it became obvious that it would take several more years to acquire a sample of engaged couples large enough for such a procedure to be entirely legitimate in terms of the rigorous standards insisted upon by some statisticians. There are those who insist that the sample size at least equal the number of correlations to be computed, because of the supposed inflation of a number of significant correlational values resulting from the interdependence or lack of independence of one's observations.

Such a criticism would seem more appropriate when one is seeking to *extract* meaningful factors from a matrix of correlations than when one is, as here, attempting on the basis of already meaningful theoretical assumptions to predict particular correlational outcomes within such a matrix. As it is, the present study is less vulnerable to criticism on the ground of lack of independence of observations than any previous one of its type in this area of which the writer is aware. The sample here is, for instance, more than two and one-third times the size of that employed in the Banta and Hetherington 1963 study which has been so often mentioned in the foregoing. Any inflation in the number of significant correlations here would be less than any such that would be obtained with a sample of smaller size. The fact that the present study looks at all 225 possible correlations in the matrix rather than with just 15, as other studies have, makes no difference whatever, since the 15 in question in any case each come from the same "contaminated" matrix. Even given some inflation of correlational values such that an .01 significance level correlation is "really" only an .025 level one, the reduction in confidence is not so great as to occasion great dismay. The optimistic expectation in pursuing the course taken was that the major points of theory for which confirmation was sought in the correlational analysis would require almost no more. That is to say, even if no bit of attention were paid to correlational values lower than the nominal .01 level, the major theoretical contentions could almost rest their case with no more than those at such a figure.

PROVISION OF A CONTROL GROUP

None of this should be interpreted as a counsel for cursoriness of procedure, but only as one of reasonableness of same. To increase confidence, resort was also had to a control device believed to be as scientifically rigorous as any it is possible to employ in research of this nature. This contrivance consisted in the establishment of what, in effect, constitutes a comparison control group by random pairings of male and female subjects from the same sample of 71 original couples. More specifically, the contrived matings were accomplished simply by pairing a given male subject at random with a female S, who was in no case his actual love partner, although she was from the same sample of people involved in the study.

Such a procedure is, in correlational research, an attempt to approximate the function of a control group in a manipulative experiment. In one of these, some response effect that the experimenter has hypothesized to be due to or influenced by some causal agent or determinant is measured in one case, that of the experimental group, with the presumed determinant of the effect having been deliberately varied or manipulated to test for its significance.

In the other, the case of the control group, it is measured under circumstances wherein the presumed determinant has not been varied or manipulated. In this design, if the effect is measurably more present in the experimental group than it is in the control group, it is inferred that the presumed determinant produced the difference. If, on the other hand, the effect is present in undifferentiated magnitude in both groups the experimenter concludes that the hypothecated determinant was not actually an effective one.

The effect with which we are concerned here, a reciprocal condition of being in love and engaged between pairs of Ss has, of course, already occurred. The relationship obtains in its natural condition only in the "experimental" group, for the pairs of subjects in the control group are not in love with each other, even if each is in love with someone else in our "experimental" sample. What is presumed to be different between the two is that which we are employing as an index to the determinants of the effect; namely particular patterns and degrees of likenesses and differences in motivational intensities of various kinds obtaining between the love partners. These, it is expected, will be revealed to be present in the patternings of the direction and magnitudes of correlations of the partners' need scores on the test they have taken. These indices of our presumed determinants of the love obtaining between our subjects, if they truly are that, should not be present nearly to the same extent between pairs of Ss who are not in love with each other. If they were present this would indicate their lack of any power in producing the effect for which they were presumed to be responsible, since the effect itself is not present in the control group.

It should be recognized that such a procedure by no means minimizes the likelihood of similarities in patterning and values on the particular correlational indices of our determinants being found between the "experimental" and control groups. Rather, such an opportunity is maximized. And for these reasons:

1. The same condition of heightened affect of a distinctive quality, namely, being in love, characterizes the individuals in both groups. A randomly paired sample of couples *not in love* with anyone at the time of measurement would be less similar

to the *in-love* couples of the "experimental" group.

2. The age, general intellectual level, life style, cultural background, race, religion, place of residence, institutional affiliation and other personal and demographic characteristics as obtain in the "experimental" group are duplicated in the control, not on a deliberately matched basis to be sure, but, nevertheless, as a restricted pool of possibilities. Hence, they are more likely on a chance basis to match those of given pairs of actual partners than would otherwise be the case. If the control group had been a non-university, non-west coast, non-southern California or even a non-UCLA randomly mated sample of couples there would be less likelihood of coincidences of correlations between such couples and those of the "experimental" group with respect to the need variables in question.

3. There is a greater likelihood, of similarities of motivational, characteristics, abilities, aptitudes and other personality variables existing between the "experimental" and control groups than in any other case. That is, a control group selected at random from any other population aggregate would be less like the "experimental" group in these respects.

4. Any factors such as test format, non-independence of observation, procedural peculiarities of either data collection or analysis, and in fact any others that might conceivably influence a correlational finding from the experimental group in a given direction, would equally affect results in the control.

CHAPTER SEVEN

EVALUATION OF THE THEORY OF AN ORDER OF PRIMACY OF LOVE'S DETERMINANTS AND THE THEORY OF INTERMOTIVATIONAL MECHANICS

SOME GENERAL POINTS ABOUT THE OUTCOME

THE FIRST THING to note concerning the results of the study is that the revised form of administering and scoring the need measuring schedule eventuated in quite symmetrical and normal distributions of scores for both sexes on all of the 15 need variables. It is not possible to make precise comparisons between these and the EPPS originals, but in terms of Edwards' own statement (Edwards, 1959) this accords with them. Also notable is the fact that the scoring scheme used in the present study, although designed to increase the variability of scores, had no such effect, on the whole, for the signas, were quite similar to those obtained by Edwards. What is most important, it is thought, is the fact that the pattern of differences between the sexes on the various measures of needs remains quite similar to that found for the national college student sample by Edwards. In Table VII is noted the mean score on each need obtained by each sex group as well as the differences between the sexes in terms of excess of mean score of one group over that of the other on particular needs. In Table VIII are shown comparisons of the rank orders of sizes of differences between means of males and females in Edwards' normative college student samples and those obtained in the present study. While the correspondences are not perfect, they are on the whole quite close, with the notable exception of the placement of n sex, which, while first in the Edwards' sample, is only fifth in the present one. Some comment on this latter will be offered presently, but not before some note is taken of the signifi-

TABLE VII
MOST IMPORTANT NEEDS OF MALES AND FEMALES
A: In Terms of Mean Scores on Each Need, and
B: In Terms of Difference in Mean Scores From Other Sex

A: Mean Scores of Each Sex on Each Need			
Males	*Mean*	*Females*	*Mean*
Achievement	28.155	Affiliation	27.930
Sex	27.563	Nurturance	27.620
Nurturance	25.690	Change	26.592
Affiliation	25.648	Achievement	26.014
Change	25.423	Sex	25.845
Intraception	24.634	Intraception	25.789
Endurance	23.479	Order	23.972
Autonomy	23.099	Succorance	23.634
Order	22.887	Deference	22.873
Dominance	22.873	Endurance	22.296
Deference	22.577	Autonomy	21.338
Succorance	22.183	Abasement	20.465
Exhibition	19.690	Dominance	18.648
Abasement	19.000	Exhibition	18.254
Aggression	16.915	Aggression	13.563

B: Most Important Differences From Opposite Sex In Terms of Excess of Mean Score			
Males	*Mean*	*Females*	*Mean*
Dominance	4.226	Affiliation	2.282
Aggression	3.352	Nurturance	1.930
Achievement	2.141	Abasement	1.465
Autonomy	1.761	Succorance	1.451
Sex	1.718	Change	1.169
Exhibition	1.436	Intraception	1.155
Endurance	1.183	Order	1.085
		Deference	.296

cance of the generally quite reassuring correspondences in the two patterns of differences.

This is important because, did it not obtain, much of the theoretical development which has been presented in the foregoing pages and that which is to be presented later would seem to have little basis in reality. It is important, again, because the demonstration of the facts of close correspondence in patterning of differences between the sexes indicates that the elimination of the supposed control (the forced-choice format) for the social desirability factor does not in any essential respects alter the outcomes of the tests. Thus, what findings are reported here cannot be interpreted as arti-

TABLE VIII

A COMPARISON OF THE RANK ORDERS OF THE SIZES OF
DIFFERENCES IN MEANS BETWEEN MALES AND FEMALES ON
FIFTEEN NEED VARIABLES OBTAINED BY EDWARDS WITH HIS
NORMATIVE COLLEGE STUDENT SAMPLES WITH THOSE
OBTAINED IN THE PRESENT STUDY

Rank Order of Variables on Which Males Mean Scores Were Higher		*Rank Order of Variables on Which Females Mean Scores Were Higher*	
Edwards $N = 760$	Centers $N = 71$	Edwards $N = 749$	Centers $N = 71$
Sex	Dominance	Abasement	Affiliation
Dominance	Aggression	Affiliation	Nurturance
Achievement	Achievement	Nurturance	Abasement
Aggression	Autonomy	Succorance	Succorance
Autonomy	Sex	Change	Change
Exhibition	Exhibition	Intraception	Intraception
Endurance	Endurance	Deference	Order
		Order	Deference

facts of social desirability responses occurring through a lack of control for them.

As for an interpretation of the difference in the ranking of n sex, which was the most distinctively male linked need of all in Edwards' study, but only fifth in that respect in the present one, it is believed that it is essentially simply an artifact of the forced choice format of the original EPPS. In responding to it individuals are required to choose repeatedly between two alternatives wherein items indicative of the sex drive as well as other given needs are paired in each instance with one of the items indicative of one of the other needs. The following are some examples:

A. I like to praise someone I admire.
B. I like to be regarded as physically attractive by those of the opposite sex.

A. I like to keep my things neat and orderly on my desk and workspace.
B. I like to be in love with someone of the opposite sex.

A. I like to become sexually excited.
B. I like to accept the leadership of people I admire.

The writer wishes to suggest that comparisons of this sort are not very much like any choices any of us make any time, forced or otherwise. But, when one *is* forced to choose between being sexually excited or being deferent, being regarded as physically attractive to those of the other sex or being deferent, etc., there is no contest, and being sexually aroused etc. is so far more appealing that it gets the preference. This sort of thing, being done repeatedly tends, it is thought, to exaggerate or inflate males' scores on the n sex scale. The same sort of thing may occur with respect to other need scores, but this seems the most obvious instance of the presumed effect.

It is believed that the single item format used in the present study represents a more realistic and less biasing situation for accurately gauging the importance of n sex relative to the strengths of other needs. In this format the respondent simply indicates the degree of his agreement or disagreement with each of the items standing alone. If any comparison process is involved in such a procedure, it would seem to be one implicitly taking into account the whole sample of gratifying experiences of any sort that the respondent has ever known. It is thus being contended here that there would be a greater likelihood of the subject's responses being an accurate expression of the relative strengths of his various motivational orientations than in the former case.

VINDICATION OF THE POSITION ASSIGNMENTS OF DOMINANCE AND AFFILIATION

The last point is important, not alone in a general sense, but especially so with respect to its bearing upon a position taken in Chapter Four of this work, wherein the formulation of the theory of the hierarchical order of determinative importance of particular needs was set forth. It will be recalled that there, with regard to a prospective testing of the theory concerning the dynamics of the postulated need for maintenance and enhancement of sexual identity and role, that a position contrary to what would be indicated by Edwards' normative data was taken. It was predicted that the highest correlation on *different* needs between male and female lovers would be found between the need most closely linked to the male identity on the one hand and the one most closely linked to the female identity on the other. In the face of Edwards' data to the contrary, which indicates n sex as the closest male linked need, dominance, second in terms of his findings (see Table VIII) was assigned this role. Further, instead of assigning to abasement the corresponding part for the female, affiliation, again second in position in Edwards' findings, was chosen. The data under analysis now were not available then, hence the assignment of first place to dominance had to be on rational rather than empirical grounds. To have presented these there, it was pointed out then, would have been awkward. But, now, with the advantage of the preceding discussion it is less so. It was quite simply on the theoretical ground that the forced choice format of Edwards' test artifactually exaggerates the importance of n sex, and more so than is the case with pratically any other need. The data submitted in Table VIII tend to support this hypothesis, for, as noted previously, sex falls to fifth place in importance as a male linked drive in the newly obtained ranking, with dominance moving up to first. It is believed, then, on both rational and empirical grounds that this is its appropriate place.

The rationale for rejecting abasement as the most importantly female linked need and replacing it with affiliation, which in Edwards' normative data was second, was quite different. It was simply that abasement as measured by the EPPS is not a need for abasing oneself at all, but a feeling or attitude of inferiority. The reasoning for this reconceptualization has been given in previous discussions at some length, however, and hence, will not be repeated here. It is worth noting, of course, that the data acquired with the single item format of the Personal Preference Schedule fully justifies affiliation being assigned first in position of importance among female linked needs. The abasement variable drops to third place in the revised scheme.

EVALUATION OF THE THEORY OF THE PRIMACY OF DETERMINATIVE IMPORTANCE OF PARTICULAR NEEDS

The Places of Sex and the Need for Affectional Intimacy

It will be recalled that in a previous chapter a theory was presented that, drawing upon a wide base of cultural, social and psychological facts, distinguished five needs from all others as those having the greatest degrees of determinative significance in intersexual attraction and love. These were further distinguished among themselves in causal efficacy with a hierarchical ordering of importance being postulated. This was as follows: 1. sex, 2. need for affectionate intimacy (affiliation), 3. need for maintenance and enhancement of sexual identity and role, 4. need for interpersonal security, and 5. need for self-esteem (in the general sense).

The data collected in the present study, as previously noted, provides information useful for evaluating the relative importance of only the first three of these, sex, affiliation, and sexual identity. The indices by which the relative importance of the first two, sex and affiliation may be assessed are, of course, simply the correlation magnitudes between the scores of lovers on measures of these needs themselves, as derived from the Personal Preference Schedule. The index to the identity variable is far less direct. It was pointed out in the chapter where the operation of this drive was initially postulated, that the gratification of the sexual identity need was a derived one. It was noted that it was contingent upon the gratification of the important sex linked needs of the individual, which themselves differ with his sex membership. Since this was so, an indirect index of its determinative significance, employing these sex linked needs would have to be used. For the male the needs in question are, in order of importance of sex linkage, using the data of the present sample as the basis for establishing it: dominance, aggression, achievement, autonomy, sex, exhibition and endurance. For the female the most important, again in rank order, are affiliation, nurturance, succorance, change, intraception, order and deference. Abasement is eliminated for reasons previously stated.

It was maintained that an indication of the importance of the sexual identity drive in attraction could be found in the relative magnitudes of the correlations between the most saliently sex linked needs of one sex and the most prominantly sex linked needs of the other in comparison with sex linked needs of lesser importance in the respective cases. Further, it was noted that the two most importantly sex linked needs were dominance for the male, on the one hand, and affiliation for the female on the other. It was, hence, deemed critical for the plausibility of the theory that these be the two needs most highly correlated across gender of all those under consideration. It was additionally specified, of course, that the correlation be in the gendericly congruent direction, m dom-f aff, and not the reverse.

Let us now attempt to evaluate these theoretical notions in terms of the data that have essential relevance to them. In Table IX is summarized a part of the information in point. There it can be clearly seen that the correlational value for sex *is* distinctly the highest of all the correlations obtained (.64). This is followed closely by the correlation for affiliation (.56) and it, in turn, quite closely by the cross-need, cross sex correlation m dominance-f affiliation (.50). Given that each of these is an appropriate index to each of the respective motivational variables in question, and accepting the magnitude of the coefficient of correlation as an appropriate indicator of determinative significance, it is clear that the conception of their relative importance stated in the theory is supported. Certainly it at least is highly congruent with the obtained data. As anticipated, inasmuch as each of these variables was believed to be of major determinative importance, the differences in magnitudes of the correlations between them are each too small in value, in a sample of this size, to reach conventional significance levels.

Fortunately, however, an alternative way of assessing the probability of this resulting order being a non-chance outcome exists. Of the 225 correlations contained in the 15×15 matrix, the chance probability that one would find the m-f sex, m-f affiliation, and m dom-f aff correlations assuming first, second and third place in ranking by magnitude as predicted is $p = 1/225 \times 1/224 \times 1/223 = .0000000889 = 8.89 \times 10^{-8}$.

In a circumstance of this sort one can, of course, seek confirmation in corroborative data from other investigations. There have been several other studies carried out which employed the EPPS as the instrument for measuring the needs of engaged couples, and from which data indicating the relative correlational magnitudes of sex, affiliation *and* m dom-f aff might be expected to be presented. However, there is, unfortunately, a complete uniformity in their omission to do so. Hence, the placement of the sexual identity drive in relation to the other two must rest entirely on the data of the present research for the time being. With regard to sex and affiliation, the situation is somewhat better, but not as good as one would wish. Winch (1958) chose not to deal with the sex need at all in his study. Bowerman and Day (1956) did measure n sex along with the other needs, since they employed the EPPS, but they do not report correlational values for either it or for affiliation. The same is true with regard to the investigation of Schellenberg and Bee

TABLE IX

CORRELATIONS OF THE FIFTEEN *SAME* NEEDS AND THE FIFTEEN HIGHEST CROSS NEED-CROSS SEX ONES FOR BOTH ACTUAL LOVE PARTNERS AND RANDOMLY PAIRED MALES AND FEMALES

Same Needs	Actual	Random	Difference Value Fisher's Z	<p	Different Needs	Actual	Random	Difference Value Fisher's Z	<p
Sex	.64*	.12	.64	.001	M Dom-F Aff	.50*	-.08	.63	.001
Affiliation	.56*	.05	.58	.001	M Int-F Aff	.47*	-.12	.63	.001
Nurturance	.36*	-.11	.49	.005	M Dom-F Sex	.43*	.06	.40	.01
Change	.30*	-.09	.40	.01	M Exh-F Sex	.43*	-.11	.51	.001
Deference	.29*	.12	.18	ns	M Aut-F Aff	.42*	-.08	.53	.001
Order	.27†	-.02	.30	.05	M Ach-F Aff	.41*	-.13	.57	.001
Abasement	.26†	.03	.23	ns	M Aff-F Nur	.40*	.00	.42	.01
Succorance	.23†	.07	.16	ns	M Sex-F Aff	.39*	-.06	.47	.005
Exhibition	.19	-.21	.40	.01	M Exh-F Aff	.37*	.09	.30	.05
Intraception	.17	-.02	.19	ns	M Ach-F Nur	.36*	.05	.33	.025
Endurance	.16	.05	.11	ns	M Chg-F Aff	.34*	-.11	.46	.005
Dominance	.16	-.03	.19	ns	M Suc-F Aff	.34*	-.12	.47	.005
Achievement	.13	.02	.20	ns	M Exh-F Ach	.33*	-.10	.44	.005
Autonomy	.13	-.06	.19	ns	M Int-F-Nur	.33*	.01	.33	.025
Aggression	.06	-.01	.07	ns	M-Suc-F Nur	.33*	.09	.25	ns

Significance levels of rs: * = .01; † = .05.

(1960), Day (1961) and Becker (1964). The Kerckhoff and Davis study (1962), since it did not employ the EPPS, contains, of course, no data with respect to sex and affiliation.

However the findings of the present investigation are more or less corroborated in both the Banta and Hetherington (1963) study involving a sample of 29 engaged couples, and that of Murstein (1961) involving a sample of 20 newlywed couples and 48 "long-wed" couples. The Banta and Hetherington correlation on sex was .79 and those of Murstein .63 for the newlyweds and .50 for the "longweds." Affiliation in the Banta and Hetherington study was correlated .24; for Murstein it was .30 for newlyweds and .83 for "longweds." In Murstein's study sex and affiliation were the two most highly correlated variables in his "longwed" couples except for autonomy, which exceeded sex. Sex and affiliation were also the two most highly correlated variables in his newlywed sample except for dominance and change, which exceeded affiliation. What accounts for these variations is puzzling. It is probably a compound of several factors; such as size of samples, the composition of samples, the difference in the measuring instrument, and the somewhat different regional norms obtaining in the respective locations; Los Angeles in the present study, Seattle in Murstein's, Madison, Wisconsin in the Banta and Hetherington case. The present study has the merit of a much larger sample, and, it is believed, a more valid test, but can in no other important respect be clearly seen to be preferred as a basis of fact than the Wisconsin investigation. Murstein's samples were not only both smaller than the present one, but also introduce forces of an unknown magnitude in the fact that his couples were married for varying lengths of time.

Both Murstein and the Banta and Hetherington report are in agreement in finding sex more important than affiliation in their young samples and to that extent corroborate the findings reported here. The finding that sex is replaced in the first position of importance in Murstein's longwed couples by affiliation is intuitively rather simply understood as an adaptation effect in respect to the sex drive widely observed to occur with age and loss of the novelty in sexual stimulus value of a partner that also occurs over time. Murstein's longweds were on the average nearly 37 years old and had been married for nearly twelve years. His newlyweds were not quite 23 years old, as an average figure, and had been married only slightly more than one year.

What is most puzzling about these comparisons is the wide discrepancy between them in the findings with regard to affiliation. Murstein's study is much closer to the present one than the Banta and Hetherington one in this respect. The findings of the latter cannot, as can those of Murstein, be readily accounted for as a change in need strengths over time and circumstances. Further research may be able to offer some clarification of the matter, and toward this end a more adequate measure of the need for affectionate intimacy than the present EPPS Affiliation Scale provides would surely be of service.

That in this sample, at least, affiliation can be accorded a place second only to sex seems quite demanded when one examines the cross need-cross sex correlations arrayed in Table IX. In these highest fifteen such correlations only ten of the needs in the system have any representation, and the ubiquitousness of affiliation in this list is truly impressive. Into the fifteen combinations there, it enters into over one half; eight times in fact. It exceeds its nearest competitor, a close relative, an affectional need with strength property, nurturance, by being twice as frequently present. It is also, more often than the latter, present in the higher ranking combinations in terms of the correlational values. Sex appears in one of these combinations with affiliation, but is represented twice more, at still higher values, in combination with dominance and exhibition respectively. In the latter two cases it is female sex paired with each of these needs of the male. It is characteristic of these cross need-cross sex correlations of highest magnitudes that the need with the greater affectional property (sex itself has affectional property) be represented by the score of the female on the need. Affiliation conforms to this positional relationship, and in fact, in seven of the eight instances of its presence it is *female* affiliation that is involved. Only in its relationship with nurturance, the female linked affectional drive which has the highest strength property, does affiliation appear as a male need. Here, incidentally, there is either reciprocality or cocomplementarity operating as a mediating mechanism but, quite possibly, both.

Another point to be noted concerning the cross need-cross sex correlated pairs shown in Table IX is that practically one half of the 15, namely m int-f aff, m aff-f nur, m sex-f aff, m chg-f aff, m suc-f aff, m int-f nur and m suc-f nur are composed of needs both of which have some *affectional property*. Regrettably, a full discussion of the various properties of needs does not appear until the theory of intermotivational dynamics is presented in later chapters. But, if the reader can either find this assignation of affectional property intuitively obvious or can accept it tentatively, "on faith," he will be able to see that the facts noted are also supportive of the theory of the importance of the need for affectionate intimacy.

It will be recalled that in the earlier discussion of the primacy of importance of particular needs in attraction, that Murray's main affection need, affiliation, was adopted as the foremost embodiment of the posited need for affectionate intimacy, and until some better measure to represent the latter is discovered or developed, so it shall remain. But, it will be argued later on in the present work, in the chapters dealing with intermotivational dynamics, nurturance, sex, succorance, intraception and others, to a minor degree, have affectional properties. This being so, it is argued in the later context, has the consequence that in interpersonal interchanges involving these needs, exchanges of affection, along with exchanges of other gratifications uniquely pertaining to each of them, are integrant to the transactions. Thus, in other words, the need for affectional intimacy is not, as conceived of here, limited in its indicators to just what of it is embodied in the measure of n affiliation. It spreads itself as a dynamic across several particular motivational modules as its vehicle and finds gratification in a variety of guises.

Referring to the list of cross need-cross gender correlations noted in Table IX once more, it is observed that the proportion of the need appearances in the juxtapositions there which is occupied by needs with appreciable to great affectional value; namely aff, nur, sex, def, int, suc and chg, is truly large, 21/30 (70%). If one accepts the view of the writer as tenable, that all of these are at least in part expressors and conveyors of some components of the need for affectional intimacy, then the assignment, to it of a determinative power second only to that of sex seems entirely justifiable. This is strengthened as a conviction when the next highest and statistically significant 30 cross need-cross gender correlations are examined.

Table X has been prepared for this purpose, listing them in their order of magnitude. These same need variables account for 37/60 (61%) of the components there.

Finally, for further evidence for what is asserted, looking at the list of *same* needs in Table IX again, it is notable that third in magnitude behind sex and affiliation, themselves both affectional, is nur-

TABLE X

THIRTY CROSS NEED-CROSS GENDER CORRELATIONS OF NEED
SCORES FOR ACTUAL LOVE PARTNERS AND FOR
RANDOMLY PAIRED PARTNERS

Need by Gender	Actual	Random	Difference Value Fischer's Z	$<p$
M Dom-F Suc	.32*	−.06	.39	.025
M Sex-F Nur	.32	.14	.19	ns
M Chg-F Agg	−.32	−.03	−.30	.05
M Aff-F Agg	−.31	−.09	−.23	ns
M Nur-F Agg	−.30	.03	−.34	.025
M Ach-F Agg	−.30	.08	−.39	.025
M Aba-F Def	.29	−.02	.32	.05
M Def-F Aff	.28	.03	.26	ns
M Agg-F Sex	.28	−.02	.31	.05
M Aut-F Nur	.27	.05	.23	ns
M Aut-F Int	.27	.03	.25	ns
M Exh-F Nur	.27	.24	.03	ns
M Exh-F Chg	.26	−.04	.31	.05
M Dom-F Nur	.26	.17	.10	ns
M Aut-F Agg	−.25	−.03	−.23	ns
M Def-F Chg	.25	−.10	.36	.025
M Dom-F Chg	.25	−.07	.33	.025
M Def-F Nur	.25	.02	.23	ns
M Aff-F Chg	.25	.09	.17	ns
M Def-F Ach	.25	.05	.21	ns
M Exh-F Suc	.25	−.14	.40	.01
M Aba-F Nur	.24	−.15	.39	.025
M Aut-F Suc	.24	−.14	.38	.025
M Nur-F Def	.24	.21	.03	ns
M Int-F Suc	.24	−.16	.40	.01
M Ord-F Sex	.24	.02	.22	ns
M Suc-F Sex	.23	.04	.19	ns
M Int-F Chg	.23	−.10	.33	.025
M Aff-F Int	.22	−.14	.36	.025
M Aut-F Sex	.22	.00	.22	ns

*Value of r required for a given significance level: Above .28 = .01; Above 20 = .05.

turance, which is in a later chapter where the postulate of common and general properties of needs is set out, assigned affectional property second only to affiliation itself (see Table XIV). It is further remarkable, in reference to the ordering of *Same Needs* in terms of correlational magnitude in Table IX, that only one of the eight significant correlations in the list represents a need module having *no* affectional property; namely Order. The others, sex, aff, nur, chg, def, suc and even aba *do have it*. The message in this observation is quite clear. Intersexual attraction and love are responses brought into being primarily, although not entirely, in virtue of the sexual and affectional gratifications male and female exchange with each other. People, of course, have always known this, but here is now data to document the knowing. It is fitting too, that far at the bottom of the list, with an exiguous .06 correlation, is aggression; the only need with pronounced hostility property.

THE NEED FOR SEXUAL IDENTITY MAINTENANCE AND ENHANCEMENT

In Table IX, extending upward from the nadir need in apparent attractiveness, aggression, to the affectional need, succorance, is an assemblage of need modules having such low correlational values as to suggest them to be of no considerable importance in the formation of love relationships between male and female. None of their values achieve the level of .05 significance usually considered the sine qua non for any serious attention as witness of anything of much consequence in the world of psychological data. With one exception, that of n exhibition their values in the case of actual love partners, again, are insufficiently differentiated from those obtaining as correlations between randomly paired partners for the difference to reach a significance criterion. They are, then, merely chance occurrences? The writer does not think so. Many pages antecedent, in the chapter wherein the sexual identity drive was first proposed and the various aspects of the generic congruency factor were discussed, *they were predicted to be low.*

The underlying dynamic condition responsible for these several small correlations, except that for intraception, is the operation of the need for sexual identity and role maintenance. They are, each of them, to varying degrees genericly linked with masculine identity. Males, as was noted many times is the foregoing, are, in terms of their animating needs within our purview, most distinctly differentiated from females in measures of them. Further, they are typically, any of them, save perhaps endurance, when found in a female personality in high degrees of strength, not a cause of attraction toward her, but repulsion instead. High degrees of them when present in both prospective partners, other things being equal, are conflict and punification producing. The low correlations result from the requirement of unequal development here. Males encountering females with the strong behaviors that devolve upon these needs are, unless they themselves are much stronger, so discouraged or defeated in the contest of assertion and control engendered as to retreat to a more tractable relationship with a more sequatious female. Therein, and not in the former relationship, can the male establish more fully, maintain and enhance his sexual identity and role, and therein too, and not, again, in the former case, can the female do likewise. It is a confounding circumstance, too, that though the partner wanted by the female must have the behaviors that devolve upon these needs so sufficiently salient as to endow him with the puissance of maleness, he is valued highly if he is also equipped with an affectionate tenderness and perceptive understanding of her own needs and impulses. That is to say, as long as he provides the masculine strength she requires, his possession of many of the affectionate qualities she herself has makes him more, not less, attractive to her. Very commonly she wants him to have a certain measure of dependency (succorance) along with all the rest in order that she can in some measure gratify her nurturant need with him. What it all comes to, in a sense, is that the male's identity is threatened when he interacts with a female who has much development of the masculine sort of needs, but she on the other hand, is *not threatened* in relating to a male with many needs like her own. But, while not threatened by male "femininity" in the sense that the male is threatened by female "masculinity," for it to be attractive to her it must be well wrapped in a pattern of masculine strength. It is a coincidence of circumstances hitherto unremarked in this essay that affiliation, the most highly genderically linked drive in the female, is, in the theory of the attraction determinative hierarchy of motives, the second most potent of such. Males must have, along with their more masculine type needs, a great deal of the need for affectionate intimacy and the behaviors it engenders for reciprocal attraction and love relationships with females to be promoted. They do have it in this sample, else the correlation of .56 found here would not obtain.

A quite different correlational value exists between both partners with respect to the dominance drive, the preeminent male need. The limited tolerance in the male to its likeness of magnitude to his own in the female he is attracted to and in love with is indicated by its exiguousness of correlational value as recorded in Table IX. It is third from the bottom place occupied by aggression and amounts to a meagre .16.

But the attractiveness value of dominance behaviors in the male are truly great in our scale of relative values here. Where male and female discover in each other a partner whose behavior invites or permits *him* to express his dominance drive and *her* to express her affiliative need, each is thus able to maximally gratify his need for sexual identity maintenance and enhancement. Look now at Table IX and see the evidence in other cases like the foregoing, reading down the list from m dom-f aff. These cases are those wherein the cross need-cross gender correlation is one between a male linked need on the one hand and a female linked need on the other; vis, m aut-f aff, m ach-f aff, m sex-f aff, m exh-f aff, m ach-f nur. These five plus m dom-f aff represent 60 percent of the top ten highest cross need-cross sex correlations.

A further source of evidence for the operation of the identity drive is found in Table X. Combinations of the above type account for one third of those in the list. These are the sort of correlations which in an earlier chapter were identified as gendericly congruent ones. But the concept was not exhaustively developed there, and there are other types of gendericly congruent relationships that are less obvious. Take, for example, the second highest cross-need, cross-gender correlation after m dom-f aff, namely m int-f aff. Here the genderic congruency is only partial. F aff is where it should be, but m int is not, since it is not as strongly linked to masculinity as to femininity (see Table VII). But intraception ranks only sixth in the eight in the female list, whereas affiliation ranks first. Translated into somewhat different terms, this means that there is far less differentiation in terms of sexual identity for the intraception need than for n affiliation. Hence it represents a less gendericly incongruent relationship, or a more genericly congruent one, than the reverse would be; vis m aff-f int. Of the fifteen highest cross need-cross gender correlations in Table IX four more such genericly congruent ones are found; namely m chg-f aff, m suc-f aff, m int-f nur and m suc-f nur.

Still a third type of generic congruency exists. It is similar to the one just considered, but differs in that both of the needs involved are more male linked than female linked; vis m dom-f sex. This, coincidently, happens to be also third in the list in Table IX. This latter is more congruent genericly than the reverse m sex-f dom, and rather obviously so because dominance is higher in the male ranking, being first in order of importance, whereas sex is only fifth.

Altogether the three types of generic congruency account for twelve (80 percent) of the fifteen highest cross need-cross sex correlations. The three remaining, and incongruent, ones are m exh-f sex, m aff-f nur, and m exh-f ach. Inasmuch as the generic congruency factor has been previously proposed as the clearest indicator of the operation of the sexual identity drive which was postulated as the dynamic circumstance underlying it, and since the generic congruency phenomenon is here found to be present as well as pervasive in its involvement with the very highest cross need-cross sex correlations found between love partners, the postulated underlying identity drive cannot but be regarded as a very powerful force.

A useful index to its power is the *generic congruency effect*, a phenomenon observable when the congruent relationship is reversed, such as, instead of m dom-f aff, we have f dom-m aff. The effect in question is identified with the diminution in the correlational value found to accompany the reversal. Examples, and further evidence of the potency of the sexual identity drive are presented in Table XI.

In Table XI are arrayed, in order of magnitude, the 30 highest cross need-cross sex correlations together with the value each has when the correlational direction is reversed. Typically, since most of these 30 highest *r*s are genericly congruent ones, the reversal represents a genericly incongruent relationship. A simple method of arithmetically stating the magnitude of the Generic Congruency Effect is to subtract the value of the incongruent correlation from that of the congruent one; thus, m exh-f aff: .37 minus f exh-

TABLE XI

THE THIRTY HIGHEST CROSS NEED-CROSS SEX CORRELATIONS* OF LOVE PARTNERS SHOWN IN BOTH DIRECTIONS TO REVEAL THE GENDERIC CONGRUENCY EFFECT

Needs by Sex	r With Sexes as In- dicated	r With Sexes Reversed	Generic Congru- ency Effect	Difference Value of r in Terms of Fisher's Z	$<p$
M Dom-F Aff	.50	.04	.46	.51	.02
M Int-F Aff	.47	.22	.25	.29	.05
M Dom-F Sex	.43	.09	.34	.37	.025
M Exh-F Sex	.43	−.11	−.32	.57	.005
M Aut-F Aff	.42	.02	.40	.39	.025
M Ach-F Aff	.41	.17	.24	.27	ns
M Aff-F Nur	.40	.30	−.10	.11	ns
M Sex-F Aff	.39	.11	.28	.30	.05
M Exh-F Aff	.37	−.14	.51	.53	.005
M Ach-F Nur	.36	.16	.20	.22	ns
M Chg-F Aff	.34	.25	.09	.09	ns
M Suc-F Aff	.34	.14	.20	.21	ns
M Exh-F Ach	.33	−.14	−.19	.48	.02
M Int-F Nur	.33	.07	.26	.27	ns
M Suc-F Nur	.33	.07	.23	.27	ns
M Dom-F Suc	.32	.09	.23	.24	ns
M Sex-F Nur	.32	.10	.22	.23	ns
M Chg-F Agg	−.32	.08	−.24	−.41	.01
M Aff-F Agg	−.31	.14	−.17	−.46	.02
M Aut-F Chg	.31	.01	.30	.31	.05
M Nur-F Agg	−.30	.15	−.15	.16	ns
M Ach-F Agg	−.30	.08	.22	.23	ns
M Aba-F Def	.29	.01	−.27	.29	.05
M Def-F Aff	.28	.14	.14	.15	ns
M Agg-F Sex	.28	−.21	.49	.50	.02
M Aut-F Nur	.27	−.04	.31	.32	.05
M Aut-F Int	.27	.07	.20	.21	ns
M Exh-F Nur	.27	−.10	.37	.38	.025
M Exh-F Chg	.26	−.06	.32	.33	.025
M Dom-F Nur	.26	.01	.25	.26	ns

*Value of r required for a given significance level: Above .28 = .01; Above .20 = .05

m aff: —.14 gives a net value for the Genderic Congruency Effect of .51. This is a very large Genderic Congruency Effect as compared with that for the Effect found for the pair of needs change-affiliation, where it is only .09. Typically, again because most relationships wherein the higher *r*s obtain are genderically congruent ones, the value of the Genderic Congruency Effect coincides with the magnitude of the difference in correlational values between the two in the opposite directions. This is not always true, however. An example is the case of m exh-f ach: .33 and f exh-m ach: —.14. The difference in correlation value is .47. Here, since the first relation is an incongruent one, and the second a congruent one with an appropriate negative value, this, changed to positive and then subtracted from the higher and incongruent one leaves a net Genderic Congruency Effect of —.19. This also exemplifies an instance wherein the effect acquires a negative rather than a positive value. The computation of the value of the Genderic Congruency Effect is more than a mere academic exercise, for it facilitates important and revealing comparisons between various sets of need pairings and their resulting correlations. In a later chapter much additional use will be made of it. In examing the values for the Genderic Congruency Effect in Table XI it can be seen that it is typically quite large, being associated with correlational differences found to obtain in reversing the genderic direction which themselves are, in somewhat more than half of the instances, statistically significant ones.

These findings, it seems almost unrequired to say, are highly fulfilling to theoretical demand. They reveal by implication what was earlier claimed; that male and female would seek and find a love partner in interaction and relationship with whom there would be found also maximum gratification of the needs underlying and associated with their respective sexual identities. The gratification is not itself measured and tangibly evidenced, to be sure, but it is compellingly indicated by this indirect means; that is, in finding that the needs for which the gratification would be specifically appropriate are also fittingly associated in greatest strength in these maximally attracted persons.

One final thrust at theory confirmation is afforded in a reckoning of the proportion of occasions in which the needs most strongly linked to the sexual identities of male and female occur as members of pairs which are listed as most highly cross correlated in Table XI; first, in absolute incidence and, second, in a genderically congruent direction. The absolute incidence for various male linked needs which occur in male-female correlations on the male side for these highest 30 cross need-cross sex ones is: dom 4, exh 5, aut 4, ach 3, sex 2, agg 1. Together they constitute 63 percent of all such need appearances on the male side. The corresponding computation of incidences for female needs appearing on the female side reveals the following: int 1, aff 9, chg 2, suc 1, nur 8, def 1. Together they constitute 73 percent of the needs appearing on the female side. Only twice, in the case of m exh-f ach, and m exh-f sex does a male need enter into a relatively highly correlating incongruent relationship. This is only 6.7 percent of the 30 possible occasions. The corresponding incidence of genderically incongruent appearances for a female need is once in the 30 opportunities, or 3 percent.

Examination of the data in Table XIX (Chapter Eleven) for additional cross need-cross sex correlations meeting the .05 confidence criterion reveals that their inclusion into consideration would require no essential change in the result of the preceding analysis. Once more the data seems highly corroborative of the theory of the operation of the sexual identity drive in intersexual attraction and love, and, to accord it a determinative rank second only to the need for affectionate intimacy seems compellingly justified.

Beyond sex, affiliation and sexual identity one can seek to find in the empirical data clues to the relative determinative importance of various other interpersonal needs in the schema under examination. Using as a criterion the relative magnitude of coefficients of correlations involving particular needs, and looking at *same* needs first, then clearly nurturance, change and deference would seem to merit places 4, 5 and 6 in a list of determinants in order of importance. Nor does such a ranking seem contraindicated when the magnitudes of *r*s and the frequencies of occurrence of these needs in the cross need correlation list is scrutinized. But this same scrutiny leads to the upgrading to perhaps 7th and 8th places certain needs that on the basis of their smallness of correlations on the *same* needs comparison rank much lower. These are intraception and succorance respectively. M int has an *r* with f aff that is second only to that for m dom-f aff, being .47. Its correlation with f nur is also relatively high: .33. Succorance, both in male and female, in its correlations with "strength" needs across sex; i.e., m suc-f nur, .33 and m dom-f suc, .32, is revealed to be relatively important here. These quite significant *r*s indicate that this dependency need is only slightly less important than the need for interpersonal understanding and support to which intraception seems to be an index.

EVALUATION OF THE THEORY OF NEED MECHANICS

In appraising the utility and value of any theory in the context of science several different criteria may be employed. Three of the most important of these are the predictive power of the theory, its congruency or closeness of fit with the factual data already accumulated, and its effectancy in supplying and describing mediating causative agents or processes to account for the apparent linkage between sets of consequents and their supposed antecedents. While the appraisers may be swayed somewhat by the persuasive effectancy of the theory's advocate in the latter case, it is ultimately the evaluator's own judgment that decides the issue. In the instance of the first two criteria an effective marshalling of the evidence and its credibility are the deciding factors.

The data which are most relevant to the evaluation of the theory of need mechanisms are arrayed in Table XII, where each of the correlations the nature of which were predicted from the analysis in terms of need mechanics are revealed and other facts pertaining to each of them are indicated. The numbers of the predictions are indicated to facilitate reference to the sequential location at which each of them was put in appearance in the textual material of Chapter Five. Certain predictions, namely 5, 11, 14, 17, 19, 20, 21, 22, 23 and 28, which were advanced in the course of that chapter are omitted from those listed. The reason is that these designated ones are not predictions devolving primarily upon the principles of intermotivational mechanics. In the cases of numbers 11, 17 and 28, the predictions were based upon the principle of intermotivational dynamics previously referred to as the postulate of genderic congruency. Their positive outcomes offer additional support for the posited operation of the need for sexual identity and role maintenance rather than serving to demonstrate the efficacy of one of the postulated mechanisms.

Predictions 5, 19, 20, 21, 22 and 23 are excluded from con-

TABLE XII

OUTCOMES FOR CORRELATIONS PREDICTED ON THE BASIS OF PRINCIPLES OF INTERMOTIVATIONAL MECHANICS

Prediction No.	Needs Correlated	Direction (+ = Positive)		Magnitude		P (one tail)	Correlation in Randomly Paired Partners	Difference Value, Fisher's Z	<P	Correlation in B & H Study	Hypothesized Mediating Mechanism
		Predicted	Obtained	Predicted	Obtained						
1	M Sex-F Sex	+	+	Moderate to high	.64	.01	.12	.64	.001	.79	Reciprocality
2	M Aff-F Aff	+	+	Moderate	.56	.01	.05	.58	.001	.24	Reciprocality
3	M Agg-F Agg	+	+	Small	.06	.30	−.01	.07	ns	.16	Coadjuvancy
4	M Dom-F Dom	+	+	Small	.16	.10	−.03	.19	ns	.25	Coadjuvancy
6	M Ach-F Ach	+	+	Small	.13	.15	.02	.20	ns	−.01	Coagentiality
7	M Suc-F Suc	+	+	Moderate	.23	.05	.07	.16	ns	.36	Cocomplementarity
8	M Nur-F Nur	+	+	Moderate	.36	.01	−.11	.49	.005	.16	Cocomplementarity
9	M Suc-F Nur	+	+	Small	.33	.01	.09	.25	ns	?	Complementarity
10	M Nur-F Suc	+	+	Small	.07	.25	.02	—	ns	?	Complementarity
12	M Exh-F Exh	+	+	Small to Moderate	.19	.10	−.21	.40	.01	.39	Cocomplementarity
13	M Def-F Def	+	+	Small	.29	.01	.12	.18	ns	.52	Reciprocality

TABLE XII (Continued)

Pre-diction No.	Needs Correlated	Direction (+ = Positive) Predicted	Direction (+ = Positive) Obtained	Magnitude Predicted	Magnitude Obtained	P (one tail)	Correlation in Randomly Paired Partners	Difference Value, Fisher's Z	<P	Correlation in B & H Study	Hypothesized Mediating Mechanism
15	M Dom-F Def	+	+	Small	.19	.10	.09	—	ns	?	Complementarity
16	M Def-F Dom	+	+	Small	.15	.15	.04	—	ns	?	Complementarity
18	M Aut-F Aut	+	+	Small to Moderate	.13	.15	-.06	.19	ns	.39	Cocomplementarity
24	M Int-F Int	+	+	Small to Moderate	.17	.10	-.02	.19	ns	.38	Cocomplementarity
25	M Aba-F Aba	+	+	Small	.26	.05	.03	.23	ns	.44	Reciprocality
26	M Aba-F Nur	+	+	Small	.24	.05	-.15	—	ns	?	Complementarity
27	M Nur-F Aba	+	+	Small	.18	.10	.01	—	ns	?	Complementarity
29	M Chg-F Chg	+	+	Small to Moderate	.30	.01	-.09	.40	.01	.29	Reciprocality
30	M Ord-F Ord	+	+	Small to Moderate	.27	.05	-.02	.30	.05	.48	Coagentiality, Coadjuvancy
31	M End-F End	+	+	Small	.16	.10	.05	.11	ns	.51	Coagentiality, Coadjuvancy

sideration in evaluating the theory of intermotivational mechanics because they were based essentially on postulates concerning relationship between intrapsychic motivational dynamics and intermotivational forces. They are dealt with in considerable detail in a later chapter.

Prediction 14 is omitted too, because it is only marginally relevant to the purpose before us. It was based primarily on the hypothesis that the importance of a given need (in this case, deference) in effecting intersexual attraction is a partial function of the relative importance of the given need in the motivational structure of a particular group of individuals as compared to other groups. On the assumption that deference was a need of greater importance in a presumably more conventional Mid-Western (Wisconsin) sample than in a less conventional UCLA subject group, the correlation between fiancés was predicted to be lower in the latter group than in the former. The prediction was, it will be recalled, supported.

Attending now to the data in Table XII, and assuming that the degree of correspondence of outcomes with those predicted is an entirely appropriate criterion in terms of which to validate the postulated set of interpersonal need gratification mechanisms which collectively comprise the theory of intermotivational mechanics, the facts are, on the whole, quite supportive, indeed. The direction of each of the 21 correlations obtained is in agreement with what was predicted. This is not a highly exacting criterion, of course, and more reassuring is the fact that in practically all instances the obtained correlation also falls within the range of magnitude predicted for it. The lone exception is in the case of the correlation on succorance, wherein moderate was predicted but small was obtained.

In statistical terms the results are not as impressive as the facts just recounted, but ten of the 21 correlates are large enough to meet the conventionally respected .05 level of significance, and six additional ones equal or exceed the magnitude required to correspond to the .10 level. When one remembers that most of the correlations were predicted to be small, then the fact that they turn out to be small, and thus some of them nonsignificant in a statistical sense, is far from a discrediting finding. It is confidently believed that had the sample been twice as large as the one employed the resulting correlations would not have been appreciably different in magnitude, but one would, of course, find distinctly more of them meeting the conventional significance criteria.

A still more demanding condition for establishing that these correlational effects are attributable to the postulated causes is the existence of statistically significant differences between the correlations obtaining between actual love partners and those found with randomly paired ones. Again the smallness factor almost defeats us, for such differences as those noted must be of very substantial or large magnitude to meet this exacting statistical criterion. Only in six cases is it met. Yet there is some reassurance in the fact that in all of the remaining instances the obtained correlation for actual partners is larger than the corresponding one for randomly paired partners. Further, the former is invariably in the direction predicted, while in a good many cases, in seven of the 15 nonsignificantly different cases, the latter is in the opposite direction.

Still another evaluation operation which may be employed here is the agreement between one's own results and comparable data independently obtained. Hence, for this purpose the interfiancé correlations secured by Banta and Hetherington ten years ago in Wisconsin, using the original version of the EPPS, have been indicated in Table XII. The writer's predictions for individual outcomes were in most cases essentially similar to those reported by B and H. But the correlations in the present study were also expected to be somewhat higher because it was assumed they would be derived from an improved measuring instrument. As can be seen by inspection of Table XII this expectation was disconfirmed. Predictions at variance with the B and H findings were made in five (1/3 of the) cases, however. Affiliation was expected to show a higher correlation than theirs, as were also achievement and change. Deference and order were predicted to be lower. Only one of these variant predictions, that for change, was disconfirmed. However, with the exception of affiliation, all of these variant predictions were based on assumed differences in the importance of the several need variables in the motivational structures of the respective samples. They did not involve any question of mechanisms of interpersonal need gratification per se; hence are not of evaluative relevance.

Two outstanding correspondences in the two sets of data are with regard to the relative rankings of sex and aggression in both. In the B and H study as well as in the present one sex has the highest interfiancé correlation of all. In both, again, aggression, in correlational magnitude, is either at the lowest point on the list or near it. It is lowest in the present study, but tied with nurturance for next to lowest in the other. Close correspondences in rank order of magnitude of correlations in the two lists are otherwise lacking, but these were not, after all, either predicted or implicitly expected, given the differences in samples and instuments obtaining wherein the respective sets of response data were collected. At the very least the two sets of correlations are in agreement in showing that, considering *same* needs only, there is *similarity* rather than *difference* in partners with respect to them. For, except for the negative .01 *r* for Achievement in the B and H study, all the correlations in both lists are positive, and, in more than half the cases in each, statistically significant.

The last point, that concerning concordance of findings re similarity is in a very real sense the best validation of all those discussed in the foregoing analysis. For, it should be remembered, it was in the attempt to *explain* the fact of similarity that led the writer to develop his system of postulates pertaining to mechanisms of interpersonal need gratification in the first place. In pointing this out the writer must at the same time recognize a possible objection to his manner of representing his evidence. Since the mechanisms were proposed to explain the then already existing empirical findings, and in particular those of the B and H study, there may be to some a questionable propriety in calling what the writer has referred to as "predictions" by precisely that name. Although the so-called predictions are represented as having been developed from theoretical principles, could they not also be seen as merely reaffirmations that the same or similar pattern of outcomes as those already discovered would again be found under only somewhat different conditions? They could be. It does not really matter. Their fit with both the old data and the new is enough, it is thought, to establish a respectable degree of credibility and usefulness for them.

In drawing this conclusion it should be apprehended that in doing so the writer desires it to be clearly understood that the outcomes cited as supporting his posited interpersonal need gratification mechanisms cannot be conceived of as validation for them apart from the simultaneous validation of assumptions made concerning the dynamic properties and interactive consequences of each the need variables under consideration. In the closing section of Chapter Five the point was stressed that the mechanisms could be used effectively only in combination with an adequate understanding of these *intermotivational dynamics.* They were used that way in generating the predictions under review. Thus far, the theory of intermotivational dynamics has been required to be developed only to a very modest degree in accounting for these correlations on same needs, with few general principles (e.g., the principle of punification avoidance) being formulated. In the following chapters the number of these will be greatly augmented as the theory of intermotivational dynamics is more fully developed.

CHAPTER EIGHT

PREPARATIONS FOR A THEORY OF INTERMOTIVATIONAL DYNAMICS: INTERPERSONAL ATTRACTION & REPULSION AS A PARTIAL FUNCTION OF THE GENERAL AND COMMON PROPERTIES OF NEEDS

THE PROBLEM AND THE GOAL OF PREDICTION

"Fools Rush in . . ."

FOR THE ANALYSIS of need mechanics and dynamics operating to produce attraction or repulsion in terms of behaviors instigated by *different* needs, no such solid ground as that provided by the Banta and Hetherington data, which proved so useful for examining the instances of need relatedness for the *same* needs, was found to be available. Winch (1958), and Winch, Ktsanes and Ktsanes (1954), to be sure, present data relevant to 16 pairings of disparate needs in their various works, but cite only the directions of the correlations predicted or predicted and found. Replicative studies have typically followed their example, but in some cases some correlational magnitudes are given as well. These latter are almost always limited to merely those for the 16 need pairings reported in the pioneer study. A great lack of consistency in findings on these type II (Winch's term) complementaries obtains among the various studies, but there has on the whole been revealed a bit more support for the complementary principle for *different* needs than that for *same* needs. If anything at all can be said to have been found with any appreciable consistency it is that complementary relations hold between dominance and deference and nurturance and succorance needs.

178

For combinations, or cross correlations of need pairings other than the original sixteen, few correlations are mentioned, and the findings of Banta and Hetherington are fairly typical with regard to what has been the experience of other researchers in this respect. In addition to examining similarity between pairs of subjects with respect to the *same* need, similarity between pairs of subjects with respect to *different* needs was analyzed by them. The matrix of such cross need correlations includes n (n-1) or 210 correlations in all. For the engaged couples they found only 7 percent of the correlations to be significant at the .05 level, and, they point out, *"most of the need pairings which were significant could not be interpreted in a meaningful pattern on the basis of logic, past research, or theory"* (italics added, Banta and Hetherington 1963, p. 403.)

Such a statement implied strongly that the present enterprise was doomed to failure from the outset. But perhaps, it was thought, meaningful patterns *could* be found if a theory were supplied for that purpose. It was seen that this could be constituted of principles derived from *need motivated behavioral interaction analysis*, the guidelines for which and the application of which, as a method, were described in a preceding chapter. Still, one could expect no better than about 7 percent of the correlations to be significant. No theory could possibly alter that empirical fact. So, to make the endeavor at all worthwhile it had to be accepted at the outset that correlations below the .05 level of significance could still be of interest and value. Predictions concerning the *direction of* the correlations, while a far less rigorous criterion for evaluating hypotheses than the significance value of the rs, are nevertheless of *some* weight in this respect. Precedent for their use in this sense, and with these same motivational variables, has been quite well established, not only in the pioneer investigation of Winch, where, in fact, they constituted his major criterion for evaluating his hypotheses, but in those of his would-be replicators as well. It is, of course, not being proposed here that the .05 significance level be ignored at all, but it is being suggested that it is probably erring on the side of excessive rigor to ignore correlational values which fail to meet it in every case. For there may possibly be discerned in their *patterning* a consistency of conformity to prediction that would more than suggest that such outcomes were not due entirely to chance, but instead to the operation of the very determinative agents hypothesized to produce them. Directionality of a correlation coefficient *is meaningful* as a criterion, even if not a rigorous one. So too, is a statement that the confidence level for a correlation is only .10, .15, .20, or no more than .25, for, assuming that you predicted such a correlation, that means that in only one case out of four is the correlation you predicted attributable to so-called chance factors. Relationships of the magnitudes mentioned, moreover, even if they have quite limited and relatively noncritical value, are commonly not only noted as a 'tentative' sort of support for hypotheses, but also appreciated in an heuristic sense as well. It is generally recognized that possibly under more carefully controlled circumstances, such as those contrived to remove the suspected influence of some suppressor variable, the effects suggested by them might well be revealed to be more salient and reliable. It is in terms of these considerations that the anticipated small correlational values will be regarded here: not as a substitute for the more exacting criteria, but as useful, nonetheless. Besides these considerations, in respect to plans to test predictions with the data to be acquired and being presented in this report, better results than those found before might, it was confidently thought, be forthcoming by obtaining a much larger sample on which to base correlations and by modifying the measuring instrument in certain respects. As indicated in Chapter Six, these plans were carried out.

Even so, the expectation remained that most of the correlations would be small. But this condition has causes, just as any other, and these, too, are of interest to know about. Some of them have already been considered and noted, and additional ones will be pointed out later. Half of the Banta and Hetherington correlations with respect to strengths on the *same* needs between fiancés dealt with in the foregoing section were too small to reach the .05 level of significance. Yet this did not prove a deterrent in accounting for them meaningfully in terms of the postulated principles of intermotivational mechanics, and the predictions made on the basis of the principles was that in most cases they would again be found to be small. *There are causes for correlations being small that are no less important to identify and deal with in predictive science than the causes underlying large correlations.*

In what has preceded it was seen again and again that an important underlying cause for the smallness of the correlation in a given instance of need juxtapositioning was that needs engender behaviors in intersexual interaction that may be both gratifying, and thus generative of forces of attraction, and also punifying, with consequent forces of repulsion being produced. In such cases the obtained correlation could be understood as a net resultant of these conflicting forces. In the task confronting us still more such forces obtrude themselves. But, by identifying them, and understanding their modi operandi, predictions might still, it was thought, with some confidence be made.

Some Dissonance Reduction

A question which may arise in the minds of some readers is that as to why the writer, realizing the severe limitations intrinsic in the circumstances discussed in the foregoing, is insistent upon pursuing such an enterprise as this. Would he not be better advised to attend in his analysis to only those few need variables which have been revealed in previous research to be significantly cross correlated between dyadic partners? It is not thought so. Little that is new could be learned by such a limited analysis. Full exploration may reveal relationships hitherto unsuspected because of previous investigators having concentrated their attention upon and having directed their scrutiny mainly toward those variables and relationships they supposed relevant to evaluating their own theories, without adequate attention to other possibilities. Also, by reporting the correlations of the entire matrix the writer maximizes the opportunity for another theorist to offer opposing or alternately plausible formulations to explain the findings. Also, those wishing to replicate the study have a maximum access to data for comparisons. Moreover, to deal only partially with the intercorrelations available to his analysis leaves one open to the criticism that one has selected, to fit his hypotheses, the data he does reveal. Further, critics could argue that there were more or less severe limitations in his theory, if it were unable to account for all of the data; which, it might be implied, was the case if he evaded consideration of the total array.

Another question which may arise is why one should focus attention upon the Murrayan need variables measured by the EPPS. As was indicated earlier, there are several quite excellent reasons. One of them is that the only theory on any comprehensiveness dealing with intersexual attraction hitherto presented, the complementarity theory of Winch, and the research enterprises it has spawned in consequence, has been built around these very need variables. Hence by concentrating upon them anew, with different theoretical formulations, the theorist is able to maximally relate his own theory to and test its value against the formulations constituent to the previously established one. Further, these need variables comprise a large sampling of those which have been for over a third of a century the most prominent, or certainly among the most prominent of, motivational constructs of concern to students of personality and social behavior. It is, further, around them that the largest body of information and theory has been accumulated; all of which is fundamental to constructing hypotheses as to how and to what degree these motivational variables are related as dynamic factors in intersexual attraction. Further work using other motivational schemas, such as that of Centers (1948, 1949) and Shutz (1958), is already in progress and subjects these to scrutiny in relation to formulations of the instrumental theory being developed here with the Murrayan one. But the appropriateness of the priority in treatment and analytical processing given to the latter seems inescapable.

A Macroanalytic Approach: The Postulate of General or Common Dynamic Properties of Motives

In the chapter wherein the theory of the order of ascendancy of particular need gratifications in intersexual attraction and love was presented, and where the need for sexual identity maintenance was postulated, intensive consideration was given to the genderic congruency factor, or the sex linkage of needs. Genderic congruency can readily be thought of as a particular *property* which all needs can be found to have in greater or lesser degree. The writer found it extremely useful both for understanding and demonstrating the plausibility of the posited need for maintenance and enhancement of sexual identity.

A further discovery as analysis directed by consideration of the generic congruency property proceeded was that other forces were cross-stitched and interlaced with the congruency factor in such a fashion as to complexly and markedly influence attraction and repulsion and thus to affect the direction and magnitude of correlations to be expected. In addition to the fact that all the needs have quite different properties, giving each its unique character, they also contain implicit common properties in certain cases. Affiliation, intraception, nurturance, sex, succorance and deference all embody various qualities and quantities of *affection*, while needs such as ach, aut, and dom might be seen as *friendly strength* in contrast to agg and exhibition which are more *hostile strength*. Finally, there is the property of *weakness* in succorance, deference and abasement, giving them common property.

Such properties as the aforementioned, on further reflection, were seen to be only those most outstanding and obvious. Further analysis revealed several more which could be plausibly assigned. Studied from the orientation of searching for properties relevant to explaining and predicting cross need correlations in intersexual attraction, which, with a matrix of 210 relations to be accounted for presented an appalling challenge, many possibilities were considered.

The purpose mediating their consideration was this: to find an economical and meaningful way of effectively reducing fifteen unique motivations and the vast variety of behaviors generated by them to some smaller set of factors which could be conceived to have instrumental exchange values in reciprocal need gratification. In the earlier portion of this enterprise, wherein the concern was to discover mechanisms of exchange between persons with homogamous needs, there was little necessity for going beyond the specific and unique properties of any given need which was being analyzed, for there was not diversity, but sameness, to be dealt with there. Now, however, diversity of unique properties is the problem before us. For example, in the correlation matrix with which we are confronted there is a possible correlation of n sex and n order. The unique properties of these respective motivations are so mutually irrelevant as to preclude any *direct* relationship or engagement of the two in an interaction sequence of reciprocal exchange of gratifications such as have hitherto been presented for the purpose of exhibiting and exemplifying the mechanisms heretofore identified. One would, on this reasoning, expect no correlation other than one of chance value. But, it is at least conceivable that there is some dynamic and a not merely chance relationship between them. After reflecting repeatedly upon such a possibility the writer was led to postulate that a dynamic relationship between such seemingly unconnected and mutually irrelevant motivational variables could indeed exist in virtue of the *general and common properties* of such needs, as distinguished from their *unique properties*. The *Postulate of General and Common Properties of Needs* now proposed asserts: *needs actuate behaviors possessing general as well as unique properties which have specific instrumental exchange values, and hence can mediate interpersonal attraction.*

Obviously, if this is true, then, discovery of the most significant of the properties of needs which function in this way and identification of the interpropertal dynamics permits far more generalized postulates to be formulated and tested with predictions of correlational character. Further, if the latter are validated by the facts, a quite substantial increment in our knowledge of how needs function in interpersonal attraction and repulsion will thereby be obtained.

The Common and General Properties

Eight properties aligned in four polarities of opposites were finally decided upon as the optimum number for prediction of intercorrelations among the needs embodied in the EPPS. These were 1. *strength-weakness*, 2. *beneficence-suppliance*, 3. *affection-hostility*, and 4. *excitement-sameness*. Each was seen as possessing dynamic properties with respect to interaction with its opposite that would be productive of either attraction or repulsion in interpersonal, but especially, intersexual relations. While specific in applying to the fifteen needs the interrelations of which understanding was sought, *they were also conceived of as forces operative in respect to needs not included in the present purview.* That is, as forces making for attraction or repulsion in a general or universal sense. It was seen, further, that in terms of the inter-relationships obtaining among these forces a theory to accompany and integrate with that of intermotivational mechanics; in this case one of *intermotivational dynamics*, might be developed. Finally, it was seen that the postulates comprising such a theory could be used to derive predictions with regard to the directions and magnitudes of the correlations that should obtain between interattracted persons, not only on the Murrayan need variables, but with other motivational entities as well. It was not supposed that they would be sufficient for all such cases, to be sure, but rather that additions to the list might be required if and when further research or the failure of these dynamisms to account for findings anticipated in the present project proved their inadequacy. It was not expected either that the specific and unique properties of each need could be thus transcended or ignored. The specific is meaningless without the general and vice versa. But system always aims toward generalization and abstraction from particulars, for otherwise we have only a catalogue, not a science.

As stated before, a careful analysis of the properties of the needs in the EPPS assortment revealed several more than the four sets of polarities mentioned. Ascendance-submission is a property which several of the needs clearly have. So is assertiveness-receptiveness, as well as positivity-negativity. Yet not any of these polarities was found appropriate for embracing the entire assemblage of needs, for with the use of any single one of them, one or several needs could not be included. For example, although achievement, autonomy, exhibition, aggression and dominance could all be conceptualized as having the property of ascendance, and deference, succorance and abasement as having the property of submission, only slightly more than half the needs are thus encompassed. Endurance, order, nurturance, intraception, affiliation, sex and change are not plausibly so described. Assertiveness-receptiveness fits and fails to fit to a practically equivalent degree.

Activeness-passiveness was another polarization of properties which was considered. Activeness-passiveness, while somewhat more embracing, accomplishes its inclusiveness at the price of a vagueness and murkiness of meaning found too high. Also, while all fifteen needs could plausibly be assigned to either the active or passive category, almost all of them were seen as having relative amounts of activity property, with only abasement being truly passive in quality. Moreover, not much *instrumental exchange value* could be found in these relatively undynamic properties. The dimensionality was seen as little more useful in this sense than a gradation in a series from white, through shades of grey, to black.

With some reluctance, for the concepts are value laden in the popular as well as scientific minds, and the terminological difficulties and literary awkwardnesses in their use distasteful, the strength and weakness properties were selected from the possibilities as one set of properties best meeting the requirements of the intended goal.

Strength and weakness are readily exchangeable behavioral commodities in the context of interpersonal interaction, where one is instrumental in the exercise of or occurrence of the other, but they are likewise instrumental in the case of strength vis-a-vis other strength and in the case of weakness vis-à-vis other weakness. Further elaboration of these points will be presented later on. It is worth noting, in suggestion of how valuable the behavioral commodity of strength is, that, within the contexts of purchasable behavior transactions, its price is typically high. When one hires a person of expertise and know-how as he is regularly accustomed to doing when he has a problem with his health, his psyche, his income tax return, or for that matter the stopped drain in his kitchen sink, he is buying *strength* in one form or another and he expects to pay dearly for it. But the strong need the weak, also; no less than the weak need the strong. The professional expert who lives on his specialized strength needs his clients, who are weak in the sense of lacking the particular kind of competence they typically pay so handsomely for in the marketplace of professionalized behavioral resources.

The strength-weakness properties of needs so overlap the assertiveness-receptiveness and ascendance-submission attributes of needs, as, in effect to contain these. Thus they derive meaning from these less abstract and more explicit concepts. For example, at least some of the needs of high strength value could be de-

scribed meaningfully as having the properties of either assertiveness or ascendancy, or both, as well as, in addition, other properties identified in one way or another in the semantics of the
psychologically unsophisticated person with strength. Indeed
strength and strong, as well as weakness and weak the writer has
observed, are in high frequency of use by laymen in talking about
factors of significance in attraction between persons of opposite
sex. They are seldom more explicit in defining their meaning for
the terms; mostly, it is supposed, because they feel anyone under-
stands what they mean by them when they use them. The terms
may be somewhat vague to a psychologist, accustomed as he is
to greater precision in speech and meaning, but laymen are less
demanding.

In a sense this correspondence with popular conception is an
advantage for what must to some, at least, seem an "abstraction"
too broad and general to be useful. On the contrary; if people
perceive, respond to, interact with and engage in instrumental
behavioral interchange with each other in terms of 'strength' and
'weakness' in a sense that is similar to the conceptions of them
being employed here, then such a conception cannot be denied
its appropriateness for the purpose at hand. A wealth of meanings and synonyms exist in our language for both terms. Strength
is, indeed, a many splendored thing, as is suggested in Table XIII
where each of the 15 needs is listed and one or more outstanding
aspects of its strength or weakness noted.

The attributed characteristics are not presented as an exhaustive
or comprehensive description or guide, but simply as illustrative
of some of the ways in which the behaviors activated by these
motivations may be described. That they are perceived and cog-
nized by people in general in *precisely* these ways is not, it is
thought, either likely or necessary for the purpose here. But it
is being proposed that people implicitly attribute many of these
meanings to behaviors devolving upon the needs in the imprecise
currency of their thoughts and feelings and that this process is
intimately involved in a mediating sense in their feelings of attraction or repulsion to each other. This proposal is intimately
bound up with a postulated process of need-resource resonance
which will be discussed later.

TABLE XIII

SOME CHARACTERISTICS OF NEEDS HAVING STRENGTH
OR WEAKNESS PROPERTIES

I: Needs Having more Property of Strength than Weakness
  A: Achievement: Competence, mastery, *able strength*
  B: Aggression: Combative strength, sometimes hostile strength
  C: Autonomy: Unfettered strength, sometimes defensive strength, self-sufficient strength
  D: Change: Venturesome, strength, playful strength, joyous strength
  E: Dominance: Controlling and directing strength
  F: Endurance: Durability, perseverative strength
  G: Exhibition: Cocksure strength, narcissistic, attestatory strength, conceited strength
  H: Intraception: Understanding, sympathetic, comprehending, empathic strength
  I: Nurturance: Sympathetic, helpful strength, sheltering, protective strength
  J: Order: Planful strength, organizing strength
  K: Sex: Erotic strength, lusty, passionate strength

II: Needs Having more Property of Weakness than Strength
  A: Abasement: Self-effacing, submissive, abject weakness
  B: Affiliation: Friendly, affectionate, insecure, somewhat anxious weakness
  C: Deference: Friendly, respectful, admiring, cooperative, subordinating weakness
  D: Succorance: Appealing, dependent, supplicant, helpless weakness

Ordering the Needs on a Magnitude Dimension

Table XIV shows the a priori orderings of the several need variables on the strength-weakness, the affection-hostility, the beneficence-suppliance, and the excitement-sameness dimensions or propertal polarities. These orderings were arrived at by a judgmental process far too elaborate to be made fully explicit here, but taken into account in their ordering was all the theory and facts known to the writer, both specific to them, as contributed by Murray, and that which has accrued in the many years since his 1938 monograph. Schacter's (1959) work on affiliation is an example of this latter. The matrix of intercorrelations of the needs presented in the EPPS manual was used also, and every research report that could be found which presented correlations of these needs with other need variables and personality traits. It involved more than anything else an intensive and searching scrutiny of the nature of the items comprising the index to each need, with an eye to determining what an affirmative response to it implied, not only with regard to latent motivational forces of the endorser of it, but also with regard to its stimulus value

TABLE XIV

A PRIORI ORDERINGS OF NEEDS ON THE STRENGTH-WEAKNESS,
AFFECTION-HOSTILITY, BENEFICENCE-SUPPLIANCE, AND
EXCITEMENT-SAMENESS POLARITIES

	Strength	*Affection*	*Beneficence*	*Excitement*
HIGH	DOM	AFF	NUR	AGG
	AUT			
	AGG	NUR		SEX
	ACH		DOM	
MODERATE	EXH	SEX		EXH
	SEX	DEF	ACH	ACH
	NUR	INT		CHG
	END	SUC	INT	DOM
LOW	INT	CHG		AUT
	ORD	DOM	AGG	AFF
	CHG	ABA		
ZERO		ACH	AUT	SUC
			SEX	
		AUT	ORD	NUR
		ORD	END	INT
			EXH	
		END	CHG	DEF
LOW	AFF		ABA	
			AFF	
MODERATE	DEF		DEF	
		EXH		
HIGH	SUC			ABA
				END
	ABA	AGG	SUC	ORD
	Weakness	*Hostility*	*Suppliance*	*Sameness*

and behavioral effects in an interaction episode.

A common discovery in this process was that the name assigned to the collectivity of the items purporting to measure the given need seldom captured the full richness of possibility the collation contained. Obscured by the name exhibition, for example, which unsuspectingly interpreted, connotes simply a need to show off, to capture people's attention, and thus, presumably, to win their approval and applause, is a hateful and hostile intent. That is, an intent to make them suffer from feelings of inadequacy and inferiority in contrast to the show of brilliance or wit or wisdom on the part of the performer. And what underlies motivation such as that at a still deeper level of search is often, one finds, a lurking feeling of inadequacy and inferiority in the self that its victim seeks to exorcise by the compensatory magic of putting other people down.

The process of thought exemplified here was applied intensively to each motivational variable in the sample in turn, amounting to, in its thoroughness of execution and penetration, a far greater effort along such lines than any heretofore encountered. Contingent upon the successful comprehension of the true nature of each need thus expedited, it was realized, was the whole validation of the conceptions advanced here. The properties posited and assigned are thus in no sense simply intuitive hunches, as some might think, but rather, ones abstracted by virtue of searching cognitive analysis. Inevitably, in the end, the orderings are, in the absence of numerical mensuration, judgmental. They are presented here, then, simply as another theoretical postulate of the instrumental framework, and it is thought, to attempt to adequately defend them and to further justify them would be both too expensive of time and energy and far too distracting from the main task to be worthwhile. Their usefulness and validity are best tested by the confirmation or disconfirmation of the predictions that will later be derived from them.

However, one empirical check on the orderings on each of the dimensions was made. This was by means of a questionnaire study of the sematic-differential type (Osgood, Suchi and Tannenbaum, 1957), wherein a sample of 206 students in a class in social psychology were asked to rank each of the fifteen need variables along each of the defined continua.

The agreements and disagreements of their positionings with those of the writer, in terms of the rank order of the variables in the strength-weakness dimension, are shown in Table XV.

While the agreements in rankings are far from perfect, with only seven correspondences in position out of 15, the displacement is rarely more than one location point in the respective cases. The greatest discrepancy is in the instance of sex; sixth in the writer's ranking, but eleventh in that of the students. Affiliation's ranking, while twelfth with the writer, was ninth with the students. Autonomy was ranked second by the writer, but positioned as fourth by the students. Notable, too, is the exact correspondence of the

TABLE XV

COMPARISON OF TWO RANKINGS OF NEED VARIABLES ON THE
STRENGTH-WEAKNESS DIMENSION

Writer's Rank N = 1	Position	Student's Rank N = 206
Dom	1	Dom
Aut	2	Ach
Agg	3	Agg
Ach	4	Aut
Exh	5	Exh
Sex	6	End
Nur	7	Nur
End	8	Int
Int	9	Aff
Ord	10	Chg
Chg	11	Sex
Aff	12	Ord
Def	13	Def
Suc	14	Suc
Aba	15	Aba

last three in both lists. The agreement in rankings for the affection-hostility, beneficence-suppliance and excitement-sameness dimensions was of somewhat lesser magnitude in each instance as compared with that for the strength-weakness one, although still generally supportive.

While there exists a certain amount of reassurance in the finding of reasonably good agreement between the two sets of rankings the decision was made to nevertheless adhere to the original a priori positionings as the basis for predictions in the present study rather than to adopt the student-derived ones for the purpose. For, it was believed that they had a far greater amount of psychological information and theory behind them, and that it would, hence, result in a greater amount of predictive success if they were used.

The stance taken does not preclude some discussion of the positions assigned various needs, and, indeed, this seems required in the instance of n affiliation being categorized as one with the predominant property of weakness rather than strength. The work of Schacter, previously cited and commented on early in this present work, it should be more or less obvious, is the main ground for assigning to it the characterizations of insecurity and anxiety. Schacter's research documented the point that persons who were made highly anxious by being given the expectation of later experiencing pain or unpleasantness manifested a stronger desire to be with others in a similar plight than did persons who were less anxious. According to his interpretation, being with others in a similar predicament serves at least two important functions for the anxious individual. First, the company of and simply physical presence of others in a like circumstance is anxiety reducing in itself, and secondly, being with others and exchanging communications with them may provide the individual with information and interpretation that will help him give clarification and meaning to his own feelings. Schacter, in effect, extends the Sullivan and Festinger notions of the drive for consensual validation to include comparison and validation of affective and emotional experiences. The latter two had stressed, instead, simply cognitive and perceptual products, such as beliefs, attitudes and values, and evaluations of one's abilities and self-worth.

There is no quarrel with either Schacter's findings or his interpretation as far as they go. They have not only been supported by other experiments conducted along the same lines as his own, but findings from other lines of research are also congruent. For example, Edwards (1959) reports a small positive correlation between scores on n affiliation and scores on the Taylor Manifest Anxiety scale (Taylor, 1953). Yet, n affiliation as defined by Murray and measured by Edwards is conceived of far more broadly and somewhat differently than the highly specific manifestation of it studied by Schacter. Affiliation is association, yes, but association out of affectional and kindred needs in the Murrayan conception, hence the position assignation on the strength-weakness continuum made here is on somewhat shaky ground, and for that reason must be considered even more tentative than some of the other positionings.

Another position assignation seen as one likely to be challenged by some, is the attribution of low affectional property and moderate beneficence property to dominance, which, it is observed, is a drive somewhat negatively viewed by some people. It is not seen as such here, but rather as a drive to control others with whom one interacts partly because they are perceived to be *"ask-*

ing for it," as seeking direction, guidance, instruction, etc., and partly out of a desire to benefit them by one's control. It is characteristic of leaders of all sorts that they seek to benefit their followers, and they are most admired and revered by the followers when they are able to do this in organizing and directing group action toward achievement of the group's goals.

Some may also question, it is expected, the assignment of some beneficence property to n aggression. Yet, in reflecting on its proper placement, this seemed reasonable in view of the fact that people still, even in our civilized world, do need protection. An aggressive person can supply such a benefaction in some measure, provided his abilities are congruent with his drive. Also, it is recognized, other persons, depending somewhat upon their particular relationship with an aggressive individual, may make attributions of beneficence to him, seeing him as a defender and protector irrespective of what he himself may feel.

The purpose to be served in the orderings of these properties, as has been previously indicated, was to facilitate in an orderly way the formulation of principles of as much generality as feasible in consideration of the multiplex forces operating, and from these to derive specific predictions concerning the correlations expected between given pairs of needs. In this way it was expected that understandings of the roles in effecting attraction or repulsion of the properties of the behaviors instigated by the several needs in the sense of their instrumental exchange values might be gained.

The advantage that was seen in this procedure was that of ascending to a higher degree of generality than that permitted when one is forced to analyze the consequences and effects of each of the many possible need pairings, pair by pair, as was the procedure in accounting for the similarity phenomena in the preceding part of this monograph. The prospect of arriving at predictions via the less concrete and somewhat more abstract analysis became additionally seductive after some considerable amount of such a microscopic analysis had already been accomplished. This was after it was realized that no essentially new need gratification mechanisms beyond those already proposed would be required. With the addition of an interrelated set of principles; those of intermotivational dynamics, the existing mech-

TABLE XVI

SCHEMATIC CORRELATION MATRIX FOR THE FIFTEEN NEEDS OF THE EPPS

	MF Aba	MF Acb	MF Aff	MF Agg	MF Aut	MF Chg	MF Def	MF Dom	MF End	MF Exh	MF Int	MF Nur	MF Ord	MF Sex	MF Suc
F Aba	X														
M Aba	—														
F Ach	X	X													
M Ach	X	—													
F Aff	X	X	X												
M Aff	X	X	—												
F Agg	X	X	X	X											
M Agg	X	X	X	—											
F Aut	X	X	X	X	X										
M Aut	X	X	X	X	—										
F Chg	X	X	X	X	X	X									
M Chg	X	X	X	X	X	—									
F Def	X	X	X	X	X	X	X								
M Def	X	X	X	X	X	X	—								
F Dom	X	X	X	X	X	X	X	X							
M Dom	X	X	X	X	X	X	X	—							
F End	X	X	X	X	X	X	X	X	X						
M End	X	X	X	X	X	X	X	X	—						
F Exh	X	X	X	X	X	X	X	X	X	X					
M Exh	X	X	X	X	X	X	X	X	X	—					
F Int	X	X	X	X	X	X	X	X	X	X	X				
M Int	X	X	X	X	X	X	X	X	X	X	—				
F Nur	X	X	X	X	X	X	X	X	X	X	X	X			
M Nur	X	X	X	X	X	X	X	X	X	X	X	—			
F Ord	X	X	X	X	X	X	X	X	X	X	X	X	X		
M Ord	X	X	X	X	X	X	X	X	X	X	X	X	—		
F Sex	X	X	X	X	X	X	X	X	X	X	X	X	X	X	
M Sex	X	X	X	X	X	X	X	X	X	X	X	X	X	—	
F Suc	X	X	X	X	X	X	X	X	X	X	X	X	X	X	X
M Suc	X	X	X	X	X	X	X	X	X	X	X	X	X	X	—

anisms would suffice for the present enterprise.

As noted before, originally it had seemed that, in seeking to find an understanding of intermotivational mechanics and dynamics in interpersonal attraction, one need not concern oneself with the whole matrix of intercorrelations made possible by the juxtapositioning of each of the 15 EPPS need variables. This attitude seemed, at first, an entirely justifiable one. Almost anyone not acquainted with the reasoning heretofore outlined, in scrutinizing the mock matrix presented in Table XVI, might well conclude that to expect relatedness between some of the pairings on other than a chance basis, or on factors so deviously concatenated as to defy sensible analysis, would to be engaging in sheer folly. Better, it was originally thought, to confine one's attentions and efforts to only those most clearly interpersonal needs, as had previous examiners. Yet, as the possibilities of fruitful analysis and prediction along the channels heretofore delineated became more hopeful, and the advantages intrinsic in this which were discussed earlier in this chapter were reflected upon, the prospect became ever more engaging. It was decided to attempt to predict the outcomes of all the need pairings in the entire remaining matrix with this mode of operation.

MACROANALYSIS AND THE POSTULATE OF NEED-RESOURCE RESONANCE

The economy of this procedure, as compared with the more microanalytic one was further justified by a realization perhaps implicitly contraindicated by the previous use of the latter procedure. This was that, in order for needs to have an influence in interpersonal attraction and repulsion, they do not always require direct engagement with one another in particular interaction situations such as those which have been exemplified. They may have great stimulus significance to persons also by virtue of these persons' opportunities to observe the potential partner or incipient lover in para-personal and meta-personal behaviors. Conscious or unconscious registering and reregistering of them may lead to attraction or repulsion on the basis of the perceived potential for gratifying the interacting or observing one's needs or by virtue of vicarious gratification already having been received. No impairment of principle, it is insisted, is necessitated by thus shifting perspective from the micropersonal to the macropersonal sort of relatedness, or, in other words, from the specific and direct momentary interaction sequence of events to the global, longer time-spanning picture. Need gratifications or punifications must be exchanged still, though not necessarily in a penny by penny kind of transaction. This process could not otherwise by an integral and corporate aspect of instrumental theory as here conceived.

It is in virtue of this more global approach in examing the inter-active effects and consequences of varieties of inter-motivated behaviors, moreover, that a transition is accomplished, in a sense, to a *trait level of analysis*. Traits, as conceived here, are essentially those relatively stable and recurring qualities of behavior that are born of the underlying needs of the person. They are, like attitudes and beliefs the manifest side of the need mechanism, open and available to the perception and apprehension of others, and thus it is in them that are resident the cues and stimulus properties which trigger the responses of others. This is no more than to say that people attribute to others the qualities the behaviors emitted by them imply. If one observes an individual on repeated occasions to behave in a friendly way he is strongly inclined to consider him a friendly person. If the viewer's need for affiliation exists in some strength, this friendly person may well be seen as a potential source for gratifying that need, and, hence, feelings of attraction would be readily generated.

A less common sense way of stating this is to assume, as a working hypothesis, that persons are motivated (one might say "sensitized") by their needs to be selectively attentive to, and to be perceptually discriminative with regard to, the cues provided in the behaviors of others. That is, they are motivationally sensitized in such a manner that a conscious or subconscious "resonance" may occur in the event that behaviors produced by the others is "sensed" or consciously perceived as potentially gratifying to their needs. Thus, for example, a girl with a strong sex drive and strong need for deference to masterful and dominant males may be conceived to be consciously or subconsciously highly "attuned" (receptively sensitized) to certain relevant cues. Given these conditions she could be expected to readily "resonate," consciously or subconsciously to behavioral cues indicative of a plentitude of these resources in a male, and to, ceteris paribus, experience fairly powerful feelings of attraction to this fortunate one on those bases. To put it less combersomely, "needy" people are always on the look out for those with the resources to satisfy their needs, and are automatically attracted to those they discover to have them.

This is unquestionably a conscious process in great part, but also, without doubt an automatic, unconscious process to some considerable extent. This latter is said in simple recognition of the fact that people often have no real awareness of their needs, don't really know what they want, have only much of the time vague unlabeled feelings born of them. These vague feelings, nevertheless, by the person's experiencing satisfaction or pleasantness (by their needs being fulfilled) on the one hand, or unease or unpleasantness on the other (by their needs being unfulfilled) serve to direct or guide their interactions and associations with others in such a fashion as to maximize their gratifications and minimize their punifications. We are, thus, strongly attracted to those subceived, perceived, imagined or known by us to have the behavioral resources which our own needs require for our gratification, and this is so even when our needs are not consciously recognized by us. That the process is not conceived to be a necessarily conscious one is not because it is supposed that awareness of the needs has, because of their unacceptibility to the self, been repressed. To be sure, repression is compellingly indicated as at least a probability for almost any particular need for almost anyone, given the enormous variability in the human psyche. But the more probable reason is that man is simply, by and large, a simple, ignorant, uninsightful being, unaccustomed to analyzing his motives and often utterly uninterested in doing so. He is, more often than not, simply guided by the currents of his feelings, without clear cognitive labelling either of the nature of his motives or the characteristics of their consumatory affects. He knows a need gratifying behavioral resource when he sees one even when he doesn't know that he knows it, or that he has seen it.

Here is a mediation process, a construct, which will be referred to as *need-resource resonance*. It may be either recognized in consciousness or not, depending upon many possible variables. It operates in such a way as to generate forces of attraction, indifference or repulsion depending upon whether the cues existent in the behaviors of the other person are sensed as potentially gratifying, irrelevant, or punifying to whatever needs are activated by those cues in the senser. It is presumed to be operative too, whether direct interaction is occurring or there is merely contemplation of it, and whenever observation of the other's para-personal and meta-personal interactions and behaviors has occurred or is occurring.

Let us summarize all that has just been said in *the postulate of need-resource resonance.* Every person is assumed to be consciously and unconsciously sensitized by his needs to the perception and subception of resources in others that have potentialities or actualities for gratifying these needs. In encounters with others he will respond to them with either feelings of attraction or repulsion in keeping with his conscious or unconscious "sensing" of their actual or potential resources for his gratification or punification.

PROCEDURE IN APPLICATION OF THE THEORY

Thus, in most of the subsequent analysis, on the assumption that needs are "acted out" or expressed in behaviors congruent with them, the question becomes, essentially, that of asking whether males (or females) with given need X will find females (or males) attractive or repulsive if the latter manifest behaviors instigated by need X, or Y, or Z, etc. This is only putting the question, of course, in the way we prefer to put questions in science, where we prefer to set up the independent variables, the antecedents, and observe the dependent variables, or consequents, and that, of course, is precisely reversed in the data to be confronting us. Attraction, the consequences will have already been observed, the sample of persons already having been, in these necessarily correlational studies, selected because the attraction was known to have already occurred. So, what is essentially being done is retroactively inferring the kinds of processes, the mechanisms and dynamisms of attraction, that functioned to produce this outcome. In these terms the question to be asked repeatedly becomes this: given the fact that M and F are lovers, and examining the possible relatedness of need X in M to need Y in F, would a correspondence in need strengths between them or a difference in need strengths be expected to have produced this result? Then, from what is inferred to have been the requisite relation, a prediction will be stated in as precise terms as possible as to the direction and magnitude of the correlation necessary to be compatible with the mutual attraction known to exist.

For this procedure to be carried out with a great assurance of success would require, of course, that such predictions will have been derived from secure knowledge of need mechanisms and dynamisms and their modi operandi in interpersonal attraction and repulsion. This ideally would have been based on previous intensive research. Here, however, is terrain untrodden, jungle unpenetrated, chaos unordered. There is an intuitively obvious necessity for having a theory of intermotivational mechanics and dynamics for understanding and predicting interpersonal interaction outcomes. One that could account for them in terms of the motivational forces brought into contrapositional interjunction and interdigitation in the process is surely to be desired. Yet, none by such a name, nor by any other that would apply itself to the opportunity and challenge here presented, as yet exists. Hence, all being wanting, the successful consummation of the intended objective outlined in the foregoing could only be expediated by the essentially no more than trial and error testing, and which, in plain, the writer intends, himself, to use.

Regretfully it is realized, with such an inadequate base in information from which one must start in developing such a theory, it is almost certain to be crude. Crude theories, crudely tested, can only produce crude data outcomes and crude statements of relationships, which constitute, then, no more than crude representations of realities. Since even this modest achievement, however, is as yet unrealized, one should feel profited by his venture if only this were gained. Actually, we do not at present even have very much secure knowledge concerning either the nature of the need system or the manner in which the various needs function *intrapsychicly* in the individual personality. Even less is known as to how they function in interpersonal interaction. That is not to say we have no relevant theories at all, but these are essentially no more than theories about particular individual needs, not of inter-need relations. Theories of some elaborateness have been developed concerning a few of the needs we are concerned with here, such as achievement (McClelland et al, 1953), affiliation (Schacter, 1959), and aggression (Berkowitz, 1962; Buss, 1961). Approval

(Crowne and Marlow, 1964), is another need which has been the subject of some theorizing also, although it is not one of those included in the EPPS set. The theories which have been mentioned, of course, represent only some of the most systematic and better documented efforts, with an abundance of unchecked hypotheses and interpretations concerning these needs being found in the psychological literature. These constitute a plethora of useful additional possibilities. To some extent all of these theories, interpretations and hypotheses have been influential in the theorizing offered here, but by far the most respected guide has been the ideas of the pioneer conceptualist and systematizer, Henry A. Murray (1938), for the measures of the needs, which operationally define them, were essentially adaptations of his formulations, and are so intimately tied in with them that to depart too widely from these would seem both unnecessary and unwise.

In effect, what will be done here is to adhere more or less closely to Murray's own conceptions as, in a sense, mini-theories about each need, but to add to or otherwise modify these as necessitated by the insights added since his analysis and the requirements of the context of the relations under study. The present work is addressed to simply accounting for intersexual attraction and repulsion on the basis of needs as they mediate behaviors with instrumental exchange value, rather than to need theory itself. Hence, whatever additions or modifications in existing theories of needs occur here will not be separately and explicitly elaborated upon, but will simply be embodied in and implied in the postulates which are integral to the instrumental theory.

In what follows, these are to be developed and summarized in generalizations, the reasoning behind them revealed, and the attempt will be made later to state predictions. These will specify the direction and magnitude of correlation coefficients to be expected on the basis of particular principles theorized to be operative in terms of the dynamic properties abstracted from the needs. They will be qualified as little as possible by considerations of unique qualities of particular needs and particular juxtapositions of them. If the predictions are later validated with congruent outcomes the total theoretical structure will have received some support. If the predictions fail, on the other hand, little credence can be assigned to the ideas involved in their generation.

THE THEORY OF INTERMOTIVATIONAL DYNAMICS

SOME NECESSARY ASSUMPTIONS: THE POSTULATE OF ISOMORPHISM OF MOTIVE AND BEHAVIOR

INTERACTIONS between individuals occur, *observably*, only in terms of behaviors verbal and nonverbal, not in terms of motives. In making the inferences to construct a theory concerning the inter-dynamic forces of the interdigitations of the contrapositioned needs of interacting males and females, the writer's informational and cognitive resources are extremely limited. Those which are to be employed in it are *the assumed or imagined behaviors instigated by the respective needs and the reciprocal consequences of them for each of the interactors.* No data, no observation of such behaviors are actually, available. Nor has there been an observation of the needs themselves. Nor will there be.

Needs themselves are not observable. Hence, it has to be assumed in the operations to follow that the samplings of behavioral preferences indicing them on the EPPS constitute valid and reliable samples of responses indicative of the action of each of them in varying degrees of strength in the persons who have taken the test. These are not small assumptions. While it is known that the reliabilities of the various component scales presumed to measure each of the needs in the modified form of the EPPS used in the gathering of the data in the investigation range between .72 and .91 in correlational terms, the validities of these as well as of those of the unmodified original form are much less than certain. Perhaps the most one can say is that the scales have high plausibility as measures of these needs. At least, they are the most valid objective measures we have for them. But our theorizing and predicting about the interactions of these *inferred variables*, since they take place prior to actually administering the measuring instrument, have not even the observations to be provided by the, as yet, unobtained scores to start from; hence it is a very much "as if" situation all the way through. In brief, we start, then, with the hypothesized properties, general and specific, of each of fifteen motivational variables which we plan to later measure, and imaginatively reconstruct the behaviors instigated in the interattracted persons by each of them as well as their reciprocal consequences for the interactors. From this we then construct a system of dynamic principles descriptive of the forces seen as interdigitating, and, finally, from all this, predict the direction and magnitude of the correlations for each of the fifteen motivational scores for one of the partners with each of the fifteen scores of the other. That is, to say the least, a rather elaborate inferential process; and it could only succeed if certain basic assumptions which will be specified have been reasonably well substantiated. One of these is what will be called *The Postulate of Isomorphism of Motive and Behavior.*

For any theory of intermotivational dynamics to be credible or useful it has to be postulated that the needs of a person as indicated by his test scores have each instigated responses more or less isomorphic with them or at least meaningfully congruent with them in his past interactions and exposures to the person known to be attracted to him. Further, that the other person's needs have, fulfilling this same principle, done likewise. A further assumption is that each person in this process has been able to more or less accurately interpret the other's behaviors and to respond more or less appropriately to them in interactions with the other. Let us discuss this postulated isomorphism first, then attention can be given to the latter assumption.

There are five conditions seen as ones upon which the assumption of isomorphism is contingent. These are the following.

1. The *intrapsychic inhibitions* of conflicting motives which may obtain; thus preventing the occurrences of the expected behavior or in some way compromising its character.

2. The *intrapsychic costs* incurred in making the responses or engaging in the expected behaviors; a. *irrespective* of the characteristics of the stimulus person or, b. *with respect to* the characteristics of the stimulus person,

3. The *abilities* of the person motivated toward the particular

behavioral goal to actually effectively behave in that motivated way.

4. *Interpersonal deception*; a person's behaving in a way calculated by him to induce another to perceive either, a. *that he does not have* a particular need he actually does have in some strength, or, b. *that he does have* a particular motive in considerable strength, whereas, in fact, he does not.

5. *Conformity to the Socially Desirable in Behavior*: A person's behaving in a manner and style determined in part by outside social influences; hence only in the residual part behaving in keeping with his particular needs.

These five continguencies are not, probably, all that could be identified, but they seem at least the most obvious. There is no intent to be comprehensive on this point, but only to emphasize it to the extent seen necessary for the difficulty of fulfillment of the isomorphic condition to be appreciated.

Examples of each of the five mentioned in the foregoing may further assure this. As to the first, *intrapsychic inhibitions of conflicting motives*; these are extremely common in the case of the sex drive. They are well known to operate so strongly that a person having high strength of such a drive may have his outward behavior so thoroughly under the control of some restraining motive force, such as that stemming from his moral ideology or religious beliefs, that he does not behave in a manner or style either isomorphic to or congruent with his actual strength of sexual motivation. Hence, he will fail to meet our condition. His behavior will not have the sexual stimulus value a person of the opposite sex, not suffering from the inhibitory influence himself, would require for the evocation of his sexual interest in the person in question.

Another example could be found in the instance of a person who, although scoring high on n exh, was blocked in his behavioral effort to realize his goal of showing off by virtue of coexisting strong feelings of shyness and inferiority, lack of confidence, etc. Thus a person, who might otherwise be attracted to him because of his exhibitionism if it were outwardly expressed, would not be likely to be attracted, because of its absence from his actual behavioral repertoire. Other examples are abundant.

Examples of the second contingency mentioned above, *intra-*

psychic costs, refer to punifications incurred in engaging in the behavior the person is motivated toward because of the embarrassment occasioned by the accompanying realization that the behavior may evoke disapproval or censure or even worse consequences. Other examples can be seen in the cases of fear, anxiety or other emotional states being aroused when behaving in the particular way. There is much similarity between this second contingency condition and the first, of course, but here the response *does occur*. Also, whereas in the first named condition it is motivational conflict that is seen as the cause, in the present instance it is the price paid in punifying emotional states that accompany the behavior and which are set off more by the interpersonal stimulus than by the person's own conflicting motive. The behavior may nevertheless occur in either undiminished strength or even with a compensatorily exaggerated emphasis. Another intrapsychic cost incurred is in the effort and energy expended in making the response. Although it is difficult to separate this from an involvement with the third contingent condition, the abilities consideration, which will be discussed later, the position taken here is that independently of the magnitude of ability to make the given sort of motivated responses, say exhibitionist behaviors, the costs incurred will vary with other (non-ability) factors. These are such conditions as energy levels of the person, fatigue, and temporary satiation of need.

For this second condition, two subcontingencies were noted, the first of which has been adequately exemplified, but the second of which has not been. The intrapsychic costs will vary with the stimulus person the behavior is addressed to, and in many ways, the elaborate elucidation of which is too costly for the purpose here. Hence, only one will be mentioned. M, let us say, is motivated by high n dominance, a drive which instigates managing other peoples' behaviors, and is in a relationship with an extremely succorant and dependent F. By and large M enjoys (is gratified by) managing her life, advising her, instructing her, etc., but she is an exceptionally undocile (unteachable) girl, and is so difficult to advise effectively that M engages in much less of this behavior with her than would be the case with a more apt partner. He will not, then, be behaving in high congruence with his true drive strength in n dom; the reason being, in this instance, that the intrapsychic costs in respect to effort and energy expenditure are greater than they typically are for him in alternative interactional relationships.

Examples of the third contingency condition, the abilities factor are quite abundant. To consider one: the case of a male, high in exhibition drive, which he seeks to gratify by saying witty and clever things, making puns, telling amusing stories, etc. But his histrionic abilities are so limited that his audience is only bored, his jokes fall flat, his puns only provoke punification. M, assuming he is not stupid, soon learns his limitations, and characteristically adopts or affects behaviors that could not be easily seen as exhibitionist, but, instead, as those characteristic of a rather unexciting but amiable fellow. It does not follow that this change is internalized to the point of modifying his drive strength on n exh, however; and on a test given him to measure it, he might well be found to have, still, a high score. His behavior would not in such a case as this be isomorphic with his drive strength.

The fourth factor frustrating the occurrence of motivational and behavioral isomorphism is probably the most perfidious and powerful of all those that might be mentioned: namely interpersonal deception. It is perhaps best summed up in the folk saying: "All's fair in love and war." Men and women seem to have practiced it on each other since humans can remember; with not uncommonly tragic consequences. But, to take a familiar example, an attractive F with high n sex *and* high n dom learns early in the dating and mating game that any very appreciable display of or exercise of dominating behavior by her drives males away. She doesn't give up her dominance need, but being smart, she does stop *behaving* dominatingly, and adopts instead the pose and role of a very amiable and compliant and even moderately deferent girl. She not only lets her boyfriend make most of the decisions about where they go, who they see and what they do on their dates, but she also asks him occasionally for advice about important things. M, who is engaged to her now, will not learn perhaps until the wedding music is only a vague memory of a few months back that he has married a veritable tyrant, who will seek to manage and control every facet of his life with her and apart from her. Her behavior was not isomorphic with her dominance drive then. It is now. The deceptive behavior was, of course, isomorphic with another motivation, say the desire to ingratiate, to win his love, which was temporarily ascendant over her more characteristic and enduring dominance need.

The fifth and final contingency condition noted above was referred to as *conformity to the socially desirable in behavior.* Here the individual modifies the quantity of or the qualities of his behavior motivated by a given need because of an outside pressure he feels upon him. This stems from the particular membership or reference groups to which he belongs or from the society as a whole, and is experienced as a demand to conform more or less closely to what is collectively and consensually regarded by the group as its norms or standards of behavior. The aggressively motivated person, the strongly sex driven person, the exhibition seeking person, are each of them likely to feel such a conformity demand more strongly than others, and to have their behaviors trammeled in relatively large degree by it.

The second large assumption made explicit in the preceding was that each person in his interactions and relationships with others "has been able to more or less accurately interpret the other's behaviors." Common observation bears out this assumption sufficiently, it is thought, to make it more or less axiomatic. If people couldn't do it more or less accurately, couldn't discriminate the cues indicative of affiliative and affectionate behavior from those indicative of aggression and hostility, and distinguish both of them from sexual overtures, etc., people, to say the least, 'would be in real trouble.' One, in fact, finds it difficult to understand how man or any other species would have survived if it were not so. That is not to assert that people are very precise in the accuracy they exhibit, for there *is* frequent misunderstanding and misinterpretation. The consequences can sometimes be tragic, but seem more often than not merely comic. Our TV programs thrive on the possibilities found in such situations.

The writer in the preceding chapter went somewhat beyond what is stated in these remarks, in postulating a process called *need-resource resonance.* This is conceived to be a special sort of sensitization that heightens the ability of persons to discriminate, on the basis of observed behaviors, between those with the potentials or resources for meeting their needs and those not having such characteristics. It is recognized that it is a highly tentative hypothesis the validity of which *may* seem contraindicated by abundant research findings bearing on the accuracy of social perception depending on how that information is interpreted. Obviously it is being interpreted here as favorable to the hypothesis of need-resource resonance, but to review the voluminous literature both pro and con as to the issue of accuracy-inaccuracy, to cite supportive material for the position taken here, and to criticize the non-supportive research would require another book. The methodological and conceptual problems heretofore encountered by quite competent psychologists in their research on the various aspects of accuracy-inaccuracy have resulted in a plethora of results that are extremely difficult to interpret and almost impossible to compare. Hence the question still begs for an answer.

But even with the confidence that a process of need-resource resonance does exist and does function in the way supposed, it has never been supposed that such a process could be free of error, and to the extent that error exists the predictions to be made here about interpartner need correlations are subject to one more hazard. Given all of these contingencies as antecedents, all of them known to be as tenuous of fulfillment as they are, there is no surprise at all that the correlations yielded in research affected by them are almost uniformly small and recalcitrantly inconsistent.

CONTINGENCIES INTRINSIC IN THE CIRCUMSTANCES OF THE LOVE AND MATE MARKET

At least one more set of circumstances of unmeasurable proportions must be recognized as arrayed against us. People do not have 'the world to choose from' in their seeking of a mate or love partner. Their circles of acquaintances are quite limited in the typical instance, and their contacts beyond the narrow confines of the situations in which they find themselves are few. Given that the concatenation of need strengths in each is *special*, the *supply* of persons with the right resources for gratifying any large number of their needs may typically be quite small. Moreover, the *demand* for persons of his or her resource characteristics may be so in excess of the supply that a highly competitive love and mate market is thus created. Each must bargain competitively in it; bidding, in effect, his own resources against those of other buyers, who are, at the same time, sellers, of course. No one has really studied this circumstance with any care as yet. So we have no information as to the probabilities of people's being able to actually find and fall in love with, successfully court, and eventually marry someone who with high precision possesses the behavioral and other resources that would maximally gratify and minimally punify their needs. What they probably eventually do obtain in most instances is simply the closest approximation they can find and keep. But this may represent a more or less severe compromise both with their need requirements and their *deserts stances.*

Despite all of the foregoing it is resolutely being believed that the patterning of need correlations which will be predicted to exist between people who have chosen each other as mates will, in fact, be found.

PRINCIPLES OF INTERMOTIVATIONAL DYNAMICS

Intermotivational dynamics refers to the system of reciprocally operating cause and effect processes occurring between the contrapositioned and interdigitating motives of two interacting persons which exists in virtue of certain dynamic properties of an exchange sort that the behaviors instigated by these motives are found to have. Since it is the dynamic properties of the *behaviors* instigated that *directly* interact to produce the effects, the processes in our attention, could with equal or more propriety be termed *interbehavioral dynamics,* or more simply, *interactional dynamics.* However, since it is the accounting for the relationships among the quantitative values of a sample of motives with which we are concerned here, the term *intermotivational dynamics* seems most appropriate.

In the sample of fifteen motivational variables, or needs, with which we are occupied at present, four sets of two properties representing polar opposites having an exchange value with respect to each other have been identified. These are strength-weakness, affection-hostility, beneficence-suppliance and excitement-sameness.

Contrapositioned motives of any given pair of interactors produce behaviors in each of them which, actually, have a great variety of properties, each more or less unique. However, there are some properties that may be found common to many particular behaviors. The several that are seen to occur with the greatest frequency, so as to attend most of the interactions which appear relevant in the engendering of attraction or repulsion between interactors, consist of the four pairs of behavioral values previously identified.

The individual members of each pair are found to have, in each of the respective four, values quite opposite to each other, with each of them, in fact in each case being defined and given meaning only in reference to its opposite; the other. But, what is more important, in each instance, a dynamic relationship exists between each pair of qualities which is coinstrumental in significance. This arises from the fact that, in interactions between two persons whose contrapositioned motives produce behaviors with the properties in question, reciprocal gratifications or punifications are effected for the respective persons. The consequence of the experiencing of these, in turn, is that, in the respective cases, either attraction between the persons or repulsion between them is engendered.

The nature of the dynamic coinstrumental relationship between different motives giving rise to behaviors possessing properties which are members of the four sets of these varies. In some cases, as between strength and weakness, and between beneficence and suppliance, it is a complementary coinstrumentality that exists. Each motive, being different in property, produces different gratifications for the respective interactors.

In most of the other cases of interactions actuated by the behaviors arising from the contrapositioned motives of the interactors the coinstrumentality is reciprocal in nature. In such cases the respective motives, being similar in property, produce the same kind of effect for each of the interactors. If these effects consist of gratifications, attraction between the persons is engendered, but, if the effects consist of punifications, repulsion between the persons is the consequence.

Reciprocal attractional coinstrumentality obtains in the interactions of affection and affection, excitement and excitement, sameness and sameness, weakness and weakness, and in some cases of strength and strength, for in each of these instances gratifications are reciprocally experienced by the respective interactors. In the case of the last one mentioned, however, this outcome is contingent upon the presence of accompanying special circumstances and the operation of the coadjuvance mechanism.

Reciprocal repulsional effects, on the other hand, are produced in the interactors in situations wherein their contrapositioned motives are both, whether alike or different, productive of reciprocally punifying behaviors; as in the case of hostility and hostility, excitement and sameness and *some* cases of strength and strength, and weakness and strength; with the outcome in the latter two cases dependent upon the accompanying special properties of the behaviors related to the needs.

In instances where the contrapositioned motives of the respective interactors are productive of behaviors of opposite and nonreciprocal or noncomplementary effects, such that only one person experiences gratifications while the other experiences punifications, repulsion rather than attraction between the two is engendered. Affection vis à vis Hostility is the classic example.

Finally, in situations where the properties of the contrapositioned motives of the respective interactors are such as to instigate behavioral products which cannot be exchanged between them, there are neither gratifications nor punifications effected, and hence, the result is indifference. This situation obtains in the cases of beneficence and beneficence and of suppliance and suppliance.

Since this last outcome may not be entirely clear on the basis of assumptions previously stated, it should perhaps again be made explicit that attraction between persons is a function of the gratifications experienced in their interactions and that repulsion between them is a consequence of the punifications experienced in such interactions. More specifically, in order for the interactions mediated by the contrapositioned motives of two interactors to produce *either* attraction *or* repulsion between them, the properties of the behaviors in the respective cases must be such as to effect *either* gratification *or* punification in both interactors. Further, in order for attraction to occur the properties of the behaviors of one interactor must be such as to produce effects having an exchange value with respect to the effects produced by the behaviors of the other.

Nothing was said in the preceding account with regard to the determinance of the magnitude of the attraction or repulsion which would result from the various cases described. The following postulate makes explicit the dynamic circumstances upon which this depends.

Ceteris paribus, the attraction or repulsion engendered through the interactions instigated by the contrasituated motives is proportional to the magnitudes of the dynamic qualities characterizing the behaviors instigated by the respective motives. That is to say, for example, if the affectional values of the respective behaviors are high, more attraction is produced than when either or both of these values are low. But, since it is the magnitudes of the gratifications or punifications that most directly and specifically determine the magnitude of attraction or repulsion, it is necessary to state that the greater the magnitude of reciprocal gratification experienced the greater the magnitude of the reciprocal attraction engendered. Also, the greater the magniture of reciprocal punification experienced the greater the magniture of the reciprocal repulsion resulting.

There is still another point to be noted. Insofar as in behavioral interactions subject to these contrapositioned interdigitating motives both gratifications and punifications are commonly produced in the respective interactors, whether attraction or repulsion is engendered is contingent upon the respective magnitudes of these, and the magnitude of the excess of one over the other. More specifically, in order for attraction to be the result, both parties must experience more gratification than punification in the interaction so as to receive a profit. The magnitudes of attraction toward the other experienced by each will be proportional to his profit in each case.

These principles have been stated in the foregoing in an extremely general sense and one intended to be applicable to accounting for relationships expected to obtain with regard to the phenomena of interpersonal attraction in general. However, we are dealing here with specifically intersexual attraction, and, as will be seen in the more detailed discussion to follow, this complicates the situation a great deal. We need to examine this more carefully.

THE DYNAMIC PROPERTIES AS ASSOCIATED WITH MASCULINITY AND FEMININITY

The properties described in the foregoing were also seen as interacting with masculinity-femininity in such a manner that the forces of attraction or repulsion generated by them might be either dampened or augmented by the generic congruency dynamic. This is additionally and especially complicated, in that, besides the more or less readily understood attraction relationship posited between strength and weakness, there are others not so obvious, and all also cross-cut with generic congruency dynamics. These are the relationships between *strength and strength* as well as those between *weakness and weakness*. Some discussion, it is thought, may make this complexity less confusing.

Strength-Strength Repulsion

In a preceding chapter there was discussed the circumstance that in interpersonal encounters two persons each instigated to high degrees by motives impelling assertive and aggressive behaviors might well so punify each other in the conflict likely to be engendered that repulsion would result. This was formally recognized in the *postulate of punification avoidance*. In the present context this reciprocal repulsion between such persons will be referred to as the phenomenon of *strength-strength repulsion*.

Strength-Strength Attraction

But it was further noted that empirical data revealed engaged persons to have at least modest positive correspondences in the measured strengths of their various assertive drives. To explain and account for this evidence of attraction in the face of the repulsive forces presumed to be produced in interactions devolving upon these drives, the *postulate of coadjuvance* was adduced. In effect, it was asserted that under circumstances where this mechanism obtained that the gratifications accruing to the respective adversaries could so exceed the punifications involved that a profit would result, with attendant attraction. Thus there is also *strength-strength attraction*.

The attraction to the strong by the strong is no mystery when one remembers that to feel and to enjoy (gain gratification from) one's strength, as such, it must be used; tested against opposition; thus defined both by its limits and its extent. The affinity of strength for strength thus resides in need for testing and retesting and a gratification in overcoming obstacles to define the extent of one's strength and a gratification of succumbing resident in thus knowing one's limits. There is, too, the excitement of competition and combat, the challenge of an adversary against whom one may prove one's mettle.

But a male does not play this game with great pleasure intersexually. Strength is male, and male prefers to play it with male. Victory over a female is relatively empty in comparison to what it would be with another male. He does not want to fight her but to kiss her, embrace her, pet her, fondle her and copulate with her, for it is in that latter act, especially that he defines his strength, yes, even his very maleness, with a female. Still, he and she do enjoy a good argument now and then, and provided the drive strengths toward assertiveness and aggression are only moderate the gratifications outweigh any punifications in it and there is a profit, and hence attraction.

But there is still another kind of strength-strength attraction wherein the reciprocal principle applies, for here, it is no conflict that is engendered, but affectionate appreciation of each other's behaviors. It is a *compatible strength*.

Order, endurance, nurturance, change, and intraception are, all of them, needs with considerable strength property in terms of the behaviors they engender, and they are also, most of them, more feminine than masculine. Further they are not assertive or aggressive and hence do not produce punifications to associates, but rather, more often than not, carry affectional property. That is, they give rise to affectionate sorts of behavior which are gratifying to associates. Males and females both of whom manifest these kinds of strength can reciprocally exchange many gratifiers, not only on the basis of the accompanying affectional properties that obtain in the cases of nurturance, intraception and change, but also in terms of strength property itself in the instances of endurance and order. For example, ord and end in any well-established and continuing relationship with others are almost certain to have resulted in mutual gratifications of many sorts involving time and tasks and cooperation. They are reciprocally agential and reciprocally facilitatory (coagential and coadjuvant) to gratifying various other more specific needs not in our sample here; ones like getting tickets to plays and concerts, working or studying together and a host of other such. More than this, people generally value and esteem individuals who display the qualities of orderliness and endurance in their behaviors. An exchange of appreciation for possession of such valuable attributes is, then, a reciprocally gratifying event also likely to occur between persons who both have such attributes. This gratification to the need for self esteem of each is of no negligible importance in interpersonal attraction, as has been remarked before.

There are instances, however, where *incompatibility* would obtain due to the accompanying properties of certain of these need pairings vis a vis one another. Order and endurance have high sameness property, while change has moderate excitement value. Excitement and sameness are mutually repelling forces we noted earlier. Here, of course, is a *mediated* strength-strength repulsion, not one arising from the interaction in terms of strength values per se.

The foregoing circumstances contain examples of one kind of *compatible strength* relationship, one between low to moderate strength needs. But another is found between all of the above mentioned needs when they are found in a female on the one hand and the needs of great strength value such as dominance and aggression when they are found in the male partner in the love relationship. The circumstance is a highly genderticly congruent one. The needs do not engender conflict behaviors, but behaviors that are by one need gratifying mechanism or another, as will be seen later, reciprocally gratifying to M and F; with their main gratification, of course, lying in that to their respective sexual identity drives. But the reversal of this, with high strengths of need on dominance, aggression and other assertive drives on the female's part obtaining, is a highly incongruent and genderticly punifying and repelling one. That is, these other, and characteristically masculine kinds of strength when found in a female are generally repugnant to the male. Her dominance and aggression conflict with his and force him to avoid her, for, again, there is little or no gratification to be gained by him in such combat. Further, they conflict with his essentially affectional and erotic drives in respect to her and for which her reciprocation of such feelings toward him is the goal. It is romantic, perhaps, but nonetheless true also, that for her to be too strong robs him of any purpose to which his strength may be put in relating to her, for he achieves gratification for it there in functioning as her guardian and protector, her companion and provider. It is to castrate him of his maleness if such functioning is denied him by vying with her for the role he feels his birthright. The stronger the male, of course, the less threat offered him by a male-like female, for he can still retain his male role and even enjoy, much as he enjoys a game, her occasional or perhaps even frequent testing of his mastery. But even so the prospect holds no great attraction for him. There is little or no satisfaction for most men in the taming of a shrew, even if she has an extraordinary compelling sexual allure, which few do.

Strength-Weakness Attraction

So, the structure of the forces of attraction and repulsion are such, in the main, as to conduce to a circumstance wherein *he* is attracted more to weakness in a female and *she* more to strength in a male. Each has for the other a valuable behavioral commodity to exchange and it functions as a powerful dynamic in intersexual attraction.

That is not to say that the male wants only weakness or abject weakness in his woman *unless he himself is weak,* for he both respects and prizes strength in her (which is another way of saying that it is of instrumental value to him), but only up to a point tolerable to his maintenance of his masculine identity of self and role. To the extent that he is himself strong in the traits born of his socialization to the masculine role he can tolerate, respect, admire and even be strongly attracted to a strong female. *However, he can be confidently predicted in choosing a marital partner to tend to pick one weaker than he himself is.* Those "strength behavior producing needs" which are congruent with the feminine identity and role, namely change, order, nurturance and intraception, moreover, should give rise to traits such as vivacity and venturousness, orderliness and planfulness and sympathetic understanding in the respective cases. These would be attractive to males who are themselves strong and not plagued by feelings of low self-esteem.

The female; specifically, the more or less average female, will have quite different preferential biases. Unless she has rejected her femininity or received a socialization making her overmasculine in her needs, she wants a man with all the "strength behavioral traits" identified culturally with maleness, for it ideally is such a man that can most powerfully gratify her own needs to fulfill her feminine self-identity and social role. The more feminine her need constellation the more attracted she will be to the male whose own need constellation complements her own. It follows, of course, at least up to the point where she has such strong masculine needs that she has more or less compromised or rejected her femaleness, that the greater the magnitude of the masculine-type needs she herself has the more masculine the male must be. Only such a one would be able to allow and promote the maintenance of her femininity and still preserve his own sexual identity and role.

Weakness-Weakness Attraction

Having dealt with the forces of attraction and repulsion in terms of strength as they are bound up with masculinity-femininity, let us look now to weakness and its forces of attraction and repulsion in these same terms. Weakness in males, by and large, leads them to be attracted, not to a stronger female, although that will sometimes occur, but more often to a female who is also weak, and preferably weaker than they themselves are. For, to maintain the masculine identity and social role, their partners must be as weak or weaker, rather than stronger than they are. If one finds it difficult to understand that the weaker female would be reciprocally attracted, let him remember that the needs which instigate behaviors having weakness properties are commonly, but not invariably, simultaneously investing these same behaviors with *affectional properties*, maximum reciprocation of which, as such, can best be obtained from one with similar needs. It is these latter who can best give them acceptance, understanding sympathy, affection and the kindred gratifiers that in some cases only persons with need structures similar to their own can supply. Only another coward can truly understand the experience of being afraid, and cowards seem to know that. Schacter, remember, found that one fearful, anxious person was more strongly attracted to (desired association with or the company of) another person presumably also anxious and fearful than he was to one not so aroused.

To be sure, the female in interacting with such a weaker male is not interacting with one whose resources provide as great an opportunity as those that the stronger male would for the maintenance and enhancement of her sexual identity and role. Hence, the attraction would be diminished somewhat by this circumstance, and the correlations between the "weakness behavior producing needs" (excepting n aff, of course) of existing partners in a love relationship would reflect this by never being truly high, but only moderate or small in magnitude.

Strength-Weakness Repulsion

So far we have dealt somewhat with strength-strength repulsion, strength-strength attraction, strength-weakness attraction and weakness-weakness attraction, but there remains at least one more dynamic relationship to be commented on: namely a *strength-weakness repulsion*.

In interpersonal encounters where the behaviors instigated by the need of one person have mainly properties of weakness with little or no affectional properties attendant, and the behaviors instigated by the needs of the other have moderate or great strength qualities, mutual punification, and hence repulsion are likely to result. More concretely, whenever an abjectly weak, self-effacing, 'mousy,' or inferiority ridden person finds himself or herself confronted with a strong, dominant, assertive, aggressive other, the likelihood is that each would be repelled. The repulsion would be caused by behaviors activated by the threat to the weak one's sense of adequacy, his embarrassment, fear of rejection, etc. on the one hand, and the strong one's lack of any likelihood of experiencing excitement of contest with and sense of triumph over so submissive and inadequate an adversary on the other. A strong male is probably frightening or even terrifying to a mousy, inferiority ridden female, and she is, to him, utterly unchallenging and uninteresting, and, almost certainly, *unsexy*. The same statements could be made with the genders reversed.

There is, of the needs measured by the EPPS, only one weakness type of need that motivates feelings and behaviors which represent such a special case, however; one wherein no affection or other benefits (except for some sympathy or pity) are either sought by the weaker from the stronger or found in relating to him. This is the so-called abasement need, commented on at some length in an earlier chapter. This need is easily misunderstood as to its aim, for one might at first-hand assume that to abase oneself is what is implied, just as one assumes, and correctly, that n dominance is a need to act dominant and *to be* dominant in interpersonal relationships. The abasement items on the EPPS elicit only feeling responses (e.g. "I feel depressed by my own inability to handle various situations"), not preferences for behaving in particular ways, as the items measuring other needs do. High scores on n aba mean, then, simply that the one so scoring feels inadequate, inferior, and afraid of others whom he perceives as stronger, superior, or more capable than himself. Interacting with persons whose behavior devolves upon needs productive of strength qualities of appreciable magnitude is punifying in varying degrees to such an inferiority ridden person. And, since there are no accompanying gratifications to offset the punifications he incurs by it, he can be predicted with high confidence to avoid forming relationships with such strong persons. It is, then, in the relationships between n aba and needs that produce strong behaviors that we are most likely to see the prediction fulfilled, and the principle of strength-weakness repulsion exemplified. This would be evidenced by negative correlations between partners on these needs.

Of relevance here is a study conducted by Kidd (1951) on the characteristics of persons most likely to lead to rejection by others. He asked 639 male students in a residence hall to name those individuals among their acquaintances who they found least acceptable as friends and to give their reasons for their aversion to them. The most frequently stated rejection involved either behaviors associated with an assumption of superiority; such as being egotistical, overconfident, sarcastic, domineering, etc., or their opposite; those behaviors associated with the assumption of a role of inferiority, such as being too timid, too quiet, too retiring; in short, *too abasive.*

Jennings' (1950) study on the friendship choices of about 400 adolescent girls, employing Moreno's sociometric procedure to ascertain the patterns of choice and rejection, and interviews with the girls to determine the causes of attraction and repulsion, is highly consistent in its findings with those of Kidd. The girls in the Jennings' study, like the boys in Kidd's, tended to reject not only bossy, domineering, aggressive, egotistical acquaintances, but also those too abasive. For example, in commenting on one rejected girl, another says, "She gets along with people, but they tease her because she doesn't fight back. She's so quiet that if I talk to her, it's mainly a conversation with myself: *I wouldn't get anything out of being associated with her*" (italics added). Another girl remarks, "There's nothing definite about her. She never takes sides on issues that come up. She's slow and sort of not interesting. There's nothing against her, but nothing in her favor much either. You don't feel she's around hardly." (Jennings 1950, p. 168)

There are additional complications involved in connection with strength-weakness forces of repulsion that are not as obvious or as readily understood as the sort of case just described. For, even where the weak are attracted to the strong, certain repulsive forces must be overcome for this condition to exist. It should be realized that in interpersonal interactions, individuals instigated by motivational processes which give rise to behaviors with weakness properties in encounters with persons driven by needs which promote behaviors with strength properties may experience varying amounts of punification from a variety of causes. For example, if social comparisons occur, as they almost certainly will, and they perceive the other as stronger than they themselves are, as they probably will, they are likely, depending upon the magnitude of the contrast, to experience, even along with their attraction, feelings of threat, shame, embarrassment or even mortification.

Such punifications are probably produced to some degree in all relationships involving the strong and the weak, and in proposing that the weak are attracted to the strong, as has been done in the foregoing, a recognition of their presence was not made explicit there. It would have been inconvenient and inexpedient to have done so, given the complexities attendant upon describing the essential conditions even in the simplified case. But it should be made clear now that the likelihood of their presence exists. That is to say, then, that the attraction generated by the gratifications accruing to the weak in their interactions with the strong is dependent upon such gratifications being in *excess* of whatever punifications are incurred, and thus representing a profit. This may readily occur in strength-weakness transactions wherein the weaker seeks something from and gets what he seeks from the stronger, as the succorant one does from the nurturant or the deferent one does from the ascendant, achieving or dominant one.

One may well ask here, of course, what gratifications the stronger one in the transaction receives in exchange that makes the attraction reciprocal rather than simply a unidirectional phenomenon. Some remarks pertinent to this question were made much earlier, but perhaps should be reemphasized. The answer, of course, is that much of the gratification to the stronger accrues in the very exercise of the strength he has. That is, strength to be enjoyed must be used, and one use lies in helping, leading, comforting, directing, informing, teaching, supporting, advising, etc. a person who needs these behavioral resources; that is, one who needs to be helped, led, comforted, directed, informed, taught, supported, advised, etc. Recall the nurturance-succorance model here. Besides this, the weaker one is, in return for these benefactions, grateful, appreciative, affectionate, admiring or even adoring, all of which are powerful gratifiers.

Weakness-Weakness Repulsion

One other possible relation between strength and weakness in interpersonal affectional orientations remains. Is there *weakness-weakness repulsion?* It is conceivable that there could be, because neither person, in encounters wherein each was under the control of needs motivating behaviors with weakness properties, being able to appreciably gratify the other, because of his passivity, self-effacing mode of response, lack of stimulation value, etc. However, the empirical support for this seems wanting; for recall that there was a positive and significant correlation of .44 obtained in the Banta and Hetherington study between fiancés on n abasement, the variable with the greatest weakness property of all. Further, that the magnitude of this correlation was systematically diminished in dyads composed of persons whose relationship was increasingly less intimate. All of this was in a preceding chapter interpreted as evidence of attraction. However, it is quite reasonable to interpret this attraction as an outcome of a situation in which the gratifications reciprocally experienced in the relationship exceeded the quantities of punification of the sort suggested above, which would also have been involved. Hence, a weakness-weakness force of repulsion *is* posited. But the expectation is, on the basis of the evidence cited above, that its operation would be obscured from view by the overridingly more potent forces of attraction simultaneously in process.

THE BENEFICENCE-SUPPLIANCE DYNAMICS
Beneficence-Suppliance Relations

Although certain of the strength needs such as dominance and nurturance motivate their possessors to supply certain benefactions like advice, direction, help and emotional support to others and thus have beneficence property, certain others, such as autonomy and aggression (although it has some beneficence property of a protective sort) lack this. Hence, largely because of this circumstance, the exchange value of various strength needs differs, and to take account of the consequences of their differing exchange values in this sense the various needs have been ordered along a polarized dimension in accordance with whether they possess as a predominant property that of either beneficence or suppliance. Inasmuch as a person motivated to benefit others requires appropriately motivated others to receive his benefactions he is inevitably able to gratify his motive only with such others and will hence be attracted to them. Those motivated to obtain benefits by receiving them from others, that is, ones whose needs carry the property of suppliance, being able to receive them only from persons motivated to supply such benefits, will be attracted in return.

The attraction engendered by this kind of complementariness is in intersexual relations, of course, also influenced by the factor of genderic congruency, the attraction being enhanced when the congruency is high, but depressed when the congruency is low. Some comments relevant to this point have been made in previous discussion, but probably should be replicated here. Consider the relationship wherein the male prospective partner has a high dominance drive (rated high in beneficence property), while the female prospect is instigated by strong succorance or deference needs (rated high and moderate respectively in suppliance property). The genderic congruency factor is highly favorable for attraction between them to obtain. This is so because each not only is able to gain gratification for his respective particular need, but at the same time behave in a way congruent with his sexual identity and role requirements, thus gratifying the sexual identity and role maintenance drive as well.

With the situation reversed, there is high genderic incongruency, and while the male, now the one with the deference or succorance needs, in relating to the female high in dominance may receive the benefactions needed from this source, his need for sexual identity and role maintenance and enhancement would be punified. This would result in lowering his profit in the relationship, so that its attraction value for him would be diminished, the degree of such diminution depending upon the relative strengths of the drives in question and the relative strengths of the gratifications perceived in prospect or experienced by him. Conceivably there could result from this an actual *beneficence-suppliance repulsion*. It would be a mediated repulsion, in this instance, of course.

Another possibility of mediated beneficence-suppliance repulsion is seen in the case of dominance vis à vis abasement. Here, the strength-weakness relation would be the mediating factor. It is in this instance one of strength-weakness repulsion due to the reciprocally punifying behaviors activated by these respective needs. In this case, too, the very low value of the suppliance property of n aba is such that whatever meagre gratifiers it produced for n dom and n dom for it would be so far exceeded by the reciprocal punifications as to result in a *loss*, with attendant repulsion between persons in terms of these two needs. This would be reflected in a negative correlation being found between interattracted partners on n aba and n dom.

Beneficence-Beneficence Relations

Are two persons of opposite sex, both possessed of strong drives productive of benevolent behaviors attracted to each other on that ground in itself? Does a nurturant and/or dominant male find a female high in these same needs attractive on that account and vice versa? The answer is not simple. First of all, however, it would seem clear enough that, considering only the gratifiers each produces for others that stem from beneficence per se, no attraction would be created, for neither has (in his beneficence, per se) a need for what the other is producing. Yet empirical evidence (Banta and Hetherington, 1963) indicates that persons in a love relationship are, at least to modest degrees, similar in need strengths for both dominance and nurturance as well as for intraception, with the r for the latter being highly significant. The positive correlation on intraception, however, was in a previous chapter interpreted, in terms of the reciprocal and complementarity mechanisms, as produced by the affectional properties of this drive. It was seen that, in so far as it seemed to be a need to both produce and to consume affectionate understanding of self and others, it could function in a reciprocal way. Also, that it could, for both of these reasons, function as a complementary need to needs in the partner such as dominance, nurturance and affiliation.

Hence, whatever attraction value attends a beneficence-beneficence relation is always mediated by the simultaneous functioning of other properties of the needs in the relationship. There are a variety of possibilities.

1. Each may be presumed to possess attitudes and beliefs supportive of his drive, to the effect that he or she values the kind of behavior in question as an estimable way of relating to others, and such agreement obtaining between them would constitute reciprocal reinforcement for the needs of each for consensual validation of personal effectancy.

2. Needs such as dominance, achievement, nurturance, and intraception, the beneficence ones, do not exist in isolation, but in a personality structured by the simultaneous existence of other needs having suppliance properties (affiliation, deference, abasement, succorance), each person in a relationship, possessing both sets of needs. Each, then, produces gratifiers for the other in the form of beneficence behaviors, on the one hand, and suppliance behaviors on the other. The mediating process is reciprocal complementarity of previously mentioned varieties; intrasituational and transituational in particular.

3. The need for achievement motivates people to make money, win status, etc. Although in the Murrayan schema there is no need posited for receipt of gratuities of this sort, we can with high plausibility, it is thought, assume one to exist. Hence, it is hypothesized that n ach, the provider of such gratuities has, either because of its possessor's intending to be a provider or without his so intending to do so, a very considerable magnitude of beneficence property. There is in all of this, of course, complementarity; but also agentiality or coagentiality.

Still another need, this one explicitly in the schema, which can be seen to be in some part gratified in a complementary or agential sense is n change. Recall that it is indexed by preferences such as, "I like to travel and see the country," "I like to eat in new and strange restaurants," "I like to participate in new fads and fashions." Now all these behaviors are maximally possible only if one has money, and a prospective mate perceived to have a high n achievement is the one most likely to provide it—agentiality.

4. Drives such as achievement and dominance actuate behaviors that win praise, acclaim, admiration, etc. from others. The person in an ongoing or prospective relationship with someone having high strengths of such needs, if he or she has similar strengths, or even more modest strengths, of them, also can receive vicarious gratification for them by virtue of his or her identification with the actual or prospective partner. The mechanism of vicariousness here mediates the attraction between two persons, both with appreciable need strengths on needs with beneficence property.

There are in all of this, of course, cross-cutting factors of the genderic congruencies of the needs and their strengths with regard to the sexual identities of the respective partners. Since by now the reader is presumably sufficiently familiar with the principle, perhaps it suffices to point out simply that when the genderic congruency is high the attraction will be augmented, but when low diminished, and that correlations between the beneficence needs of interattracted persons would reflect these effects.

Beneficence-Beneficence Repulsion

Is there, it may now be asked, a force of beneficence-beneficence repulsion? It is posited that there is none in respect to the properties themselves in interactions between them, for neither in itself produces punifiers, but only gratifiers. But repulsive forces, stemming from the strength properties that certain of the needs high in beneficence property, such as achievement and dominance also possess, could, if activated strongly enough, produce punifications perhaps of great enough magnitude to negate or cancel out the gratifications and/or even result in a loss, instead of a profit. The repulsive forces, in brief, do not inhere in the beneficence property of the respective drives but beneficence-beneficence repulsion could be mediated by the assertiveness (strength) properties of the needs in question.

SUPPLIANCE-SUPPLIANCE RELATIONS
Suppliance-Suppliance Attraction

Like beneficence property, suppliance property is in itself without power to effect attraction in the case of suppliance vis à vis suppliance, for, in such a case, two consummate consumers, as supplicants are, have nothing to exchange in the way of gratifiers in interaction with each other. Neither person, in other words, produces what the other wants, namely benefactions such as emotional support, guidance or advice. These are supplied only by persons actuated by needs with beneficence character; in this case, nurturance and dominance.

Suppliance-suppliance attraction is like beneficence-beneficence attraction, always mediated by other properties which the needs with suppliance property have. One of these is weakness; the other affection (abasement also has sameness). It is chiefly via the various sorts of affectionate exchanges, and via a *reciprocal mechanism* that such interchange is carried on. Sympathy, understanding, emotional support, and amelioration of loneliness by virtue of perceptions of being in the same boat ("misery loves company," as folk wisdom expresses it) are the sorts of gratifications exchanged.

Suppliance-Suppliance Repulsion

Is there suppliance-suppliance repulsion? Yes, possibly there is, but again a mediated and phenotypically suppressed or hidden one, for it seems that what punifications might be involved would almost always be exceeded by the gratifications mentioned in the preceding paragraph. As to what these punifications might be, the most obvious ones are, 1. the greater gratifications foregone, that the supplicant person consciously realizes he might receive by interacting with and relating to a person whose drives actuated benevolent behaviors, 2. the constant and possibly unpleasant reminder that one is behaving in a weak sort of way and is, hence, at least slightly despicable—presuming, of course, that the person in question shares the negative evaluation society consensually places on weakness, 3. further likely reminders of weakness in association and interaction with a similarly weak person, who is likely to inappropriately make implicit or explicit demands for strength. This the highly supplicant person, as such, is not able to supply, and is thus, made to feel inadequate. But, to repeat, it is believed that the punifications would be exceeded by the gratifications produced by interactions of other properties, thus resulting in a profit, and hence some attraction. This would be evidenced by the finding of small positive correlations between interattracted partners in a love relationship on these variables carrying high suppliance values.

AFFECTION-HOSTILITY DYNAMICS

Most of the interpersonal need variables in the EPPS are characterized further by their carrying varying values of either affectional property or hostility property, the relationship of which to each other is, of course, exactly opposite. The responses instigated by them have utterly different consequences in each case, with affectionate behaviors begetting attraction and hostility responses evoking repulsion. There has been discussed at length and at various points earlier the paradox of attraction existing between persons both motivated by n aggression, a quite hostile drive, so it should be realized that the exchange relations between the behaviors instigated by needs with this hostility property are to some extent, at least, complex ones. Phenomologically at any rate, we do find *hostility-hostility attraction*. This we do not need to discuss further, for it has already been covered under the rubric of *strength-strength attraction* and accounted for via the *coadjuvant mechanism*. The same may be said with respect to what we all would expect, *hostility-hostility repulsion*, a circumstance so readily and intuitively understood as an outcome of reciprocal punification as to require, it is thought, no analysis or further comment. The postulate of punification avoidance formally states the rationale for the ensuing repulsion in such cases.

Similarly, with respect to the fact that affection attracts affection; the reciprocally gratifying mechanism inhering in a circumstance wherein interactors are producing gratifiers for each other, is obvious. No evidence is known to the writer that would suggest that interactions produced by needs having high or moderate affectional values would ever result in an *affection-affection repulsion* effect. But, submerged and hidden, it could be found as previous analysis has shown, in circumstances where the drives of the respective interactors, while carrying definite affectional property in each case, also possess additional or secondary characteristics which could result in some mutual punification of the respective parties. Certainly there is no reason to punify the reader with a duplicative discussion of the hidden costs attendant by virtue of the fact that at least half of the needs having appreciable affectional property also possess varying magnitudes of weakness property, while the other half have appreciable amounts of strength property. Nothing new could be added here.

Affection-Affection Repulsion

But two cases of motivation having modest or minor affectional property, dominance and change, require comment by reason of their relationship with n abasement, which also carries a meager measure of this property. In these cases the punifications are seen by the writer as sufficiently great to exceed the minor gratifications to be expected from the interactions instigated by these needs with such exiguous affectional values. Both n dom and n chg are so sufficiently high in strength property as to set up, vis à vis n aba, a need at the nadir on the strength-weakness continuum, a mutually repellant force. This is created by the reciprocal punifications produced through heightening of inferiority feelings, provoking fear, etc., on the one hand, and evoking disinterest, boredom, contempt responses, on the other. In other words, there would be a loss; with repellant forces between such combinations as dom-aba and chg-aba the result. This latter would be shown by at least small negative correlations being found between interattracted persons in a love relationship on these need pairings. Phenotypically, at least, we have here instances of *affection-affection repulsion*, but ones mediated, of course, by the dynamics involved in weakness-strength repulsion.

Affection-hostility repulsion is another sort of need relationship one would expect almost inevitably to result from an encounter or interaction where one person was motivated by a hostile need like n aggression and the other by an affectional need, such as affiliation or sex. Yet, supposing the n agg to be found in a male, with the n aff in a female, the genderic congruency factor is so high that one might expect some degree of attraction to obtain, and that it would be manifested in a correlation of a small positive value between the respective needs of the persons in question. In effect, if this were so, we would have an instance of what could be called *affection-hostility attraction*! But with the roles of the needs reversed, that is with the high strength of n agg being found in the female and with the high n aff in the male, this almost maximally generically incongruent circumstance would beget not attraction, but repulsion. This would be evidenced by a negative correlation in interattracted partners on f agg-m aff.

Once more, it has to be pointed out that whatever correlational cognation between affection needs and hostility needs obtains is always likely to be influenced by the involvement of the generic congruency or incongruency properties of the respective needs. When the generic congruency is high the correlation will be higher and more positive than it will be when the generic congruency is low or there is incongruency.

EXCITEMENT-SAMENESS DYNAMICS

A final set of intermotivational dynamic relationships postulated as of determinative significance in interpersonal attraction and repulsion are those that obtain between responses characterized by excitement on the one hand, and lack of excitement, or sameness, on the other.

Opposites do not attract here any more than they do so in the case of affection and hostility; they repel each other. Another, and more familiar and common sense way of putting it is that people who like (or are motivated toward) excitement in their lives are attracted to each other, but not attracted to persons liking sameness. Each provides excitement to the other in a reciprocal way in the first case but not in the second. The stimulus value of sameness behaviors is just not such as to get exciting responses aroused in an interacting or interrelating other, hence there is no gratification, but punification (of the rewards foregone sort). On the other hand those who like (or are motivated to) sameness behaviors like to interact with and have relationships with others who also like sameness, because each thus reciprocally gratifies the other's need by providing the condition or state of affairs that was sought; namely sameness. People with strong motivations to behaviors with excitement properties are not attractive to these "sameness people" because the behaviors they emit have strong excitement stimulus values and hence disturb and destroy the sameness the person motivated toward it was seeking and would be gratified by effecting or maintaining. In short, it is posited that other things being equal, people motivated toward exciting behavior are attracted to each other but are actually repelled by people motivated toward sameness behavior. Exactly the same can be said with regard to those motivated toward sameness of behavior with regard to "excitement people."

Excitement and sameness relationships then, consist essentially in excitement-excitement attraction, excitement-sameness repulsion, and sameness-sameness attraction. To be sure, it could be pointed out that instances of sameness-sameness repulsion, excitement-sameness attraction and excitement-excitement repulsion are found. But these are phenotypes and always mediated by other properties the behaviors of the interactors have. So overriding are these other properties, moreover, in accounting for attraction and repulsion in intersexual relations, that only minor and occasional use is found for the excitement-sameness dynamics in predicting what correlations are to obtain between partners in a love relationship. Like all of the other intermotivational dynamics, moreover, their operation is always strongly contingent upon the cross-cutting effects of the genderic congruency dynamic; which, as it has been pointed out again and again, may either augment or diminish the attractive or repulsive forces set up by other properties of the needs.

HOW THE DYNAMIC SYSTEMS ARE TO BE USED

Are there not possibly also dynamic relationships obtaining between properties placed on disparate polarized continua; that is, say, between strength and beneficence or affection and sameness, that might be hypothesized? Yes and no. Yes, one could *possibly* set up such hypothetical dynamic relationships, but as seen here, there is no meaningful way of doing so, unless the properties overlap in quality and are not truly independent of each other. However, it is believed that they are. They were conceived as such by discernment and design. But it is acknowledged without remorse, and even with a possibly pardonable pride of discovery, that the strength-weakness dimension has such a general breadth of meaning given to it here as to be able, almost, to contain the properties of beneficence-suppliance, as strength on the one hand, weakness on the other. Also, this could be said with respect to excitement-sameness to a definite, but lesser degree. For, note in Table VIII that sameness is not at all identical with weakness, even though excitement *is very like strength* in being a posited property in varying degrees for many of the same needs in the respective cases. But notice that order and endurance;

needs that have low or moderate strength property, also have maximum degrees of sameness property. Finally, while there is overlap of need membership between the strength-weakness and the affection-hostility continua there is less containment by the strength-weakness scaling for affection-hostility than for any of the other dimensionalities. Affection is not always strong and hostility is not always weak. Aggression and exhibition are needs with high or moderate strength values, but they are at the same time the only two of the fifteen needs under scrutiny that have hostility property.

But the strength-weakness dynamics, as the next chapter will reveal, are so general in the utility of their particular, even if complex, intermotivational dynamic relationships, as to make it possible, with understanding of them alone, to predict correlational directions and magnitudes for almost the entire matrix which looms before us.

The four systems of dynamics are conceived of and employed in stating particular hypotheses and making specific predictions as supplementary to one another, but mainly to the strength-weakness dynamic principle. A prediction, for example, made primarily in terms of the principles pertaining to strength-weakness properties for any two given needs, may be increased in precision by the realization that an important relatedness also obtains for them in terms of one of the affection-hostility dynamics. This in given cases might cause a prediction of greater positivity of value for the r, or in others, a prediction of lesser positivity for it to be made. In other words, there can be forces augmentative of the effect in question or forces decrescent of it, and the several dynamic systems are designed to allow all of them to be taken into account.

Beyond, of course, the supplementarity obtaining among the four postulated systems of intermotivational dynamics which have been dealt with above, there is a fifth supplementary factor of such overriding importance, as to be seen again and again in the foregoing presentation as able to reverse the magnitude and direction of a correlation otherwise predicted; namely, the factor of genderic congruency.

In the next chapter the four dynamic systems will be applied to the prediction of the directions and magnitudes of all of the 210 cross sex, cross need correlations that should obtain for a sample of couples in a love relationship with each other. Those who have thoroughly studied the assigned propertal magnitudes of each of the fifteen needs on each of the four polarized continua representing the four dynamic systems, and who are thoroughly familiar with the principles set forth with regard to them, could, actually, probably predict the outcomes themselves. They will also, need, or course, to be thoroughly conversant with the principles of intermotivational mechanics, have an intimate knowledge of the *unique* properties of each of these needs, *and* be able to fully grasp and use the principle of genderic congruency.

In other words, a reader might be expected to predict the nature of the correlations in question with fair accuracy if he has truly mastered the material which has been presented and has the same or similar understandings of the unique properties of each need as those which have been presented by the writer. These latter, it must be reiterated, cannot in some cases, at least, be ignored or transcended. But the writer is assuming, he regrets to say, no high degree of consensual plausibility for his own characterizations of these unique properties, and will be unsurprised if not a few of his colleagues criticize this effort with the unanswerable charge that his predictions were based on "intuitive" judgment. Denial that some "judgment" (although it would be insisted that it is *rational* rather than *intuitive*) is involved would be impossible to sustain, for the entire enterprise has been of necessity a judgmental process in default of the possibility of actually measuring any of the mediating variables and forces presumed to be involved. One would hope that someday, when they could be measured, the principles would work as well with these measured values as they will be shown to have done with the judgmentally assigned ones.

CHAPTER TEN

PREDICTIONS DERIVED FROM THE THEORY OF INTERMOTIVATIONAL DYNAMICS AND THEIR OUTCOMES

PREDICTIONS FOR CORRELATIONS OF THE PREEMINENT STRENGTH NEED: DOMINANCE

Predictions Based on Strength-Weakness Hypotheses

ALTHOUGH IT REPRESENTS a somewhat uncommon departure from the conventional format of reporting research in works of this type, wherein hypotheses and predictions are all first stated in one section of the report and the results or outcomes later presented in a separate division, both predictions and their outcomes in terms of the data are presented together in the present chapter. This is especially practical or even necessary because of the great number of details being dealt with. A summary reference table (Table XIX) listing all of the predictions and outcomes is provided in the succeeding chapter, wherein a discussion evaluating the theory as a whole is also presented.

The potency-impotency property, linked to every need variable in the sample here being considered, is rich in the system of intermotivational dynamic relations obtaining between its opposite extremes, as well as its adjacent values on the continuum it defines. This being so, the hypotheses embodying its dynamics in combination with the postulate of sexual identity maintenance are almost sufficient as a basis for predicting the entire 210 item correlation matrix. It will be employed, however, with generous supplementation by other dynamics, and sometimes, when it is more meaningful to employ one of these, even relegated to a supplementary role itself.

Let us look first at what may be expected to be the characteristics of correlations wherein n dominance is correlated across gender.

Dominance begets behaviors with social, but especially intersexual stimulus value of such high potency that it has been here assigned the position of first in this respect among the total array of needs. It is further characterized as strongly congruent with masculine identity and social role. Males scoring high n dom should be highly attractive to females, which would be evidenced in the present indagation by at least small to moderate positive correlation coefficients between m dom and those weakness variables most congruent with the female sexual identity, such as aff, def, and suc. Abasement, however, as indicated in reference to the *threat principle* of weakness-strength repulsion, would be excepted.

Weakness-Strength Attraction

All of the following several predictions are based on the principle of weakness-strength attraction.

Prediction 32: The correlation between f aff and m dom will be positive in direction and moderate to high in magnitude. The prediction of moderate to high for this pairing is derived from the hypothesis concerning the operation of the sexual identity drive. *This is the maximally genderically congruent pairing of needs.*

Prediction 33: The correlation between f def and m dom will be small to moderate in magnitude and positive in direction.

Prediction 34: The correlation between f suc and m dom will be positive in direction and small to moderate in magnitude.

All of the above relationships are genderically congruent ones. When reversed in direction, they in each case are predicted to be still positive but distinctly smaller in magnitude because here the dynamic force of weakness-strength is compromised by the genderic incongruency obtaining in each case.

Predictions 35, 36, 37: The correlations between m aff and f dom, m def and f dom, and m suc and f dom will be positive in direction but negligible or small in magnitude.

Insofar as each of the aforementioned need pairings involve different needs, each with somewhat different goals, each can be considered an instance of complementarity. In the case of f def and m dom the relationship is a *genderically congruent direct complementarity*. In the case of m def and f dom we have a *genderically incongruent direct complementarity*. In the cases of f suc-m dom and f aff-m dom, where the probable basis of the relationship is a need for emotional security and support latent in n aff and more or less manifest in n suc on the one side and a beneficence drive latent in n dom on the other we have examples of *diffuse complementarity*. In the instances of f aff-m dom and f suc-m dom this is *genericly congruent diffuse complementarity*, whereas with m aff-f dom and m suc-f dom it is *genericly incongruent diffuse complementarity*.

Outcomes: Of the foregoing set of six predictions, all were confirmed in direction and magnitude and 32 and 34 were above the conventional .05 level of significance.

Strength-Strength Attraction

The drives of nurturance, change, order, and intraception are ones with strength property of low or moderate degree and ones also linked more clearly to the feminine personality structure than to the masculine. On the basis of the principle of strength-strength attraction, i.e., *compatible strength* dynamic relations obtaining between high strength property and strength values of lesser and non-threatening values, each of them would be expected to be positively correlated with dominance, but especially so where coincidence with generic congruity obtains. Hence.

Prediction 38: There will be a positive correlation of small magnitude between f nur and m dom.

Prediction 39: There will be a positive correlation of small magnitude between f int and m dom.

Prediction 40: There will be a positive correlation of small magnitude between f chg and m dom.

Prediction 41: There will be a positive correlation of small magnitude between f ord and m dom.

When correlations in the opposite direction are being considered, that is, where the correlations between m nur-f dom, m int-f dom, m chg-f dom and m ord-f dom are involved, the correlations, while still positive in direction, will be smaller to negligible in size. These are *Predictions* 42, 43, 44, *and* 45.

Outcomes: All the foregoing eight were confirmed as to direction and magnitude. Two, 38 and 40 were significant.

The needs for endurance and exhibition are ones with low to moderate strength property, and while both are more strongly associated with masculinity than femininity, the linkage as indicated by Edwards' data, reproduced in Chapter Four in Table III, is the least strongly evidenced in his samples than that for any of the other male-linked motives. The principle of strength-strength attraction would still apply, but with the factor of genderic congruency now being merely one of degree of masculinity with respect to the correlated variables, since all are tied in with maleness rather than with femaleness. Since the tie to masculinity is much stronger in the case of n dom, the principle of genderic congruency would still be operative.

Predictions 46 and 47: There will be small positive correlations between f end-m dom and between f exh-m dom. Also,

Predictions 48 and 49: There will be small positive correlations between m end-f dom and between m exh-f dom. These will be smaller than those in the more gendericly congruent direction.

Achievement is strongly bonded with masculinity, although not as distinctly so as is dominance, and, as was noted earlier in the discussion out of which the predictions being made emerged, a female with high n ach requires a male who is very high in masculine traits in order for her to meet her needs for feminine identity and sex role maintenance. The stronger the female, the stronger the male required for gratification of the female's sexual identity drives. Hence there would be expected to be a positive correlation between f ach and m dom. *Prediction 50*: The reverse goes more strongly against the forces implied in the congruency principle, for a high achieving male who would find his own masculinity unthreatened by a female whose behaviors were to a high degree determined by her high n dom would have to be a pretty secure and self-confident specimen. They do exist, but are rare. *Prediction 51*: There will be a small negative correlation between f dom and m ach.

Outcomes: Of the just preceding six predictions, four were confirmed as to direction and magnitude. The other two, 48 and 51 were both exactly zero. None was significant.

Strength-Strength Repulsion

When we come to dominance vis à vis either autonomy or aggression we are in need conflict territory. In terms of the principle of strength-strength repulsion deriving from the conflicting goals of certain high potency needs, as well as from the dynamics associated with genderic incongruity, there should be repulsion between persons of opposite sexes with respect to these needs. A male with high n dom would find a female whose behaviors devolved to a high degree upon either n agg or n aut a highly intractable partner and she would find him repellent as well, for his dominance would frustrate her needs and result in punification, rather than gratification. Persons of either sex would not tend to choose persons whose needs and the behaviors dependent on their operation were very like their own. Such tendencies would be reflected in negative correlations between them on measures of these needs. Hence:

Predictions 52, 53, 54, and 55: There will be small negative correlations between m dom-f aut, m dom-f agg, f dom-m aut and f dom-m agg.

Outcomes: All were of the predicted direction and magnitude. None was significant.

Weakness-Strength Repulsion

It is an interesting peculiarity of the potency polarity that each extreme of the continuum of needs arrayed along this axis is characterized by repelling forces. Impotency does not attract potency or vice versa, but as noted earlier in the discussion, for quite different reasons in each case, one is repelled by the other. In accordance with the principle of weakness-strength repulsion, a small negative correlation is predicted between f aba-m dom and another of like characteristics for m aba-f dom (*Predictions 56 and 57*).

Outcomes: Both were as predicted. Neither was significant.

SEX

Although it would perhaps be more appropriate to reserve the discussion of correlates of the sex drive for consideration under the affection-hostility dimension, its relation to n dom can be predicted with equal facility in terms of the potency polarity. Here surely is a kind of strength each sex cherishes in the other, and in keeping with the principle of compatible strength-strength attraction there should be a positive correlation in both directions on sex and dominance. In fact, one would expect a moderate or even quite substantial correlation between m dom and f sex, for a male whose behavior is mediated to a high degree by n dom is about the sexiest creature imaginable for a highly sexed female (*Prediction 58*). For the reverse direction, however, the correlation is predicted to be positive and not much more (*Prediction 59*). The typical male is "turned off" by a highly dominant female, for she is too much like one of his own sex; his masculinity is threatened, and moreover he has been socialized to *expect* to be dominant in sexual interactions, just as in practically all others. But here clearly and unequivocally so.

Research findings are ambiguous on the point, but what evidence there is suggests that *the highly sexed female is often a moderately dominant one.* Maslow's (1937, 1942) studies of dominance in women revealed it to be positively associated with acceptance and enjoyment of sexual activities. If the sexy female, as suggested, is one high in dominance then the sexy male has perhaps often had an approach-avoidance conflict to resolve, possibly being often attracted to females on a sexual basis who turned out to be a bit "too much" for such a male on the dominance dimension. The survivors would be those males with high enough dominance to cope with that little serpent in Eden.

Outcomes: As predicted, m dom-f sex was .43 (p < .01). F dom-m sex was .09 (ns).

The predictions made for sex and dominance need correlations are consistent with generic congruency in strength-strength attraction but the predicted positive correlation for m sex-f dom might well have been a negative one on the basis of the principle of repulsion based on generically incongruent strength. This indicates that "males are repelled rather than attracted in response to manifestations of strength (read dominance here) in a female to the degree that the behaviors so characterized are socially identified with the definition of masculinity." The principle was not considered quite applicable because of the assumed linkage of sex drive and dominance in the female need system. With regard to the several other needs most strongly associated with masculinity; namely, achievement, aggression, autonomy and exhibition, no compromising factors are known which would forestall the invocation of this principle, hence: *Predictions 60, 61, 62, and 63*: There will be small negative correlations between m sex-f ach, m sex-f aut, m sex-f agg, and m sex-f exh. The negative correlation should be larger for m sex-f agg and m sex-f exh, moreover, because they also exemplify the operation of the principle of affection-hostility repulsion. What all of this results from in behavioral terms are the tendencies of males as instigated by their sex drive to have avoided choosing females as partners whose behaviors were strongly instigated by needs for aggression, autonomy, achievement and exhibition, for these behaviors would be strongly inhibitory, if not punifying, to male sexual impulses. They would be responded to as either too hostile or too masculine, or both.

Outcomes: All in direction as predicted; one significant at the .01 level (m sex-f aut).

But one sex's poison here is the other's meat. On the basis of the principle of attraction in terms of genderricly congruent strength, females' scores on n sex are predicted to be positively correlated with males' scores on each of these need variables.

Predictions 64, 65, 66, and 67: Correlations for f sex-m agg, f sex-m ach, f sex-m aut, and f sex-m exh will all be small to moderate in magnitude and positive in direction.

Since n agg has hostility property as well as strength, its inclusion in the foregoing list may be regarded as of dubious wisdom. But it was thought that the highly sexed female would be so resonant to the *masculine strength* involved in this behavioral resource that the male selected by her would tend to be highly endowed with it, despite its high hostility property, which, she may perceive, is not directed toward *her*.

Outcomes: All in direction as predicted with all but f sex-m ach significant.

Endurance, a male-linked need, and order, a female-linked one, but in both cases only to statistically significant degrees in the general adult population sampled by Edwards, should be, both of them, because of their strength property, correlated positively with n sex, also a drive with strength property. This is in accordance with the *principle of compatible strength*. The correlations should be small in both cases. Since neither n end nor n ord are in college populations strongly sex-linked, genderricly congruent effects would not be expected.

Predictions 68, 69, 70, and 71: There will be small positive correlations between m sex-f end, f sex-m end, m sex-f ord, and m ord-f sex.

Outcomes: Direction as predicted. Only m ord-f sex was significant (p < .05).

Sex is obviously distinctly more permeated with affectional property than it is with strength, but, as previously noted, this is more true when said of sexual impulses as they appear to function in the motivational structure of American college women today than of their male counterparts. The latter, however, often *are* represented by males who share with females an ideology of sex which justifies its expression essentially as an act of love and considers its value in the context of a loving relationship as an essentially *moral* act as well. Females of the college type tend to see sexual activity more often than not, also, as *only* moral and legitimate within the context of marriage. A recent review of the dozens of studies carried out in the last decade or so on the point reveals that two-thirds of American women still graduate from college as virgins. One-third of American males will do likewise. But more to the point is the continuing existence in some representatives of our male population, both off campus and on, of a double standard of sexual behavior and morality together with an exploitative orientation toward the female on this basis. This factor seriously dilutes the affectional property of the sex drive for males as compared with females. Although the blanket prediction is that all needs carrying appreciable affectional property will be positively correlated with n sex across gender there will be systematic differences in correlation magnitudes. It is predicted that those most distinctively affectional needs of the female, namely n affiliation and n nurturance will be more strongly correlated with the sex need measure of the male than will n def, n suc, n int, or n chg. This will be, for the reasons suggested in the preceding discussion, not true of correlations between f sex-m aff or f sex-m nur, which exemplifies once again the operation of the genderic congruency principle.

Predictions 72, 73, 74, 75, 76, 77, 78, 79, 80, 81, 82, *and* 83: There will be small positive correlations between m sex-f def, m sex-f aff, m sex-f suc, m sex-f nur, m sex-f chg, and m sex-f int; also, f sex-m def, f sex-m aff, f sex-m suc, f sex-m nur, f sex-m chg, and f sex-m int.

Outcome: All rs were in the direction predicted, but only one was significant.

There remains only the relationship of n sex and n abasement to be dealt with to complete the picture of sex drive relationships in this scheme of needs. As has been stressed already, strength and abject weakness are mutually repellent forces. It is difficult to imagine, with this as a conviction, that these lovers would have, on the basis of their respective sex needs, matched themselves with partners with strong abasing behaviors or those given to inferiority feelings, feelings of guilt, etc. It would be expected, rather, that a male with a strong sex need would avoid choosing a partner on this basis, but would seek instead a female with relatively high self-esteem. The same would apply in the case of the female as selector. She too would be expected to find a male with abasing qualities rather unattractive to her if she had a strong sex drive. Hence *Predictions 84 and 85*: The correlations between m sex-f aba and f sex-m aba will both be small negative ones. Such a relationship as these exemplify may be described as a *mutually repellent* need relation.

Outcomes: As predicted as to direction and magnitude. Not significant.

ABASEMENT

Since abject weakness and strength are mutually repellent, as already indicated for both dominance and sex in relation to abasement, the same should be the case for abasement with regard to other need variables having substantial strength property, especially where there are not other properties attached to the need which might override this tendency by the generation of stronger forces of attraction. The only need with sufficient other such properties is that of nurturance, which, while considered to have moderate strength property, also has high beneficence property and high affectional property as well. For these reasons a positive (and complementary) relationship to n aba should obtain. Hence, *Predictions 86 and 87*: There will be small positive correlations for m nur-f aba and m aba-f nur. A gendericly congruent effect should also be present, with the correlation of m aba-f nur being the larger one.

Outcomes: As predicted. M aba-f nur significant at .05 level.

For achievement, autonomy, aggression, exhibition, endurance, change, intraception, and order, all of them drives which generate behaviors having varying amounts of strength property, the correlations with abasement should be negative, indicative of mutual repulsion.

Predictions 88, 89, 90, 91, 92, 93, 94, 95, 96, 97, 98, 99, 100, 101, 102, and 103: There will be small negative correlations for m ach-f aba, m agg-f aba, m aut-f aba, m chg-f aba, m end-f aba, m exh-f aba, m int-f aba, and m ord-f aba, as well as for f ach-m aba, f agg-m aba, f aut-m aba, f chg-m aba, f end-m aba, f exh-m aba, f int-m aba, and f ord-m aba.

Outcomes: Of the sixteen predictions all but m aut-f aba were in the predicted direction. None was significant.

Of need variables not yet considered in relation to abasement there remain only affiliation, deference and succorance, all of which, unlike abasement, carry high to moderate affectional property. But it is primarily the weakness property of these latter variables and not their affectional property that creates forces of attraction between each of them and abasement. A person high in n aba is most likely to find one high in n def or n suc, and probably to a lesser degree one high in n aff, attractive, as they will him, because of the mutual weakness and nonthreatening characteristics of each other's behavior. Hence, *Predictions* 104, 105, 106, 107, 108, *and* 109: There will be small positive correlations between m def-f aba, f def-m aba, m suc-f aba, f suc-m aba, m aff-f aba, and f-aff-m aba. These seem best described as either reciprocative or coadjuvant need relations.

Outcomes: F suc-m aba was not as predicted, but not significant. The others were as predicted, and one, f def-m aba, was significant at the .01 level.

AUTONOMY

If abasement has an opposite on the strength dimension the most likely candidate would seem to be autonomy. Dominance, to be sure, has been assigned even greater strength property, but it has also some considerable affectional property, or at least affiliative property, for one cannot easily gratify his dominance drive except in associating with people, who will accept or welcome his managerial and directive services. Although dominance can be exercised in hostile ways, it need not be at all, and is frequently, if not mainly, accompanied by or fused with warmth, concern, solicitude, affection, and a beneficent style of response. Autonomy behavior does not have such qualities; but, like abasement behavior, is affectionately more or less neutral. It is neither affectionate nor hostile. Autonomy has essentially the aim of going one's own way without the interference or restraints of others, assertive to be sure, but not aggres-

sive unless threatened by the attempt of others at control or restraint of the freedom and independence sought.

Autonomy is strongly sex linked in popular conceptions with
masculinity, and this is borne out in the EPPS differences in means
between males' and females' scores on it. In considering its correlations with other high strength male-linked need variables, namely
achievement, aggression, and exhibition, the likelihood of conflict
seems quite great in the case of aggression, but less clear in the instances of n ach and n exh. Each of these needs had best be considered in relation to autonomy in terms which take as much account of the unique properties of each individual pairing as possible.
Take first, m aut-f ach: *Prediction* 110: There will be a low positive
correlation. Autonomy has somewhat greater strength value, than
n ach, and, moreover, the achievement motive, at least as measured
on the EPPS, does not appear to involve much control property, so
that a strong male—as indicated by scoring high in n aut—would not
be repelled by a female with high n ach. The reverse, m ach-f aut,
placing the greater strength value on the female side, would, on this
reasoning, call for at least a small negative correlation, indicative of
repulsion. This is *Prediction* 111.

Outcomes: Both are confirmed as to direction and magnitude.
neither reached significance.

With regard to aggression and exhibition in relation to autonomy,
not only are both extremely masculine, but one is also high and the
other moderately high in hostility property. The generalization has
already been made in an earlier context, that, while hostile behaviors
in females are repellent to a high degree for males, the reverse does
not hold. Females, associating hostility with masculine strength, not
only are tolerant of it in the main, but often feel consciously or unconsciously attracted to it. The net resolution of these forces leads
to *Predictions* 112, 113, 114, *and* 115: There will be small positive
correlations between f aut-m agg, and f aut-m exh, but the correlations between m aut-f agg, and m aut-f exh will be small negative
ones.

Outcomes: All confirmed as to direction and magnitude. M aut-
f agg was the only significant one.

Coming down the strength scale and skipping n sex, which has
already been considered, there remain nurturance, intraception,

change, endurance, and order to be related to n aut. Only order, although of comparatively much lesser strength property than autonomy, should generate repulsive forces. A person high in n aut would, with his demand for freedom from responsibility, conformity, planning and organization, find a person with high n order not just unattractive, but repellent. *Predictions 116 and 117:* There will be small negative correlations between m aut-f ord and f aut-m ord.

Outcomes: Both as predicted, but neither significant.

Autonomy and endurance are both congruent with masculinity, but they differ sufficiently in salience of sex linkage to make it likely that the difference will be manifest in the size of the positive correlations in the respective directions. That is to say, it is expected that females who score high on n end will be more strongly attracted to males scoring high on n aut, than will be the case for females scoring high on n aut with regard to males scoring high on n end. In fact, this latter relationship, since it places the more distinctly masculine resource on the female side, might almost be predicted to result in a negative correlation were it not for the fact that both autonomy and endurance vis à vis each other are relatively "live and let live" sorts of needs, neither generating behaviors that are likely to be punifying to persons motivated by the other. Further, because each lets the other fulfill itself without restraint, a mutually facilitatory condition obtains. *Predictions 118 and 119:* There will be small positive correlations for both m aut-f end and m end-f aut.

Outcomes: Both as predicted, but neither reached significance.

Nurturance, intraception, and change, each more linked to femininity than to masculinity, all give rise to behavioral resources of attractiveness values for males high in the masculine trait of autonomy. That is, they activate very feminine behaviors, which strong males find gratifying in diverse ways. And, of course, the autonomous male facilitates the gratification of the female's sexual identity drive. The same cannot be said in reverse. Females high in n aut would not be expected to find males highly attractive because they, the males, were high producers of nurturant, intraceptive and change sorts of behavior. And males would not find such females affording much gratification for *their* sexual identity drives. The positive correlations should differ to a marked degree in keeping with the factor of generic congruency.

Predictions 120, 121, *and* 122: There will be small positive correlations between f nur-m aut, f int-m aut, and f chg-m aut.

Predictions 123, 124, *and* 125: There will be small positive correlations between m nur-f aut, m int-f aut, and m chg-f aut, but these will be much smaller in magnitude than those with the greater genderic congruency.

Outcomes: All predictions were confirmed as to direction and magnitude except m nur-f aut. Predictions 120, 121 and 122 were all confirmed with significant rs.

There remain the needs affiliation, deference, and succorance to be considered in relation to autonomy. These are all needs with relatively high affectional property, but since n aut is so lacking in this same property, the relatedness is best treated in terms of the weakness property of the three in respect to the strength of aut. The genderic congruity will again be quite noticeable. More concretely, males high in n aut have the kind of behavioral resources prized by females high in aff, def and suc because of the gratifications accruing to their sex identity maintenance drive in such a relationship. Beyond this, of course, there is diffuse complementarity obtaining between aut on the one hand and aff, def and suc on the other. Hence, small to moderate positive correlations should be found. Males, on the other hand, who are high in these weakness and suppliance needs, confronted with females who are high in n aut are countenanced with ones who are manifesting a masculine behavioral pattern repellent to males. Yet the strength property is very great; there is the diffuse complementarity dynamic operating. Males will thus have an approach-avoidance dilemma because strength is a resource they seek. It is predicted that the forces of attraction are slightly stronger, resulting in very meagerly positive correlations in the several cases.

Predictions 126, 127, 128, 129, 130, *and* 131: There will be small to moderate positive correlations between m aut-f aff, m aut-f def, and m aut-f suc. There will also be positive correlations, smaller in magnitude, between f aut-m aff, f aut-m def, and f aut-m suc.

Outcomes: Only f aut-m def was not in the predicted direction. It was not significant. M aut-f aff and m aut-f suc were both significant.

The several most recently considered relationships all seem to be within the accepted definition of diffuse complementary ones. Those who like giving names to things will delight in these: the first set represent instances of *transituational bi-directional gendericly congruent diffuse complementarity*. The second set exemplify the phenomenon of *transituational unidirectional gendericly incongruent diffuse complementarity*. But that is not all. For a set of relationships such as m aut-f suc and m suc-f aut, we can, with semantic and lexicographical precision, refer to it is *transituationally reciprocal diffuse complementarity*. It is doubtful that such terminology will ever become very popular. The reader may be reassured to know that it will also find no further use here.

ACHIEVEMENT

Diffuse complementarity should also be found for two of these three recently discussed affectional needs (n aff, and n suc) and the achievement drive. The relationship between deference and achievement is a specific and direct complementarity. These statements are made on the assumption, of course, that n ach has already promoted some visual and actual achievement, although it is at least possible that a high n ach person's mere airing of his hopes and plans and aspirations for accomplishment might have stimulus value enough to evoke deference responses in some people. The following predictions are logical deductions from the principle of weakness-strength attraction.

Predictions 132, 133, 134, 135, 136, and 137: There will be small positive correlations between m ach-f def, f ach-m def, m ach-f aff, f ach-m aff, m ach-f suc, and m suc-f ach.

Outcomes: All of these were correct as to directions and magnitude, and the correlations for m ach-f def, f ach-m def, and m ach-f aff all reached significance.

The high n ach person of either sex should, in accordance with the principle of compatible (or nonthreatening) strength attraction, ceteris paribus, find those with behavioral resources deriving from needs of considerably lesser strength property, namely, nurturance, intraception, order, change, and endurance, attractive to him or her.

Predictions 138, 139, 140, 141, 142, 143, 144, 145, 146, and 147: There will be small positive correlations between m ach-f nur, m nur-f ach, m ach-f int, f ach-m int, m ach-f ord, f ach-m ord, m ach-f chg, f ach-m chg, m ach-f end, and f ach-m end.

Outcomes: Of the ten predictions, 9 were correct as to direction and magnitude. The r was negative for m ach-f ord, but not significant. M ach-f nur was significant at the .01 level, and f ach-m ord was at the .05 value.

These many last mentioned coinstrumental need relationships are not complementary ones, but, rather, coadjuvant or coagential ones.

There remain to be related to achievement only aggression and exhibition, both male-linked, high and moderate strength needs with hostility property. Their relationships with n ach are essentially similar, determined by the same principles, as those obtaining in the instances of their relationships with n autonomy. Females high in n ach will be attracted to males manifesting aggressive and exhibitionist behaviors because these are masculine and strong. Although repelling forces may be emanating from these behaviors, they are counteracted in all but the weakest of females (those high in n abasement), and are dampened and overridden by the counterforces of attraction. Males, on the other hand, high in n ach or otherwise, will experience repulsion when these masculine and hostile traits appear in a female. Hence the females chosen by the males in a sample of fiancés will have been those with low scores on these needs. The tendencies should result in negative correlations. Therefore, *Predictions* 148, 149, 150, *and* 151: There will be small positive correlations between f ach-m agg and f ach-m exh, but small negative correlations between m ach-f agg and m ach-f exh.

Outcomes: All the rs were in the predicted direction and of the predicted magnitude. Two of the four, f ach-m exh and m ach-f agg had correlations significant at the .01 level.

AGGRESSION

Aggression has already been considered in relation to all of the other strong masculine motives except exhibition, the only other need with which it shares the property of hostility. The hypothesis that is most likely to suggest itself to one in considering the two drives vis à vis one another is that repulsion would be the result of the confrontation of a male and female each high in one of these needs. The data from which was derived the principle of coadjuvance, however, contraindicated such an outcome. Recall that in the Banta and Hetherington data exhibited in Table V that the correlations between m agg-f agg and m exh-f exh are both positive, and the latter significantly so. Also in the early part of this monograph it was pointed out that the correlations for both n agg and n exh became *less positive* or *more negative* with the decreasing degree of intimacy of the relationships presented in Table V. The girls the boys left behind were not hostile enough. Hostile people need other hostile people to fight with, for fighting is enjoyable and exciting and gratifying to them. Probably it would be closer to the truth, of course, to say that some of them some of the time like a good scrap. It was also noted in the context of discussion of the assertive drives that it would be unreasonable to expect extremely high scoring persons on them to be found attractive to one another. This would be because of the possibilities of punifications mutually deliverable by such extremes being so great as to negate the forces of attraction arising from the enjoyable features of combat. More moderately scoring n agg and n exh people can be attracted. Extreme n aggs or extreme n exhs cannot. Thus, since only the more moderate scorers are mutually attracted and are found in samples of afiancéd persons, while the very high scorers are mutually repelled and are not found in such samples, the correlations obtaining for such samples would inevitably be low.

Predictions 152 and 153: There will be small positive correlations between m agg-f exh and m exh-f agg.

Outcomes: The prediction for m agg-f exh was confirmed as to direction but failed to reach the .05 significant level. The value for the other r was 0.

While it is true that one wart hog looks "real good" to another wart hog, the beast is not beautiful to others. Only a male fairly high in hostility himself is likely to find a *hostile female* attractive. Males' scores on the affection needs, such as affiliation, nurturance, deference, succorance, and intraception, would be expected to have negative correlations with females' scores on n agg. The reverse will not hold however, for females are attracted to high n agg males both because of the strength value and the masculinity property of this behavioral resource. It provides gratification for their sexual identity drives.

Predictions 154, 155, 156, 157, 158, 159, 160, 161, 162, and 163: The correlations between m aff-f agg, m nur-f agg, m def-f agg, m suc-f agg, and m int-f agg will be small negative ones. However, the correlations between f aff-m agg, f nur-m agg, f def-m agg, f suc-m agg, and f int-m agg will be small positive ones.

Outcomes: Nine of the ten predictions were borne out as to direction and magnitude, and of these, the rs for m aff-f agg and m nur-f agg reached the .01 significance level. The mispredicted m suc-f agg was not significant.

Change, which is considered to have low or moderate affectional property, was not considered in the preceding set of affectional needs because it is also related to n agg along the excitement-sameness dimension. The shared property of excitement generates forces of attraction between n chg and n agg, but these it is believed, will not be strong enough in the case of the male to override the repulsion generated in him by an aggressive female. This leads once again to a genderícly congruent type of prediction.

Predictions 164 *and* 165: There will be a small negative correlation between m chg and f agg, but a small positive correlation between f chg and m agg.

Outcomes: Both were confirmed as to direction and magnitude, but only the r for m chg-f agg was significant.

Order and endurance needs are related to aggression on the excitement-sameness dimension as well as in the strength-weakness mode, and while in the latter case the strength positions are favorable for forecasting positive correlations, repulsion forces are likely to be generated because of the disparate values on the former (excitement-sameness) polarization. These are strong enough, it is judged, to indicate the resulting correlations to be negative for these two variables and n agg.

Predictions 166, 167, 168, *and* 169: There will be small negative correlations between m agg-f ord, m agg-f end, f agg-m end, and f agg-m ord. The latter two correlations should be larger negative ones because of the genderic incongruity involved in the case of f agg.

Outcomes: All except the f agg-m ord prediction were confirmed as to direction, but at little better than chance values. The misprediction was a failure at a similar level.

EXHIBITION

Much of what has been described for the relatedness of n agg to the needs of the opposite sex in intersexual attraction and repulsion could be almost duplicated for exhibition; for, as has been noted, it is similar in properties, having moderate strength value, moderate hostility property, and moderate excitement character. Exhibition takes second place, however, on all three dimensions.

Other things being equal, as has already been noted, males find the behaviors based on this need repellent rather than attractive when embodied in a feminine personality. At least two cases where other things are not equal are found in males with high n deference and n succorance respectively. Like n ach, one of the goals of n exh is recognition and another is superiority. These, plus its strength property, all unite to create a relation of complementarity between it and n deference and it and n succorance. This complementarity dynamic, it has frequently been noted, is a very powerful one. It is judged capable in this instance of overriding the genderic incongruency sufficiently strongly to result in meagerly positive rs in both directions, although those in the more congruent direction should be somewhat larger.

Predictions 170, 171, 172, *and* 173: There will be small positive correlations between m exh-f def, m def-f exh, m exh-f suc, and m suc-f exh.

Outcomes: All four were in the predicted direction. One, m exh-f suc had an r large enough for significance at the .05 level.

Affiliation, although it has been characterized as having weakness property, does not have either the still greater dependency quality of n suc or the unique properties that give n def its requiredness for n exhibition. If the n aff is an aspect of a feminine person's need system and the n exh is found in the make up of the male partner, the correlation would be expected to be positive, and hence could be regarded as an instance of gendericly congruent diffuse complementarity. With the roles reversed, however, the direction of the correlation will also be. This is to say, in other words, that males who score high in n aff will not seek to affiliate with females scoring high in n exh, but being repelled, will choose as partners females scoring lower in n exh. These are *Predictions* 174 *and* 175.

For the remaining motives with high affectional property, namely n nur, n int, and n chg, exactly the same statements and patterns of correlations should be found.

Predictions 176, 177, 178, 179, 180, *and* 181: There will be small positive correlations between m exh-f nur, m exh-f int, and m exh-f chg, but small negative correlations will be found between f exh-m nur, f exh-m int, and f exh-m chg.

Outcomes: Of the eight foregoing predictions, eight were confirmed as to direction and magnitude. Three, f aff-m exh, m exh-f nur, and m exh-f chg, reached at least the .05 level of significance.

Since endurance and order have no excitement value but sameness property instead, whereas exhibition does have the former, negative correlations would be expected on that basis. However, the strength values are compatible, and attraction on the strength dimension might be expected to counteract what repelling forces are set up by the disparate positions on the other axis. This leaves the only secure basis for prediction the differential in terms of gender; in terms of the operation of the sexual identity drives of each. In short, males are repelled, ceteris paribus by exhibition behaviors in females, whereas females are attracted to exhibition behaviors in males.

Predictions 182, 183, 184, *and* 185: There will be small positive correlations between m exh-f end and m exh-f ord, but small negative correlations between f exh-m end and f exh-m ord.

Outcomes: The r for f exh-m ord was the only one of the four not conforming to expectation. None of the correlations reached significance.

NURTURANCE

Nurturance, ranked somewhat lower than n exh on the strength-weakness dimension, is a need of quite a different character to it; one having high beneficence quality along with high affectional property. Many of its intersexual relationships with other needs have already been described. Its complementary role in relation to succorance has already been several times noted. On the basis of the beneficence property it has, it should also be regarded as complementary (diffuse) with deference and affiliation, both of which have suppliance property.

Predictions 186, 187, 188, *and* 189: There will be small to moderate correlations between m nur-f def, f nur-m def, m nur-f agg, and f nur-m aff.

Outcomes: All were as predicted and all significant; two at the .01 level.

In terms of the principle of affection-affection attraction the correlations of nurturance with intraception and change should also be small positive ones (*Predictions* 190, 191, 192, *and* 193). These latter are not complementary relations, but are better seen as reciprocal ones mediated by the affectional properties of these motives.

Outcomes: All four rs were in the expected direction. One, m int-f nur, was significant at the .01 level.

Since neither order nor endurance have affectional property, the most meaningful way of relating them to n nur is in terms of the strength dimension. At the places they severally occupy on that scale, within the domain of compatible strength, all the correlations should be small positive ones.

Predictions 194, 195, 196, *and* 197: There will be small positive correlations between m nur-f end, f nur-m end, m nur-f ord, and f nur-m ord.

Outcomes: All were in the expected direction. None was significant.

AFFILIATION

Affiliation has few relationships left to be examined; specifically those with n def, n suc, n int, n chg, n end and n ord. The affectional principle applies to the first four of these. All of the correlations should be small positive ones. These are *Predictions* 198, 199, 200, 201, 202, 203, 204, *and* 205.

Outcomes: All but the r for m aff-f def were significant in the predicted direction.

The relationships of n aff with n end and n ord are not, in terms of their positions on the strength-weakness polarity, or in terms of genderic congruency factors, in any way so incompatible as to create forces of repulsion, but neither are they such as to generate powerful forces of attraction on the basis of differential strength. Nevertheless, end and ord have sufficient strength property to function as complementaries, in a diffuse sense for n aff, and, hence, some attraction is generated, so:

Predictions 206, 207, 208, *and* 209: There will be small positive correlations between m aff-f end, f aff-m end, m aff-f ord, and f aff-m ord.

Outcomes: All but m aff-f ord were in the predicted direction. One, m aff-f end was significant at the .05 level.

DEFERENCE

Deference is another essentially affectional need. There remains to be noted only its relations to three other affectional needs; n suc, n int, and n chg, and its relations to two minor strength needs, endurance and order. With regard to the three affectional needs, the affection-affection dynamic principle is applicable. Hence, all correlations should be small positive ones. These are *Predictions* 210, 211, 212, 213, 214, *and* 215.

Outcomes: Of these last six, five were correct as to direction and magnitude with two of them significant. Mispredicted was m def-f int, but it was not significant.

With respect to n ord and n end, the statements made above vis à vis n aff and these needs seem about equally applicable here.

Predictions 216, 217, 218, *and* 219: There will be small positive correlations between m def-f end, f def-m end, m def-f ord, and f def-m ord.

Outcomes: All outcomes except m def-f ord were in the direction expected. None was significant.

SUCCORANCE

Succorance remains to be related only to n chg, n int, n end and n ord. With the first two the principle of affection applies and positive correlations indicative of attraction should be found.

Predictions 220, 221, 222, *and* 223: There will be small positive correlations between m suc-f chg, f suc-m chg, m suc-f int, and f suc-m int.

Outcomes: All in predicted direction. Two, m suc-f chg and f suc-m int, were significant at the .05 level.

With regard to endurance and order, both low strength drives, and n suc, a high affectional dependency need, no attraction forces of any consequence obtain. Succorance is a "needy" need, and although n end and n ord do have some strength, the behavioral resources generated by these needs are quite irrelevant to what the highly succorant person is seeking. Persons high in n suc would not tend to select mates who had high scores on either n end or n ord. About the only basis that can be found for predicting anything in these cases is the possible appeal that a person with some strength of any kind might have for someone as dependent as a person high in n suc. This is suggested by the phenomenon of diffuse complementarity to be at least a plausible hypothesis.

Predictions 224, 225, 226, *and* 227: There will be very small positive correlations between m suc-f end, m suc-f ord, f suc-m end, and f suc-m ord.

Outcomes: Two of the four were as predicted. None even approached significance. In retrospect, it would seem that this was pushing the strength-weakness principle too hard. It would have been wiser to have invoked *the postulate of irrelevance.*

CHANGE

Change has the properties of excitement, affection and minor strength. On the affection dimension it has been examined in relation to all needs except intraception. To this it should be positively correlated because affection attracts affection.

Predictions 228 *and* 229: There will be small positive correlations between m chg-f int, and m int-f chg.

Outcomes: As expected, with m int-f chg significant.

Looking at change in juxtaposition with n end and n ord respectively, it is noticeable that the former has moderate excitement value, whereas the latter two are high in sameness property. The correlations should be negative in accordance with the dynamic principle of excitement-sameness repulsion.

Predictions 230, 231, 232, *and* 233: There will be small negative correlations between m chg-f end, m chg-f ord, f chg-m end, and f chg-m ord.

Outcomes: As expected, but none was significant.

INTRACEPTION

Since the only property common between n int and n end and n ord respectively is on the strength-weakness continuum, and all are found closely similar in value, compatible strength is the basis of positive attraction between persons high in n int and n end and n ord respectively.

Predictions 234, 235, 236, *and* 237: There will be small positive correlations between m int-f end, m int-f ord, f int-m end, and f int-m ord.

Outcomes: All except f int-m end were in the expected direction, but none significant.

ENDURANCE

For n endurance, whose relationship to n order is the only one remaining to be accounted for, positive correlations with order are predicted on the basis of compatible, mutually valued strength resources, as well as in terms of the reciprocally gratifying sameness property both needs have.

Predictions 238 *and* 239: There will be small positive correlations between m end-f ord and f end-m ord.

Outcomes: Both as expected, but only the second one significant.

CHAPTER ELEVEN

EVALUATION OF INSTRUMENTAL THEORY AS A WHOLE AND OF THE THEORY OF INTERMOTIVATIONAL DYNAMICS IN PARTICULAR

PREDICTIVE POWER OF INSTRUMENTAL THEORY AS A WHOLE

THE MOST RIGOROUS TEST of any set of theoretical formulations is its usefulness in prediction of outcomes or relationships between variables. Hence, it is essentially upon demonstrating efficacy in this respect that support and validation for the instrumental theory can rest most firmly. Let us briefly give some attention to the question of predictive power of the theory as a whole, and then of that of the theory of intermotivational dynamics in particular.

The correlations for all variables with all others obtained in the current study are presented in Table XVII. Table XVIII exhibits a correlation matrix obtained for the same variables with a sample of 71 couples randomly constituted from the same pool of males and females who served as subjects in the present project. Clearly, the two correlation matrices are not much alike in pattern, even though the magnitudes of many correlations in Table XVII are not distinctly greater than those in Table XVIII. The inference from the comparison which seems compelled is that the dissimilarity is due to the operation of different concatenations of causal circumstances and forces in the respective cases. The patterns of correlations in Table XVII are a reflection of causal conditions believed to be in highly close correspondence to the description it has taken many pages to give of them in terms of the instrumental theory, while those in Table XVIII are the outcomes of so-called chance factors.

TABLE XVII

CORRELATION MATRIX FOR THE FIFTEEN NEEDS

	Aba		Ach		Aff		Agg		Aut		Chg		Def		Dom		End		Exh		Int		Nur		Ord		Sex		Suc	
	M	F	M	F	M	F	M	F	M	F	M	F	M	F	M	F	M	F	M	F	M	F	M	F	M	F	M	F	M	F
F Aba	.26		-.05		.04		-.04		.02		-.17		.01		-.04		-.19		-.14		-.09		.18		-.14		-.11		.04	
M Aba				-.03		.04		-.09		-.17		-.12		.29		-.07		-.07		-.13		-.14		.24		.02		-.04		.04
F Ach			.13		.17		.08		.15		.16		.25		.17		.13		.33		.06		.16		.21		-.18		.13	
M Ach						.41		-.30		-.11		.18		.21		.00		.08		-.14		.14		.36		-.03		.19		.19
F Aff					.56		.14		.42		.34		.28		.50		.04		.37		.47		.30		.06		.39		.34	
M Aff								-.31		.02		.25		.14		.04		.21		-.14		.22		.40		-.01		.11		.14
F Agg							.06		-.25		-.32		-.12		-.14		-.09		.00		-.17		-.30		.01		-.21		.02	
M Agg										-.06		.08		.14		-.04		-.01		.10		.17		.15		-.14		.28		.05
F Aut									.13		.01		-.11		-.02		.03		.12		.07		-.04		-.08		-.06		.02	
M Aut											.30		.25		.25		.02		-.14		.27		.27		-.11		.22		.24
F Chg											.31		.08		.09		.08		.26		.23		.14		.13		.15		.22	
M Chg													.12		.19		.15		-.06		.15		.17		.06		.14		.11
F Def												.29		.15		.05		.17		.25		.24		.13		.08		.18	
M Def															.16		.00		.09		-.11		.25		-.04		.15		.08
F Dom														—		.09		.19		.04		.01		.15		.09		.09	
M Dom																	.16		.10		.15		.26		.18		.43		.32
F End																—		.13		.17		.12		.21		.08		.04	
M End																			.19		-.03		.12		.09		.07		-.01
F Exh																		—		-.05		-.10		.07		-.11		.05	
M Exh																					.11		.27		.02		.07		.25
F Int																				.17		.07		.06		.19		.15	
M Int																							.33		.01		.19		.24
F Nur																						.36		.09		.32		.33	
M Nur																									.07		.10		.07
F Ord																								.27		.03		-.08	
M Ord																											.24		.05
F Sex																										.64		.24	
M Sex																													.16
F Suc																												.23	
M Suc																														—

TABLE XVIII
CORRELATION MATRIX FOR RANDOMLY MATED MALES AND FEMALES

The table is a triangular correlation matrix among 15 variables. Column headings give each variable with Male (M) and Female (F) entries; the left‑hand stub lists the paired rows (F Aba, M Aba, F Ach, M Ach, … F Suc, M Suc). Each cell below is shown as **M value / F value**; a dash (—) marks the diagonal.

	Aba (M/F)	Ach (M/F)	Aff (M/F)	Agg (M/F)	Aut (M/F)	Chg (M/F)	Def (M/F)	Dom (M/F)	End (M/F)	Exh (M/F)	Int (M/F)	Nur (M/F)	Ord (M/F)	Sex (M/F)	Suc (M/F)
Aba	.03 / —	.02 / -.06	.07 / -.10	.15 / .08	.22 / .13	-.02 / -.11	.04 / -.02	.03 / .24	.03 / .08	.04 / .08	-.06 / -.06	.01 / -.15	-.04 / .13	-.10 / .04	.19 / -.12
Ach		.07 / —	.18 / -.13	-.09 / .08	-.15 / -.05	-.05 / -.03	.05 / -.03	.23 / -.05	-.12 / .13	-.10 / -.10	.01 / .01	.08 / .05	.14 / .04	.07 / .00	.18 / .20
Aff			.05 / —	.07 / -.09	-.08 / -.23	-.11 / .09	.03 / .23	-.08 / .04	-.29 / .01	.09 / .10	-.12 / -.14	-.11 / .00	-.07 / .18	-.06 / .12	-.12 / .06
Agg				-.01 / —	.10 / -.06	-.03 / -.20	.01 / -.03	.05 / -.06	.07 / .05	-.16 / -.14	.04 / .04	.03 / .02	.18 / .17	.06 / -.02	-.04 / -.12
Aut					—	-.16 / -.07	-.17 / -.12	-.12 / -.18	-.15 / -.18	-.13 / -.13	-.11 / .03	-.12 / .05	.06 / .04	-.12 / .00	.09 / -.14
Chg						-.09 / —	-.10 / -.01	-.07 / -.11	-.20 / -.02	-.04 / -.11	-.10 / .00	.00 / -.01	-.02 / .02	.03 / .09	-.01 / -.12
Def							.12 / —	.09 / .04	.02 / .20	.03 / -.09	-.02 / .00	.21 / .02	-.06 / .08	.04 / -.15	.07 / -.09
Dom								.05 / —	-.11 / .03	-.05 / .02	-.07 / .18	-.03 / .17	.02 / -.05	.03 / .06	.04 / -.06
End									-.03 / —	.22 / -.04	.02 / -.11	.03 / -.15	.11 / .05	.07 / -.15	.24 / -.23
Exh										-.21 / —	-.05 / .16	-.04 / .24	.04 / .04	-.07 / -.11	-.03 / -.14
Int											-.02 / —	.18 / .01	.06 / -.02	-.08 / .06	.18 / -.16
Nur												-.11 / —	.15 / .05	.14 / .13	.09 / .02
Ord													-.02 / —	.12 / .03	.25 / -.11
Sex														.12 / —	.04 / -.08
Suc															.07 / —

TABLE XIX

THE 225 CORRELATIONS WITH THE DIRECTION AND MAGNITUDE OF THE PREDICTION, THE SIGNIFICANCE LEVEL, AND THE NATURE OF THE HYPOTHESIZED RELATIONSHIP

Prediction No.	Needs Correlated	Direction		Magnitude		P (one tail)	Nature of Relationship Hypothesized
		Predicted	Obtained	Predicted	Obtained		
25	M Aba-F Aba	+	+	Moderate to small	.26	.05	Reciprocative or Coadjuvant
96	M Aba-F Ach	−	−	Small	−.03	.40	Mutually Repellent
88	F Aba-M Ach	−	−	Small	−.05	.35	Mutually Repellent
109	M Aba-F Aff	+	+	Small	.04	.40	Reciprocative or Coadjuvant
108	F Aba-M Aff	+	+	Small	.04	.40	Reciprocative or Coadjuvant
97	M Aba-F Agg	−	−	Small	−.09	.25	Mutually Repellent
89	F Aba-M Agg	−	−	Small	−.04	.40	Mutually Repellent
98	M Aba-F Aut	−	−	Small	−.17	.10	Mutually Repellent
90	F Aba-M Aut	−	+	Small	.02	.45	Mutually Repellent
99	M Aba-F Chg	−	−	Small	−.17	.10	Mutually Repellent
91	F Aba-M Chg	−	−	Small	−.12	.20	Mutually Repellent

105	M Aba-F Def	+	+	Small	.29	.01	Reciprocative or Coadjuvant
104	F Aba-M Def	+	+	Small	.01	.50	Reciprocative or Coadjuvant
57	M Aba-F Dom	−	−	Small	−.07	.25	Mutually Repellent
56	F Aba-M Dom	−	−	Small	−.04	.40	Mutually Repellent
100	M Aba-F End	−	−	Small	−.07	.25	Mutually Repellent
92	F Aba-M End	−	−	Small	−.19	.10	Mutually Repellent
101	M Aba-F Exh	−	−	Small	−.13	.15	Mutually Repellent
93	F Aba-M Exh	−	−	Small	−.14	.15	Mutually Repellent
102	M Aba-F Int	−	−	Small	−.14	.15	Mutually Repellent
94	F Aba-M Int	−	−	Small	−.09	.25	Mutually Repellent
26, 87	M Aba-F Nur	+++	++	Small	.24	.05	Complementary
27, 86	F Aba-M Nur	+	+	Small	.18	.10	Complementary
103	M Aba-F Ord	−	−	Small	.02	.45	Mutually Repellent
95	F Aba-M Ord	−	−	Small	−.14	.15	Mutually Repellent
85	M Aba-F Sex	−	−	Small	−.04	.40	Mutually Repellent
84	F Aba-M Sex	−	−	Small	−.11	.20	Mutually Repellent

TABLE XIX—*Continued*

Prediction No.	Needs Correlated	Direction Predicted	Direction Obtained	Magnitude Predicted	Magnitude Obtained	P (one tail)	Nature of Relationship Hypothesized
107	M Aba-F Suc	+	—	Small	—.13	.15	Reciprocative or Coadjuvant
106	F Aba-M Suc	+	+	Small	.15	.15	Reciprocative or Coadjuvant
6	M Ach-F Ach	+	+	Small	.13	.15	Coagential
134	M Ach-F Aff	+	+	Small	.41	.01	Diffusely Complementary
135	F Ach-M Aff	+	+	Small	.17	.10	Diffusely Complementary
150	M Ach-F Agg	—	—	Small	—.30	.01	Gendericly Repellent
148	F Ach-M Agg	+	+	Small	.08	.25	Gendericly Attractive
111	M Ach-F Aut	—	—	Small	—.11	.20	Gendericly Repellent
110	F Ach-M Aut	+	+	Small	.15	.15	Gendericly Attractive
144	M Ach-F Chg	+	+	Small	.18	.10	Coadjuvant
145	F Ach-M Chg	+	+	Small	.16	.10	Coadjuvant
132	M Ach-F Def	+	+	Small	.21	.05	Complementary
133	F Ach-M Def	+	+	Small	.25	.05	Complementary
51	M Ach-F Dom	—	0	Small	.00	.50	Gendericly Repellent
50	F Ach-M Dom	+	+	Small	.17	.10	Gendericly Attractive

No.	Pair						Classification
146	M Ach-F End	+	+	Small	.08	.25	Coadjuvant or Coagential
147	F Ach-M End	+	+	Small	.13	.15	Coadjuvant or Coagential
151	M Ach-F Exh	−	−	Small	−.14	.15	Gendericly Repellent
149	F Ach-M Exh	+	+	Small	.33	.01	Gendericly Attractive
140	M Ach-F Int	+	+	Small	.14	.15	Coadjuvant
141	F Ach-M Int	+	+	Small	.06	.30	Coadjuvant
138	M Ach-F Nur	+	+	Small	.36	.01	Coadjuvant
139	F Ach-M Nur	+	+	Small	.16	.10	Coadjuvant
142	M Ach-F Ord	−	−	Small	−.03	.40	Coadjuvant or Coagential
143	F Ach-M Ord	+	+	Small	.21	.05	Coadjuvant or Coagential
65	M Ach-F Sex	+	+	Small	.19	.10	Gendericly Attractive
60	F Ach-M Sex	−	−	Small	−.18	.10	Gendericly Repellent
136	M Ach-F Suc	+	+	Small	.19	.10	Diffusely Complementary
137	F Ach-M Suc	+	+	Small	.13	.15	Diffusely Complementary
2	M Aff-F Aff	+	+	Moderate	.56	.01	Reciprocative
154	M Aff-F Agg	−	−	Small	−.31	.01	Gendericly Repellent
159	F Aff-M Agg	+	+	Small	.14	.15	Gendericly Attractive

TABLE XIX—*Continued*

Prediction No.	Needs Correlated	Direction Predicted	Direction Obtained	Magnitude Predicted	Magnitude Obtained	P (one tail)	Nature of Relationship Hypothesized
129	M Aff-F Aut	+	+	Small	.02	.45	Diffusely
126	F Aff-M Aut	+	+	Small	.42	.01	Complementary Diffusely
204	M Aff-F Chg	+	+	Small	.25	.05	Complementary Reciprocative
205	M Aff-F Chg	+	+	Small	.34	.01	Reciprocative
198	M Aff-F Def	+	+	Small	.14	.15	Reciprocative
199	F Aff-M Def	+	+	Small	.28	.01	Reciprocative
35	M Aff-F Dom	+	+	Small or Negligible	.04	.35	Diffusely
32	F Aff-M Dom	+	+	Moderate	.50	.01	Complementary Diffusely
206	M Aff-F End	+	+	Small	.21	.05	Complementary Coinstrumental or Diffusely
207	F Aff-M End	+	+	Small	.04	.40	Complementary Coinstrumental or Diffusely
175	M Aff-F Exh	−	−	Small	−.14	.15	Complementary Gendericly Repellent
174	F Aff-M Exh	+	+	Small	.37	.01	Gendericly Attractive and/or Diffusely
202	M Aff-F Int	+	+	Small	.22	.05	Complementary Reciprocative

No.	Pair			Magnitude			Description
203	F Aff-M Int	+	+	Small	.47	.01	Reciprocative
189	M Aff-F Nur	+	+	Small to Moderate	.40	.01	Reciprocative or Diffusely Complementary
188	F Aff-M Nur	+	+	Small to Moderate	.30	.01	Reciprocative or Diffusely Complementary
208	M Aff-F Ord	+	—	Small	—.01	.50	Coinstrumental or Diffusely Complementary
209	F Aff-M Ord	+	+	Small	.06	.30	Coinstrumental or Diffusely Complementary
79	M Aff-F Sex	+	+	Small	.11	.20	Reciprocative
73	F Aff-M Sex	+	+	Small	.39	.01	Reciprocative
200	M Aff-F Suc	+	+	Small	.14	.20	Reciprocative
201	F Aff-M Suc	+	+	Small	.34	.01	Reciprocative
3	M Agg-F Agg	+	+	Small	.06	.30	Coadjuvant
112	M Agg-F Aut	+	+	Small	.06	.30	Gendericly Attractive
114	F Agg-M Aut	—	—	Small	—.25	.05	Gendericly Repellent
165	M Agg-F Chg	+	+	Small	.08	.25	Gendericly Attractive
164	F Agg-M Chg	—	—	Small	—.32	.01	Gendericly Repellent
161	M Agg-F Def	+	+	Small	.14	.15	Gendericly Attractive, Diffusely Complementary

TABLE XIX—*Continued*

Prediction No.	Needs Correlated	Direction Predicted	Direction Obtained	Magnitude Predicted	Magnitude Obtained	P (one tail)	Nature of Relationship Hypothesized
156	F Agg-M Def	—	—	Small	−.12	.20	Gendericly Repellent
55	M Agg-F Dom	—	—	Small	−.04	.40	Mutually Repellent
53	F Agg-M Dom	—	—	Small	−.14	.15	Mutually Repellent
167	M Agg-F End	—	—	Small	−.01	.50	Mutually Repellent
168	F Agg-M End	—	—	Small	−.09	.25	Mutually Repellent
152	M Agg-F Exh	+	+	Small	.10	.20	Coadjuvant
153	F Agg-M Exh	+	0	Small	.00	.50	Coadjuvant
163	M Agg-F Int	+	+	Small	.17	.10	Gendericly Attractive
158	F Agg-M Int	—	—	Small	−.17	.10	Gendericly Repellent
160	M Agg-F Nur	+	+	Small	.15	.15	Gendericly Attractive
155	F Agg-M Nur	—	—	Small	−.30	.01	Gendericly Repellent
166	M Agg-F Ord	—	—	Small	−.14	.15	Mutually Repellent
169	F Agg-M Ord	—	+	Small	.01	.50	Mutually Repellent
64	M Agg-F Sex	+	+	Small	.28	.01	Gendericly Attractive

ID	Pair	Sign 1	Sign 2	Size	r	r	Classification
62	F Agg-M Sex	—	—	Small	−.21	.05	Gendericly Repellent
162	M Agg-F Suc	+	+	Small	.05	.35	Gendericly Attractive
157	F Agg-M Suc	+	+	Small	.02	**.45**	Gendericly Repellent
18	M Aur-F Aut	+	+	Small to Moderate	.13	.15	Reciprocative, Coadjuvant
122	M Aut-F Chg	+	+	Small	.31	.01	Coadjuvant
125	F Aut-M Chg	+	+	Small	.01	.50	Coadjuvant
127	M Aut-F Def	+	+	Small	.08	.25	Diffusely Complementary
130	F Aut-M Def	—	+	Small	−.11	.20	Diffusely Complementary
54	M Aut-F Dom	—	—	Small	−.02	**.45**	Mutually Repellent
52	F Aut-M Dom	—	—	Small	−.02	**.45**	Mutually Repellent
118	M Aut-F End	+	+	Small	.16	.10	Coadjuvant
119	F Aut-M End	+	+	Small	.03	.40	Coadjuvant
115	M Aut-F Exh	—	—	Small	−.14	.15	Gendericly Repellent
113	F Aut-M Exh	+	+	Small	.12	.20	Gendericly Attractive
121	M Aut-F Int	+	+	Small	.27	.05	Gendericly Attractive
124	F Aut-F Nur	+	+	Small	.07	**.25**	Coadjuvant
120	M Aut-F Nur	+	+	Small	.27	.05	Gendericly Attractive, Coadjuvant
123	F Aut-M Nur	—	+	Small	−.04	**.40**	Coadjuvant

TABLE XIX–Continued

Prediction No.	Needs Correlated	Direction Predicted	Direction Obtained	Magnitude Predicted	Magnitude Obtained	P (one tail)	Nature of Relationship Hypothesized
116	M Aut-F Ord	−	−	Small	−.11	.20	Mutually Repellent
117	F Aut-M Ord	−	−	Small	−.08	.25	Mutually Repellent
66	M Aut-F Sex	+	+	Small	.22	.05	Gendericly Attractive
61	F Aut-M Sex	−	−	Small	−.06	.30	Gendericly Repellent
128	M Aut-F Suc	+	+	Small	.24	.05	Diffusely Complementary
131	F Aut-M Suc	+	+	Small	.02	.45	Diffusely Complementary
29	M Chg-F Chg	+	+	Small to Moderate	.30	.01	Reciprocative
214	M Chg-F Def	+++	+++	Small	.12	.20	Reciprocative
215	F Chg-M Def	+++	+++	Small	.25	.05	Reciprocative
44	M Chg-F Dom	++	++	Small	.09	.25	Compatible
40	F Chg-M Dom	+	+	Small	.25	.05	Compatible
230	M Chg-F End	−	−	Small	−.08	.25	Incompatible
232	F Chg-M End	−	−	Small	−.02	.45	Incompatible
181	M Chg-F Exh	−	−	Small	−.06	.30	Gendericly Repellent
178	F Chg-M-Exh	+	+	Small	.26	.05	Gendericly Attractive
228	M Chg-F Int	++	++	Small	.15	.15	Coadjuvant
229	F Chg-M Int	++	++	Small	.23	.05	Coadjuvant

192	M Chg-F Nur	+	+	Small	.17	.10	Coadjuvant
193	F Chg-M Nur	+	+	Small	.14	.15	Coadjuvant
231	M Chg-F Ord	−	−	Small	−.06	.30	Incompatible
233	F Chg-M Ord	−	−	Small	−.13	.15	Incompatible
82	M Chg-F-Sex	+	+	Small	.14	.15	Coadjuvant
76	F Chg-M Sex	+	+	Small	.15	.15	Coadjuvant
221	M Chg-F Suc	+	+	Small	.11	.20	Reciprocative
220	F Chg-M Suc	+	+	Small	.22	.05	Reciprocative
13	M Def-F Def	+	+	Small	.29	.01	Reciprocative
16, 36	M Def-F Dom	+	+	Small	.15	.15	Complementary
15, 33	F Def-M Dom	+	+	Small	.19	.10	Complementary
216	M Def-F End	+	+	Small	.05	.35	Complementary Diffusely
217	F Def-M End	+	+	Small	.15	.15	Complementary Diffusely
171	M Def-F Exh	+	+	Small	.09	.25	Complementary Diffusely
170	F Def-M Exh	+	+	Small	.17	.10	Complementary Diffusely
212	M Def-F Int	−	+	Small	−.11	.20	Coadjuvant
213	F Def-M Int	+	+	Small	.25	.05	Coadjuvant
187	M Def-F Nur	+	+	Small to Moderate	.25	.05	Complementary Diffusely
186	F Def-M Nur	+	+	Small to Moderate	.24	.05	Complementary Diffusely
218	M Def-F Ord	−	+	Small	−.04	.40	Complementary Diffusely
219	F Def-M Ord	+	+	Small	.13	.15	Complementary Diffusely
78	M Def-F Sex	+	+	Small	.15	.15	Reciprocative
72	F Def-M Sex	+	+	Small	.08	.25	Reciprocative

TABLE XIX—*Continued*

Prediction No.	Needs Correlated	Direction Predicted	Direction Obtained	Magnitude Predicted	Magnitude Obtained	P (one tail)	Nature of Relationship Hypothesized
210	M Def-F Suc	+	+	Small	.08	.25	Reciprocative
211	F Def-M Suc	+	+	Small	.18	.10	Reciprocative
4	M Dom-F Dom	+	+	Small	.16	.10	Coadjuvant
46	M Dom-F End	+	+	Small	.09	.25	Coinstrumental, Compatible
48	F Dom-M End	+	0	Small	.00	.50	Coinstrumental, Compatible
47	M Dom-F Exh	+	+	Small	.10	.20	Reciprocative or Coadjuvant
49	F Dom-M-Exh	+	+	Small	.19	.10	Reciprocative or Coadjuvant
39	M Dom-F Int	++	++	Small	.15	.15	Compatible
43	F Dom-M Int	++	++	Small to Negligible	.04	.40	Compatible
38	M Dom-F Nur	+	+	Small	.26	.05	Gendericly Attractive
42	F Dom-M Nur	+	+	Small to Negligible	.01	.50	Gendericly Repellent
41	M Dom-F Ord	++	++	Small	.18	.10	Coadjuvant
45	F Dom-M Ord	++	++	Small to Negligible	.15	.15	Coadjuvant
58	M Dom-F Sex	++	++	Moderate	.43	.01	Coadjuvant
59	F Dom-M Sex	++	++	Small	.09	.25	Coadjuvant
34	M Dom-F Suc	++	+	Small to Moderate	.32	.01	Diffusely Complementary

No.	Code	Sign	Sign	Size	r	r	Descriptor
37	F Dom-M Suc	+	+	Small	.09	.25	Diffusely Complementary
31	M End-F End	+	+	Small	.16	.10	Coagential
184	M End-F Exh	−	−	Small	−.10	.20	Genderically Repellent
182	F End-M Exh	+	+	Small	.13	.15	Genderically Attractive
236	M End-F Int	+	−	Small	−.03	.40	Compatible
234	F End-M Int	+	+	Small	.17	.10	Compatible
195	M End-F Nur	+	+	Small	.12	.20	Coinstrumental
194	F End-M Nur	+	+	Small	.12	.20	Coinstrumental
238	M End-F Ord	+	+	Small	.09	.25	Coinstrumental
239	F End-M Ord	+	+	Small	.21	.05	Coinstrumental
69	M End-F Sex	+	+	Small	.07	.25	Compatible
68	F End-M Sex	+	+	Small	.08	.25	Compatible
226	M End-F Suc	+	−	Very Small	−.01	.50	Diffusely Complementary
224	F End-M Suc	+	+	Very Small	.04	.40	Diffusely Complementary
12	M Exh-F Exh	+	+	Small to Moderate	.19	.10	Reciprocally Complementary
177	M Exh-F Int	+	+	Small	.11	.20	Genderically Attractive
180	F Exh-M Int	−	−	Small	−.05	.35	Genderically Repellent
176	M Exh-F Nur	+	+	Small	.27	.05	Genderically Attractive
179	F Exh-M Nur	−	−	Small	−.10	.20	Genderically Repellent
183	M Exh-F Ord	+	+	Small	.02	.45	Genderically Attractive

TABLE XIX—Continued

Prediction No.	Needs Correlated	Direction Predicted	Direction Obtained	Magnitude Predicted	Magnitude Obtained	P (one tail)	Nature of Relationship Hypothesized
185	F Exh-M Ord	−	+	Small	.07	.25	Gendericly Repellent
67	M Exh-F Sex	+	+	Small to Moderate	.43	.01	Gendericly Attractive
63	F Exh-M Sex	−	−	Small	−.11	.20	Gendericly Repellent
172	M Exh-F Suc	+	+	Small	.25	.05	Diffusely Complementary
173	F Exh-M Suc	+	+	Small	.05	.35	Diffusely Complementary
24	M Int-F Int	+	+	Small to Moderate	.17	.10	Reciprocative
190	M Int-F Nur	+	+	Small	.33	.01	Coinstrumental
191	F Int-M Nur	+	+	Small	.07	.25	Coinstrumental
235	M Int-F Ord	+	+	Small	.01	.50	Compatible
237	F Int-M Ord	+	+	Small	.06	.30	Compatible
83	M Int-F Sex	+	+	Small	.19	.10	Reciprocative
77	F Int-M Sex	+	+	Small	.19	.10	Reciprocative
223	M Int-F Suc	+	+	Small	.24	.05	Reciprocative or Complementary
222	F Int-M Suc	+	+	Small	.15	.15	Reciprocative or Complementary
8	M Nur-F Nur	+	+	Moderate	.36	.01	Compatible and/or Reciprocally Complementary
196	M Nur-F Ord	+	+	Small	.07	.25	Compatible

197	F Nur-M Ord	+	+	Small	.09	.25	Compatible
81	M Nur-F Sex	+	+	Small	.10	.20	Reciprocative
75	F Nur-M Sex	+	+	Small	.32	.01	Reciprocative
10	M Nur-F Suc	+	+	Small	.07	.25	Complementary
9	F Nur-M Suc	+	+	Small	.33	.01	Complementary
30	M Ord-F Ord			Small to Moderate	.27	.05	Coadjuvant, Coagential
71	M Ord-F Sex	+	+	Small to Moderate	.24	.05	Compatible
70	F Ord-M Sex	+	+	Small to Moderate	.03	.40	Compatible
227	M Ord-F Suc	+	—	Very Small	—.08	.25	Compatible
225	F Ord-M Suc	+	+	Very Small	.05	.35	Compatible
1	M Sex-F Sex	+	+	Moderate to High	.64	.01	Reciprocative
74	M Sex-F Suc	+	+	Small	.16	.10	Reciprocative
80	F Sex-M Suc	+	+	Small	.24	.05	Reciprocative
7	M Suc-F Suc	+	+	Moderate	.23	.05	Reciprocally Complementary

Outcomes and Specific Predictions: Some Details

Let us now examine the correspondence or lack of it between outcomes and predictions by referring to Table XIX which was prepared for this purpose. It lists the predictions by number, indicates the direction and magnitude of the expected and obtained correlations, the significance level of each, and also indicates in each case the nature of the relationship between the need variables that was hypothesized.

It is notable that 208 of the 225 correlations are found to be in the direction predicted. That is, 92.4 percent of them are. 7.6 percent of them are not. This imperfection is somewhat disconcerting; yet when it is recognized that one is dealing with correlation values known to be small on the basis of previous research and is thus operating within extremely narrow margins of error, a miscalculation of only 7.6 percent seems quite credible evidence of predictive power, and at least suggestive that some credence might be given to the theory that generated the predictions in point.

Thirty-one (14.9 percent) of the 208 correlations in the predicted direction are significant at or above the .01 confidence level, and an additional 31 are significant at or above the .05 level, making the total within the conventional limits 62 or 29.8 percent. An additional 29 correlations are significant at the .10 level or higher bringing the cumulative total above this level to approximately 43.8 percent. Going down to the .15 level, an additional 29 correlations are found. This increment raises the accumulated percentage of correlations above the .15 level of significance to 56.7 percent. Dropping to the .20 level adds 21 more. This makes the proportion above that level 67.7 percent. Still of interest are the number at or above the .25 level. There are 28, raising the total percentage at or above this level to 81.2 percent.

Of the 17 correlations not in accord with the direction predicted, none is of a magnitude large enough to meet the conventionally acceptable .05 significance level, and only five are above the .25 level of significance, the highest being one at the .15 level. Again the conclusion is that the theory has some predictive power; and, given all the conditions recognized and discussed in the course of its exposition as operating to counteract, restrain and confound the functioning of need dynamics, that it shows as much predictive power as it does suggests again that some confidence should be accorded it.

In evaluating the theory, as has been done in the foregoing, only the predictions specific to the 225 item matrix have been taken into the reckoning. But, the reader will recall, there are several more which have been made, and for which outcomes have been noted. These are not encompassed in the above accounting. These are ones which were not always identified by number and which in several cases concerned (1) differences in the magnitudes of correlations to be expected between one group of needs having threat property and another group of them, lacking this characteristic, and (2) differences in magnitude between gendericly congruent correlations and gendericly incongruent ones on given pairs of needs (11, 17, and 28). Still a third set of predictions consisted of ones drawn from an hypothesis pertaining to intrapsychic motivational dynamics as these interdigitate with intermotivational dynamics—e.g. the interactions of feelings of self-esteem and the relationship with the love partner with regard to the assertive drives (predictions 5, 19, 20, 21, 22 and 23). A final set of predictions were drawn primarily from the hypothesis that the importance of a given need in effecting intersexual attraction is a partial function of the relative saliency of this need in the motivational structure of particular groups. It was assumed that the UCLA sample employed in the present study differed from that of a Wisconsin sample used in a previous research by Banta and Hetherington with respect to the importance of achievement, change, deference and order. Hence, it was predicted that the interfiancé correlations would differ in magnitude between the two samples on these latter variables, being greater for the UCLA sample with respect to achievement and change, and being smaller for this sample with regard to deference and order. Moreover, in the case of achievement, whereas the B and H sample had revealed a negative correlation, that for the UCLA group was predicted to be positive.

Significance tests were not characteristically and consistently applied in evaluating the outcomes of all of the foregoing expectations, but with the notable exception of that for change, all of them were borne out in directional terms. It is believed that with the exception of the set concerned with feelings of self-esteem (5, 19, 20, 21, 22, and 23) such sufficiently detailed discussion of these various predictions has been given in preceding parts of this work as to require no additional commentary. Those predictions concerned with self-esteem will be intensively scrutinized in the following chapter.

The general confirmation of this rather large array of predictions, when added to that found for the 225 matrix items, measurably enhances the demonstration of the predictive power of instrumental theory already accomplished.

EVALUATION OF THE THEORY OF INTERMOTIVATIONAL DYNAMICS ALONE

The theory of intermotivational mechanics was separately evaluated in an earlier chapter, and in evaluating the theory as a whole, as has been accomplished in the foregoing, the theory of intermotivational dynamics is not thus given an equivalent treatment. But, since it was developed primarily to predict the nature of cross sex-cross need correlations it is deserving of an appraisal independent of that of any other part of instrumental theory. This can readily be accomplished by considering its performance in terms of those correlations only.

All of the 17 directional mispredictions in the 225 item matrix were those of outcomes included in the 210 correlational predictions based on this aspect of instrumental theory. Even so, its performance level of 91.9 percent directionally correct predictions is only slightly less impressive than that for the theory as a whole. Of the 193 correlations in the predicted direction 26 are significant at or above the .01 confidence level and an additional 28 are significant at or above the .05 level, making a total of 28 percent thus above the conventionally respected significance mark. Twenty-five additional correlations are above the .10 level, giving a cumulative total of those under consideration of 40.9 percent. Finally, the cumulative percentage above the .25 point is 79.7 percent, which is only slightly less than the corresponding figure cited in the evaluation of the theory as a whole. None of the 17 correlations whose direction was contrary to what was predicted even reached the .10 significance level, and in fact only one was of a magnitude great enough to exceed the .15 mark.

It is concluded that the theory of intermotivational dynamics has, in itself, very respectable predictive power.

COMPARISONS WITH THE
COMPLEMENTARITY THEORY

If a theory is to be evaluated for its predictive efficacy in comparison with others which attempt to account for a given array of phenomena, then certainly the instrumental theory must be considered far superior in this respect to its only apparent alternative, the Winchian complementarity theory. With respect to predictions of directions of correlations on *same* needs the latter theory fails completely, for it predicts negative correlations for these. The instrumental theory succeeds completely, for, as can be seen from an inspection of Tables XIX and XII (Chapter Seven) every prediction for the direction and magnitude of correlations on *same* needs is borne out, although only eight of the 15 are large enough to attain statistical significance. This represents, apparently, the strongest disconfirmation the complementarity theory has received for *same* needs since it was first presented in the early nineteen fifties.

TABLE XX

COMPARISONS OF PREDICTIONS OF WINCH AND CENTERS FOR CORRELATIONS OBTAINED ON NEED PAIRINGS SUPPOSED BY WINCH TO BE COMPLEMENTARY

Need Pair by Sex	Obtained	Predictions Winch	Centers	Need Pair by Sex	Obtained	Predictions Winch	Centers
M Aba-F Aut	—.17	+	—	M Aut-F Def*	.08	+	+
F Aba-M Aut	.02	+	—	F Aut-M Def*	—.11	+	+
M Aba-F Dom	—.07	+	—	M Aut-F Agg	—.25	+	—
F Aba-M Dom	—.04	+	—	F Aut-M Agg	.06	+	+
M Aba-F Agg	—.09	+	—	M Def-F Dom*	.19	+	+
F Aba-M Agg	—.04	+	—	F Def-M Dom*	.15	+	+
M Aba-F Nur*	.24	+	+	M Def-F Agg	—.12	+	—
F Aba-M Nur*	.18	+	+	F Def-M Agg	.14	+	+
M Aba-F Exh	—.13	+	—	M Def-F Nur*	.25	+	+
F Aba-M Exh	—.14	+	—	F Def-M Nur*	.24	+	+
M Ach-F Def*	.21	+	+	M Def-F Exh*	.09	+	+
F Ach-M Def*	.25	+	+	F Def-M Exh*	.17	+	+
M Ach-F Dom	.00	+	—	M Dom-F Suc*	.32	+	+
F Ach-M Dom	.17	+	+	F Dom-M Suc*	.09	+	+
M Ach-F Exh	—.14	+	—	M Nur-F Suc*	.07	+	+
F Ach-M Exh	.33	+	+	F Nur-M Suc*	.33	+	+

Outcome for Winch: 62.5% in predicted direction.
Outcome for Centers: 90.6% in predicted direction.

*A need pair considered by Centers to be complementary.

Table XX has been prepared for comparison of the predictive efficiency of the instrumental and complementarity theories for disparate needs, considering perforce, only those for which Winch presented data in his final (1958) report on complementarity. For the 32 possible comparisons, the complementarity theory is 62.5 percent accurate. For instrumental theory the accuracy is 90.6 percent. If the comparison for the data in Table XX is narrowed to the 16 need combinations hypothesized as complementary in terms of the conception of complementarity presented in the instrumental theory, the predictive efficacy of the instrumental theory is 100 percent.

It is perhaps both ironic and amusing to find in a work designed to test an alternative to a "single mechanism" theory like that of Winch, and one which proposes another theory as a replacement of it, so much complementarity in evidence. At the same time as the strongest disconfirmation of that particular theory is revealed, the strongest support for the functioning of the mechanism of complementarity yet discovered has also been presented. Further, the instrumental conception of complementarity presents in its direct and diffuse varieties of this mechanism 13 bidirectional and two unidirectional combinations of variables not encompassed in the Winchian scheme of "Type II" (*Different* Need) complementaries and thus more than Winch himself found. These are all indicated in Table XIX, but to save the reader the effort and time required for perusal of that lengthy listing they are extracted and presented separately in Table XXI.

Table XXI does not list any *same* need-cross sex combinations several of whose positive interfiancé correlations have been explained as due to the operation of the mechanism of *cocomplementarity*. This is not done because the positive correlation in a given case is supposed to be present by virtue of the fact that the need of each partner is present in sufficient strength to function in a direct or diffusely complementary way with an appropriate second (and different) need. That is, the positive correlation on the given same need is, in effect, an artifact of an underlying bidirectional complementary relationship between the given need and another of a different kind. Expressed more succinctly, while it is true that certain interfiancé correlations on *same* needs are accounted for as an effect

TABLE XXI

CORRELATIONS OF NEED VARIABLES (IN ADDITION TO THOSE
INDICATED IN TABLE XX) WHICH ARE HYPOTHESIZED TO BE
COMPLEMENTARY IN THE INSTRUMENTAL THEORY

Need Variables	M-F	F-M	Type of Complementarity
Achievement-Affiliation	.41	.17	Diffuse
Achievement-Succorance	.19	.13	Diffuse
Affiliation-Autonomy	.02	.42	Diffuse
Affiliation-Dominance	.04	.50	Diffuse
Affiliation-Endurance	.21	.04	Diffuse
F Affiliation-M Exhibition	—	.37	Diffuse
Affiliation-Nurturance	.40	.30	Diffuse
Affiliation-Order	—.01	.06	Diffuse
M Aggression-F Deference	.14	—	Diffuse
Autonomy-Succorance	.24	.02	Diffuse
Deference-Endurance	.05	.15	Diffuse
Deference-Order	—.04	.13	Diffuse
Endurance-Succorance	—.01	.04	Diffuse
Exhibition-Succorance	.25	.05	Diffuse
Intraception-Succorance	.24	.15	Direct

of the mechanism of cocomplementarity, that does not mean that such *same* needs are complementary to each other.

One should not be mistaken by the adduction of evidence re complementarity in Table XXI and the attendant discussion into supposing that the instrumental theory presents complementarity to be other than one of several important instrumental mechanisms in reciprocal need gratification and intersexual attraction. As has been pointed out earlier, it is only one variety of the several reciprocal mechanisms that have been discovered here. Still, it is assuredly fair to regard it as only second in importance to the simple reciprocal mechanism, if its importance may be gauged by the magnitude of the correlations associated with it.

Another way of comparing the predictive power of the instrumental and complementarity theories is in terms of the direction of correlations with regard to *all* cross need-cross gender associations. The complementarity principle as formulated by Winch more or less definitely indicates that all of these *r*s should be positive in direction. Instrumental theory, making predictions on the basis of the supposed common and specific properties possessed by particular needs, has no such blanket formulation, considering this absurd without taking the intermotivational dynamics into account in each case.

Some correlations would be predicted to be positive, others negative, depending upon what dynamics were presumed to be operative in each given case. On this basis of comparison, the outcomes again favor the instrumental procedure over the Winchian one; 92 percent correct predictions as to correlational direction for instrumental theory, 72 percent for the other theory.

The complementarity formulation as Winch presented it certainly does have one tremendous superiority over the instrumental formulations; it is far more economical. However, as men of wisdom have throughout time pointed out, you get what you pay for.

Is what has been presented in the foregoing intended as a demonstration or an argument to the effect that the concept of complementarity in intersexual relationships is a wrong idea, or only that Winch's theory about "different and complementary" needs was incorrect? Only the latter. A complementarity in the need strengths of love partners is one of the most impressive and obvious dynamic conditions underlying such relationships. But obvious though it may be, there are other things besides, and it requires a much more sophisticated set of principles to account for its nature and patterning than the Winchian formulations provide. Few theories have had as long a day in court in the face of massive and impressive disconfirmatory evidence as Winch's has. Perhaps for more than any other reason, it is because psychologists and sociologists as well as laymen have long, and "through a glass darkly," devined a vague and generalized form in the male-female mating phenomenon at least roughly identifiable as complementarity. And, convinced that it was there, were loath to dismiss a theory which asserted what they and so many others already believed. A further chapter will be devoted, in part, to giving the idea more explicit form.

CHAPTER TWELVE

MALE-FEMALE COMPLEMENTARITY AND THE ROLE OF SELF-ESTEEM IN INTERSEXUAL LOVE

MALE-FEMALE COMPLEMENTARITY

IN PREVIOUS DISCUSSIONS concerning the potency properties of need instigated behaviors it has been many times emphasized that males and females differ most saliently in those needs which instigate behaviors generally perceived as having strength properties on the one hand and weakness properties on the other. In an earlier chapter (Chapter Nine) the assertion was made that "to the extent that (the male) is himself strong in the traits born of his socialization to the masculine role, he can tolerate, respect, admire and even be attracted to a strong female. However, he can be confidently predicted in choosing a marital partner to tend to pick one weaker than he himself is." This somewhat sweeping generalization is important in the instrumental theory of intersexual attraction, especially with regard to the postulate of the need for maintenance and enhancement of sexual identity and role.

What was intended in stating it had reference to the male linked needs with high strength property, for it is in the gratification of these in particular that the male finds himself also gratified and fulfilled in the maintenance and enhancement of his sexual identity. This is difficult to accomplish with a female partner who is more strongly driven than he is toward dominance, aggression, achievement, autonomy, sex and exhibition behaviors. Hence he will find himself being gratified most strongly by interaction with and in relating to a female, who, while offering some challenge, does not threaten to defeat him in his goal of sexual identity maintenance and enhancement. That means one not necessarily weaker or less strongly developed in each single one of these drives, of course, but almost certainly one who in the net balance of strength drives is weaker than he himself is, and with rare exceptions this is the way the female wants it, too. For her to fulfill her own sexual identity drive requires a male who is stronger, not weaker; and, in this engaged sample, she can confidently be predicted to have chosen one. Only in her nurturant drive in this scheme of things is it appropriate and expected that she will be stronger than the man she chooses, and he wants it that way, too. The over-all pattern is, of course, a complementary one.

Endurance and order are drives with some strength property, also; but ones in collegiate samples not differentially emphasized in males and females; hence there should not be expected any important or significant differences in choice between males and females regarding them. But males would at least tend to be more often higher on endurance and females more often higher on order. They *are* higher scoring on them in the respective directions to significant degrees in Edwards' normative sample of general adults. Our sample is younger, yet it may well show a trend toward the adult norm in its choice pattern.

Intraception (which might be better termed interpersonal understanding) and change are additional drives with at least low strength property, but they are female linked needs, and males should be expected to have chosen females who are higher than themselves on these. This would be true not alone because the sorts of behaviors they instigate represent a kind of strength that males find entirely gratifying and compatible, but also because these behaviors carry moderate or modest affectional values as well.

It is with respect to the affectional needs, (aff, nur, def and suc) in particular that males will tend most strongly to choose females whose need strengths (scores) on them are higher than their own, and females of course, will tend to choose males not as strongly driven by these needs as they themselves are.

Finally, there is abasement, a variable highly linked to femininity. It has outstanding weakness property also; as, to lesser degrees, do succorance, deference and affiliation, also femininity linked needs. For both reasons males will choose females whose scores on them are *higher* than their own, and females will choose males whose scores are lower than their own.

If the writer is sounding like an advocate of the status quo or even a reactionary, that is an unfortunate hazard of his seeing reality as it is. He has a great deal of respect for surveys, having conducted many himself; hence some excerpts of relevant material from an article by Peggy Constantine, reporting the results of a survey conducted by the Harris Poll in the Spring of 1971, seem highly strategic.

"You'd come a long way, baby, but then you blabbed and blew it.

"At least, 3,000 women did, and they were supposed to be speaking for all American women. They answered pollsters' questions on sex, men in general, fashions, politics and family life. And from what they answered, it appears the 1970s' woman is as straitlaced as ladies of Victoria's day.

"Lou Harris pollsters questioned 3,000 women on their role in American society. The interviewees live in urban and rural areas of the East, West, South and North; they are under 30 to over 50; black and white; single, married, separated, divorced or widowed; had incomes from $5,000 to $15,000 a year, and had little to a lot of education.

MEN QUERIED ON SAME SUBJECTS

"For good measure, Harris pollsters asked 1,000 men of similar backgrounds their opinions on some of the same subjects.

"Free love—presumably fact, not wishful thinking any more—took a bad beating. An astounding 65 percent of the women interviewed think premarital sex is immoral. More astounding, 54 percent of the men think so, too.

"Also shot down as socially unacceptable: trial marriages (77 percent of the women oppose and 69 percent of the men) and bearing children out of wedlock (85 percent of the women, 82 percent of the men oppose). In fact, 89 percent of the women and 87 percent of the men think society would fall apart without the institution of marriage.

RESPECTED LADIES

"And bad news for Women's Lib. Two out of three women felt 'for a woman to be truly happy, she needs to have a man around.' Furthermore, 58 percent believe 'women will always be more emotional and less logical than men,' 67 percent think 'there won't be a woman President for a long time and that's probably just as well.' Their heroines are not all women who accomplished in their own right but rose to prominence as wives of famous husbands. The top six respected ladies of the world are Mrs. Dwight Eisenhower, Queen Elizabeth, Sen. Margaret Chase Smith (R.–Me.), Mrs. Richard Nixon, Mrs. Lyndon Johnson and Mrs. Martin Luther King Jr.

"To get down to the nitty-gritty, 53 percent of the women like being mothers and rearing children and only 40 percent even favor efforts to change women's status in society.

BUT SOME GRIPES

"Everything is not all sweetness and light, of course. The women have peevish gripes about men:

"—50 percent think 'men think only their opinions about the world are important.'—49 percent say 'most find it necessary for their egos to keep women down' " (Peggy Constantine, *Los Angeles Times*, May 13, 1971).

Yes, and yet, each will seek a relationship with a partner on the complementary basis hypothesized, for it is in it that each can gain maximum gratification for his needs, even if for women the arrangement is not quite so felicitous as one wherein they could illogically and impossibly have it both ways.*

Evidence relevant to evaluating the hypothesis is presented in Table XXII, where the percentages of males scoring higher than their fiancés is noted for each need, ordered from high to low on the strength-weakness dimension. The over-all trend is clearly supportive of the general hypothesis, with the only exceptions being the instance of n def. In the case of nurturance, a very great difference, indeed, is found, only 18 percent of males scoring higher than their partners. The specific sex linkage to femininity is such that the

---

*Not emphasized in the article quoted, but even more to the point, are these facts from the same survey reported nearly a year later in the *Los Angeles Times* (March 24, 1972). "Whatever the prospects for changing women's status, the survey showed consistently high regard—among all ages and classes of women—for a traditional role. Even half of the single women said they frequently thought that "bringing up children properly takes as much intelligence and drive as holding a top position in business or government.' Overall, 84 percent said they thought that way either frequently or occasionally.

"More women than men (58 percent compared to 49 percent) said they were 'very satisfied' with their lives.

"*And 74 percent of women frequently or occasionally thought that 'having a loving husband who is able to take care of me is much more important to me than making it on my own.'* " (italics added.)

moderate positioning of this motive on the potency dimension was from the beginning based on the recognition that the behaviors it instigates are primarily a *feminine* strength resource; hence, it was not, of course, expected that males would score higher than females on it. In the case of deference the hypothesis is only barely supported in that the direction of the choices on it is as expected, but the feminine population is not really differentiated with any prominence in terms of this variable from the masculine one.

The predictions were stated in the foregoing in terms mainly of the choices men would make, but, of course, since the choice is a reciprocal one, the predictions could have been stated in reverse for women, and would be equally as well supported by the data had that been explicitly done. It was intended to be so understood.

At this point it may be well to recall the two postulates of isomorphism of motive and behavior and need resource resonance, respectively. These choices noted in the foregoing were made, it

TABLE XXII

PERCENTAGES OF MALES SCORING HIGHER THAN THEIR FEMALE
PARTNERS ON NEEDS ORDERED FROM HIGH TO LOW
ON THE STRENGTH DIMENSION

	A	B	C	E	F	G
	Percent Scoring Higher	Percent Scoring Same	Percent Scoring Lower	Percent Scoring Same or Lower	Differ- ence A-E	Signifi- cance of Diff. at .05 level*
Dominance	60	4	36	40	20	+
Autonomy	62	4	34	38	24	+
Aggression	63	4	33	37	26	+
Achievement	60	3	37	40	20	+
Exhibition	56	1	43	44	12	—
Sex	63	5	32	37	26	+
Nurturance	18	4	78	82	—64	+
Endurance	54	5	41	46	8	—
Intraception	41	1	58	59	—18	+
Order	40	4	56	60	—20	+
Change	36	3	61	64	—28	+
Affiliation	29	3	68	71	—42	+
Deference	47	4	49	53	— 6	—
Succorance	36	1	63	64	—28	+
Abasement	34	3	63	66	—32	+

*A plus sign indicates significance of the difference at or above the .05 level.

should be recognized, not by these persons seeing each other's motives themselves, nor their need scores. *All each of them perceived was the other's behavior.* Yet by and large they reveal, in choosing, the very pattern of motivations to exist in their chosen ones that it was necessary for them to have to confirm the complementarity hypothesis.

THE ROLE OF SELF ESTEEM

Before the data for the present research was collected, although the theory for which it was intended as an evaluation had supposed the sexual identity drive to be essentially a basic and primal aspect of the need for self-esteem, not a great deal of thought was devoted to how this particular feature of the sexual identity drive might be tested by the data. The primary concern was simply to attempt to reveal the presence of and operation of the drive itself by the predicted patterning of the correlations. But as data began to accumulate, and as more thought was given to the implications of the esteem factor for the whole intersexual exchange process, various hypotheses about the interrelationship of existing feelings of (general) self-esteem and the correlation patterns to be expected when this feeling was focussed upon came to be formed. Certain predictions, it will be recalled, were made more or less in passing in the chapter dealing with intermotivational mechanics. But additional ones, not as yet made explicit, will be developed in the present chapter and evaluated in terms of the correlational data available.

In Chapter Five, first in the context of a discussion of similarity of achievement motivation of fiancés, it was predicted (Prediction 5) that males scoring low on n aba would correlate higher with their female partners on n ach than would males scoring high on n aba. Later, additional predictions were made for other assertive drives on the assumption that low scores on n aba were indicative of higher self-esteem, or at least a relative absence of low self-esteem, inferiority feelings, inadequacy feelings, etc.

The rationale indicated as underlying these predictions was to the effect that a male who was himself strong could contain and love a stronger (in the masculine sense) female to a distinctly higher degree than a weaker male could, and, hence, would have chosen one who was relatively higher in the male linked needs.

Prediction 19 held, in keeping with this, that "males who are low scorers on n aba will tend to select females whose scores on n agg are higher than those chosen by males who score high on n aba." That is to say, there should be a higher coefficient of correlation for low scorers on n aba with their female partners on n agg, than would be found in the case of males scoring high on n aba. Predictions 20, 21, and 22 were similar in nature, but had to do with the correlations of the aba score with regard to n aut, n dom, and n sex respectively.

Prediction 23, also following from the general hypothesis, was different, in that it anticipated a lower correlation on n exhibition, another assertive need, *but one that compensatorily masks low self-esteem*, between males scoring lower on n aba and their love partners. If, as the writer has hypothesized earlier, exhibition is associated with inner weakness and feelings of inadequacy, the higher self-esteem males would not be expected to have high scores on this need for exhibition, whereas the low self-esteem males would.

Extension to the Female Sample

The hypothesis, and the several predictions derived from it which have been stated in the foregoing, scrutinizes the mating process only from the point of view of the implications that possession of higher self-esteem, in the *male* has for his selection of a love partner. But what about females? Would they, if higher in self-esteem, be expected to choose males whose scores on these several masculinity linked needs would be correlated with their own in exactly this same pattern? It would seem that this would be so, and for various reasons.

1. All of these masculine type need scores are negatively correlated with abasement in Edwards' normative sample of college students. For example: dom-aba $= -.34$; sex-aba $= -.29$; ach-aba $= -.28$; aut-aba $= -.26$; agg-aba $= -.25$; exh-aba $= -.18$. The correlations for the present study are very similar to these in both magnitude and direction, and in both the subsample of males and that for females. An exception occurs in the case of abasement-exhibition, however. Exh showed a slight $-.03$ correlation with abasement in the male subsample, and a somewhat larger $-.11$ with abasement in the female one. Considering the negativity of these correlations in general, however, it is strongly suggested that females who are

higher in self-esteem (i.e., score lower on aba) will be higher scorers on these masculinity linked needs. The expectation, in the case of exhibition, is much less certain.

2. If the above is correct then these females, provided they have not rejected their traditionally defined femininity altogether, will *need* a stronger male, one whose scores on these needs more closely match their own than the male who would be needed by lower self-esteem females, these, presumably, would not score so highly on dominance, achievement, autonomy, etc. The higher self-esteem females would need such a male, more specifically, to gratify their sexual identity and sex role maintenance drive. It would not be congruent with the principles of instrumental theory otherwise.

The same pattern of correlations, then, as predicted to obtain in the male sample with respect to low and higher self-esteem individuals would be found in the female sample. *However, the correlational differences would be expected to be smaller.* There is much confusion in the social definition of the feminine role today, and females are in their own minds often confused and conflicted. The clear majority adheres to the traditional pattern, but a dissident minority rejects it. The latter are often brilliant and vocal women, who even if they convince few, unquestionably sow doubt among many. There seems no question that American women have for decades increasingly found the traditional pattern less than fully satisfying. Many exist today among university educated women who have not fully accepted the traditional feminine identity culturally thrust upon them. They hence grope now for some more satisfying identity vis à vis the male, with the solution to the problem of relating to him taking no standard patterns but being characterized instead as a highly individualistic formula in each case. And, of course, males, often themselves confused in this troubled world, exist in sufficient numbers and variety for almost any accommodation to be found; this even occasionally amounting to an almost total role reversal. Finally, it must be recognized, that, in this collegiate sample of persons under scrutiny, we have drawn from a population which at the time of our data collection was, and had for some time been, maximally exposed to the exhortations of agitators in the women's liberation movement.

It is expected that all of this will be reflected in the data.

TABLE XXIII

CORRELATIONS ON SOME IMPORTANT MALE LINKED NEED SCORES
OF LOVE PARTNERS, WITH MALES AND FEMALES DIFFERENTIATED
INTO HIGHER AND LOW SELF-ESTEEM CATEGORIES
IN THEIR RESPECTIVE SAMPLES

	Males		*Females*	
	Higher Self-Esteem $N = 35$	*Low Self-Esteem* $N = 36$	*Higher Self-Esteem* $N = 36$	*Low Self-Esteem* $N = 35$
Achievement	.44*	—.01	.17	—.13
Aggression	.25	—.10	.19	—.06
Autonomy	.23	—.11	.17	.09
Dominance	.29§	.13	.22	.12
Sex	.68*	.46*	.66*	.49*
Exhibition	.06	.28§	.06	.23

Significance level symbols: * = .005; † = .01; ‡ = .025; § = .05.

Table XXIII presents correlational data from two subsamples of male scorers on abasement, as well as that from two subsamples of females, each respectively designated there as higher self-esteem groups, consisting of low scorers on abasement, and low self-esteem groups, composed of high scorers on n aba. The male and female samples were each divided at the median to obtain these groups. The N for the low category is 36 and that of the higher is 35 in the male sample. For females the Ns are 36 and 35. Those quite numerous cases in each sex group whose scores fell on the median were randomly assigned in approximately equal number to either the higher or low subsample.

It should be recognized that the properties of the abasement scale are such that, while they do indicate, in the instance of high scorers, persons of truly low self-esteem, the reverse is not so true. That is, scoring low on the abasement items does not necessarily indicate a person with truly high self-esteem, but merely one not so low as the high scorer in this respect. He is, in other words, at least *higher* in self-esteem in terms of relative score, but that is all.

Outcome

Attending first to the male's correlations on these needs most strongly associated with masculinity, it is to be noted that the prediction regarding the differential correlations for n achievement is unequivocally confirmed. For the low self-esteem males the correlation with their partners on achievement scores is a negative one, while for the higher self-esteem males it is a substantial and highly significant positive one of .44. The difference value in terms of Fisher's Z is .48; p < .025. The other predictions tend to be supported only in that the directions are as was expected. The difference values are in each correlational comparison too low to achieve significance at the conventional .05 level. The consistency, however, with which the higher self-esteem males choose females whose needs on each of these masculinity linked variables, ach, agg, aut, dom and sex would, to the writer, be most readily accounted for by a generalization to the effect that a strong male can contain a strong and forceful woman and enjoy her challenge, whereas a weak male is repelled by her.

With respect to the prediction of a higher correlation in the low self-esteem group as compared to that for the higher on n exhibition, it also is clearly borne out in directional pattern but the difference value here, too, falls short of significance at the conventionally acceptable level.

It is unfortunate that there appears to be no unequivocally acceptable tests which may be applied to evaluate the significance of this pattern of outcomes *en bloc* in supporting the hypothesis, because certain assumptions underlying their use may be more or less violated in employing them. Since all of the correlations are indices to covariations of modules which have some at least slight intercorrelation among themselves and also are from the same respondents, the events under observation cannot be asserted to be totally independent. *Supposing that they were*, however, a sign test which seems applicable to testing this whole pattern of positive directional outcomes for the predictions is one of probability in terms of the cumulative binominial distribution (Mosteller, Rourke and Thomas, 1961). Assuming the null hypothesis, the probability of the outcomes for all six predictions being in the direction expected is .016.

Considering the general consistency of the findings with the dynamic circumstance hypothesized as operating to produce such results, what is found here does seem clearly *supportive* of the antecedent identified.

As expected the difference pattern as a whole is repeated in the female sample when it is divided into higher and lower self-esteem groups, but again, as predicted, the differences are not as great. They are, in fact in every comparison smaller. Still, they are quite consistent. The probability value of this pattern, of course, employing the same test as used for the male outcomes, is exactly the same, .016.

Perhaps it would not be too far from the truth to say, viewing all this, that just as it takes a strong man to love a strong woman, it takes a strong woman to love a strong man. The data certainly clearly suggest that such women have sought and found such men more often than the low self-esteem female has. The latter has tended to choose one whose drives for achievement, aggression, autonomy, dominance and sex are not at all like or only a little like her own.

Self-Esteem and the Affectional Motives

So far there has been consideration only of the involvement of feelings of self-esteem with the masculine linked and assertive drives, but this is only a part of the quite pervasive interaction of the self-esteem factor. Its influence can be seen in the case of all of the needs in our purview here. Let us consider, first, the next largest block of drives; female linked in the main, and all with low to high affectional properties. The one male linked affectional need, sex, has already been considered in the foregoing because of its also possessing at least moderate assertive property, and was seen there to have the highest correlation in both the male and female higher self-esteem samples. It was there consistently elevated in correlational values above those found in both of the low esteem groups, where its correlations also were in those cases the highest for those groups of those needs thus far considered. It is believed that this suggested elevation of affectional intensity in the higher self-esteem samples will prove to be a quite general phenomenon, and thought so on a variety of somewhat complex grounds.

The grounds in point are the following. 1. Motivation toward any goal is a partial function of the gratifyingness of the goal. 2. Performance level and energy expended in the effort to achieve the gratification will be greater, the more gratifying the goal is experienced as being. 3. Persons of opposite sex both initially high in affectional drives will be more gratified by the exchanges of affectional responses than those whose initial motivation is less strong (a given amount of gratification is increased in value directly proportional to need strength). 4. Individuals whose self-esteem is high are more likely to express liking and affection for others than are persons with low self-esteem (Berger, 1952; Maslow, 1942; Omwake, 1954; Stock, 1949, etc.). 5. Given all the foregoing, there appears to be maximum likelihood in interactions of an intersexual nature under such conditions that a progressive augmentation of motivation to "give more in order to get more" will occur. Recall the description of this process in connection with reciprocally functioning needs, and of affectional ones in particular, in the chapter on intermotivational mechanisms.

A final ground besides the foregoing several is an assumption implicit in the prediction of higher correlations being found for the higher self-esteem samples on the needs already considered. This is that individuals in these higher esteem groups are both obtaining more gratification sexually from one another and more gratification of their sexual identity drives as well. They are thus exchanging more gratifications of very important kinds as compared with the low self-esteem samples, and thus have elevated outcome levels (c.f., Thibaut and Kelley, 1959). It follows, if this is so, that a person in the high esteem group, in his interactions with such a gratifying partner would be induced to be increasingly more strongly motivated (short of some unknown point of satiation) toward affectionate behavior with respect to the partner. Also he or she in turn would be crescively responding in the same way toward him. In short, each would be more appreciative, understanding, nurturant and affectionate in his responses toward his partner than would be the case in the low self-esteem individual with respect to his partner. This, if it has occurred, would be evidenced by a higher correlation being found between selves and partners of subjects in the higher self-esteem groups than between those in the low group on n affiliation. Also the correlations should be higher between them on sex, nurturance, succorance, intraception and change; in short, on all of the needs with appreciable affectional property, including the most important affectional motives as well as those with only modest amounts of such a property. Dominance would also be included, but it is, of course, primarily an assertive drive and has already been seen to have the kind of relationship with self-esteem conditions posited for the ones with more salient affectional property. Possibly its correlations are elevated in the higher esteem groups partly by virtue of the modest affectionality it does have. Correlations on *different* needs having high affectionateness such as sex-aff, int-aff, and nur-suc should also be higher in the higher self-esteem group. Also, it is again expected that correlational differences will be lesser between female groups than such differences between male groups.

A consideration against the main hypothesis, of course, is that those in the low self-esteem group, presumably obtaining less gratification than those in the higher groups for both their sexual and identity needs, would thus be more needful of affection than those in the higher esteem group. And, hence, in compensation, would have secured a love partner who supplied great quantities of such gratification. Against this, again, and favoring the original hypothesis, is much clinical observation to the effect that persons who don't love themselves (have low self-esteem) have little inclination to give others much love either. The data will, it is believed, support the original hypothesis.

Self-Esteem and the Implemental Motives

With the exception of the abasement variable which it is, of course, meaningless to treat additionally as an independent variable, since it is in terms of it that all of the comparisons under concern here are being made, there remain only two needs which have not as yet been involved in any hypothesis; namely endurance, a slightly male linked need, and order, an equally slightly female linked one.

To develop an hypothesis with regard to endurance and order, it is pertinent to look somewhat more closely at what lies at the basis of self-esteem. The writer, as well as others, has stressed a sense of *effectancy* or *competence* in coping with the world, as a primary source of feelings of self-esteem; not, however, intending to say that that was its only ground. Others, far remote in time from us in the past have also tended to emphasize *success*. William James, writing in 1890 (James, 1890) is quite specific; saying, in effect, that if achievement approaches or equals aspirations in a valued area of

human competence it engenders feelings of esteem for ourselves in us, while if there is a descrepancy in this way we are caused to have a corresponding decrement in our feelings of self-worth. "Our self-feeling in this world," he says, "depends entirely upon what we back ourselves to be and do. It is determined by the ratio of our actualities to our supposed potentialities; a fraction of which our pretensions are the denominator, and the numerator our success; thus self-esteem
$$= \frac{success}{pretensions} \text{."}$$

Individuals in our higher self-esteem groups here have, unfortunately, had no observations made of them with regard to what *actual* successes or achievements they may have had. But it is known from both Edwards' data and the presently collected set that there is a positive correlation between higher feelings of self-esteem and the need for achievement (Edwards' r is $-.28$ between n ach and aba). Further, it has already been seen that higher self-esteem persons of each sex have been attracted to and have secured as love partners persons of the opposite sex whose need for achievement is more similar to their own than is the case among persons of low self-esteem. It does not, of course, necessarily follow that these subjects with high n ach have actually *accomplished* anything at all. But if the postulate of isomorphism of motivation and behavior has any validity at all it could be said that *efforts* to actually achieve would be more commonly found among these people than they would be among those whose n ach was lower.

But what has all of this to do with n endurance and n order? Essentially this: both of these drives are importantly, although not entirely, *implemental* to achieving, and, hence, people striving with any effectancy to actually achieve might be expected to have both drives fairly strongly developed in them. *In brief, this is deduced*: those Ss who are known to have higher self-esteem in all likelihood derived it from a sense of effectancy that came from actual successes. Such successes would have required higher than ordinary *endurance* in the pursuit of goals as well as planning, etc., or *ordering* one's activities. Hence n end and n order should be strongly developed in these people. One neither sticks to a project nor engages in the ordering of his activities without being motivated to do so, and while the needs for endurance and order are the immediate instigators, they are at least in part derived from the more regnant achievement drive.

It follows from all of this that an individual whose endurance at projects and whose ordering of his or her autonomous or joint responsibilities were strong characteristics would prove appreciably more attractive to a person who had a high achievement drive. Such a person could, better than another not so endowed, facilitate gratification of this drive (recall the mechanisms of coagentiality and coadjuvance). Hence, higher self-esteem males and females will be found to have higher correlations on end and ord than will low self-esteem males and females. The correlations will be smaller in the female samples.

To expedite the evaluation of the foregoing hypotheses re self-esteem and the affectional and implemental needs *en bloc* Tables XXIV and XXV have been prepared. Table XXIV orders the data with respect to *same* need correlations. Table XXV duplicates this function for cross-need correlations.

Looking at Table XXIV first, and at comparison data for males first, it can be seen that usually quite substantial correlations obtain between higher self-esteem love partners on the affectional variables. Sex has been included, of course, because it is primarily an affectional drive rather than a strictly assertive one. Other than that for n sex, the correlation for n affiliation is the highest in the array for affectional motives for the higher self-esteem group. The r for n deference exceeds that for affiliation in the low self-esteem group, and, in fact, is as high as that for sex. The differences in correlation magnitudes between the higher SE group and the low SE group, are, with the sole exception of that for deference, all in the predicted direction.

Both of the predictions with regard to the implemental needs, endurance and order, are essentially confirmed also. Not expected was such a high correlation as that for n ord that is revealed in the higher self-esteem group, for it even exceeds in value the r for affiliation.

As it is, then, eight predictions out of nine are confirmed as to direction of difference for the male comparisons; and, assuming that the sign test based on cumulative binomial is an approximately permissible test of the probability of such an outcome (assuming the

Sexual Attraction and Love

TABLE XXIV

CORRELATIONS ON SAME AFFECTIONAL AND IMPLEMENTAL NEEDS OF LOVE PARTNERS, WITH MALES AND FEMALES DIFFERENTIATED INTO HIGHER AND LOW SELF-ESTEEM CATEGORIES IN THEIR RESPECTIVE SAMPLES

	Males			Females			
	A Higher Self-Esteem N = 35	B Low Self-Esteem N = 36	C Differ-ence and Direc-tion	X Higher Self-Esteem N = 36	Y Low Self-Esteem N = 35	Z Differ-ence and Direc-tion	C-Z Differ-ence in Differ-ences and Direction
Sex	.68*	.46*	.22+	.66*	.49*	.17+	.05+
Affiliation	.61*	.42*	.19+	.48*	.29§	.19+	.00
Nurturance	.59*	.33‡	.26+	.41†	.29§	.12+	.14+
Deference	.17	.46*	.29—	.36‡	.27	.09+	.38—
Succorance	.51*	.08	.43+	.29§	.13	.16+	.27+
Intraception	.23	.06	.17+	.03	—.04	.07+	.10+
Change	.46*	.22	.24+	.35‡	.12	.23+	.01+
Endurance	.42†	—.18	.60+	.12	—.05	.17+	.43+
Order	.66*	.15	.51+	.38†	.18	.20+	.31+

Summary: Number of Differences in the Predicted Direction:

Between Higher and Low Self-Esteem Males: 8 of 9; p < .02.

Between Higher and Low Self-Esteem Females: 9 of 9; p < .002.

Between Higher Self-Esteem Males and Higher Self-Esteem Females: 7 of 9; p < .07.

Significance Levels: * = .005; † = .01; ‡ = .025; § = .05.

null hypothesis of no differences), its likelihood as a chance event is .02.

Although, as expected, the correlational values are reduced in magnitude in the female samples for most of these affectional and implemental motivational modules, and consequently the differences between the higher and low groups are smaller, the consistency of the data with what was predicted is even greater than that obtaining in the male comparisons. It has a probability as a chance outcome of .002.

Finally, the expectation that the correlational differences between

TABLE XXV

CORRELATIONS ON *DIFFERENT* AFFECTIONAL AND IMPLEMENTAL
NEEDS OF LOVE PARTNERS, WITH MALES AND FEMALES
DIFFERENTIATED INTO HIGHER AND LOW SELF-
ESTEEM CATEGORIES IN THEIR
RESPECTIVE SAMPLES

| | Males | | | | Females | | | |
| | A | B | C | X | Y | Z | C-Z |
Need Pair	Higher Self-Esteem N = 35	Low Self-Esteem N = 36	Differ-ence and Direc-tion	Higher Self-Esteem N = 36	Low Self-Esteem N = 35	Differ-ence and Direc-tion	Differ-ence in Differ-ences and Direction
Sex-Aff	.62	.34	.28+	.45	.34	.11+	.17+
Sex-Nur	.46	.28	.18+	.15	.36	.21—	.49+
Sex-Def	.21	.25	.04—	.12	.05	.07+	.18+
Sex-Suc	.16	.20	.04—	.19	.06	.13+	.17—
Sex-Int	.35	.25	.10+	.18	.07	.11+	.01—
Sex-Chg	.43	—.06	.49+	.22	—.08	.30+	.19+
Aff-Nur	.62	.34	.28+	.39	.39	.00	.28+
Aff-Def	.46	.08	.38+	.25	.18	.07+	.31+
Aff-Suc	.42	.22	.20+	.25	.42	.17—	.37+
Aff-Int	.61	.31	.30+	.42	.42	.00	.30+
Aff-Chg	.54	.07	.44+	.36	.27	.09+	.35+
Nur-Def	.36	.22	.14+	.40	.07	.33+	.19—
Nur-Suc	.49	.18	.31+	.31	.24	.07+	.24+
Nur-Int	.45	.28	.17+	.43	.23	.20+	.03—
Nur-Chg	.50	—.05	.55+	.37	.07	.30+	.25+
Def-Suc	.15	.11	.04+	.20	.07	.13+	.09—
Def-Int	.23	.16	.07+	.23	.19	.04+	.03+
Def-Chg	.27	.12	.15+	.22	.11	.11+	.04+
Suc-Int	.42	.10	.32+	.35	.07	.28+	.04+
Suc-Chg	.28	—.04	.32+	.17	—.05	.22+	.10+
Int-Chg	.38	.07	.31+	.29	—.09	.38+	.07—
End-Ord	.54	—.10	.64+	.32	.12	.20+	.44+

Summary: Number of Differences in the Predicted Direction:

Between Higher and Low Males: 20 of 22.

Between Higher and Low Females: 18 of 22.

Between Males and Females: 16 of 22.

higher self-esteem and low self-esteem males would be larger than
those found for female groups is also, on the whole, with seven of
the nine differences in the predicted direction, borne out for both
the affectional drives and the implemental ones (p < .07).

In Table XXV are arrayed the cross need correlations of each of the affectional needs with each of the others. The correlation values in only one direction across sexes is given to simplify comparisons. Also, since all of these affectional needs except sex are more strongly linked to femininity than to masculinity the correlational direction chosen for display is from female to male; thus, f aff-m nur, f nur-m def, etc. For n sex the correlational directions in each case are appropriately reversed; thus, m sex-f aff, m sex-f nur, etc.

A single cross need, cross sex correlation for the implemental needs is also shown at the lower extremity of the table. It is again, in terms of the sex linkages of the respective drives, the more gendericly congruent directionality that is conformed to. Thus, m end-f ord.

Not surprisingly, attending to comparisons of male groups first, it is in combinations of the high value affectional drives where the highest correlations tend to be found; that is for sex-aff, and aff-nur. The rs for aff-int are almost as great, however. Only in the cases of sex-def and sex-suc are the correlations in the low self-esteem group higher than those in the higher self-esteem sample, but in both cases the reversal of expected magnitudes is quite a minor one.

The confirmation of directional prediction in the instance of end-ord is outstanding, being the largest of the 22 differences found between higher self-esteem and low self-esteem males. Assuming the null hypothesis and applying the "as if" sign test, the probability of 20 out of 22 differences being accountable for as chance outcomes is .0005.

As anticipated, the comparisons between higher self-esteem and low self-esteem female groups are neither as large nor as consistent in their yield of differences. They are, however, so systematically in accord with prediction, with 18 out of 22 being in the expected direction, as to have a chance basis underlying them of only .002.

Finally, in 16 out of 22 comparisons of differences in differences between higher self-esteem males and higher self-esteem females, those for males, as predicted are greater ($p < .026$).

From this analysis, given that the statistical test applied is neither unequivocally appropriate nor an especially demanding one, the emphatic consistency in the patterning of outcomes with what was expected in terms of the underlying dynamics supposed as operating to produce these effects leads to the judgment that the latter did function as hypothesized.

Magnification of the Generic Congruency Effect

It will be recalled that in the chapter where the theory of the hierarchical order of importance of several needs as determinants of intersexual attraction and love was promulgated, the critical importance of effectancy in maintenance and enhancement of sexual identity and role in relation to *establishing and sustaining self-esteem* was asserted. It was seen there as basic and primal as a ground for a feeling of self-worth. This has not been heretofore highlighted by theorists of personality dynamics, and there appears to be no previous research data directly attesting to such a motivational force.

Although much everyday observation and clinical perception makes it eminently plausible to believe it to be a dynamic of great importance in the personality structure of the individual, and suggests its role in relation to self-esteem to be as postulated, it is highly desirable that some more adequate documentation of the position be found. Toward this end this hypothesis is deduced: *individuals who are found to be higher in self-esteem will in their choice of a marital partner have selected one whose own need structure more fully complements their own in terms of the maintenance and enhancement of sexual identity and role than will persons whose self-esteem is low.* Not only would this tend *to occur* as a function of the drive for sexual identity maintenance and enhancement, *which is at the same time a drive for self-esteem maintenance and enhancement*, but presuming its successful accomplishment, it would sustain both feelings at a relatively higher level. If this is so, then it should follow that there would be found to be a magnification of the generic congruency effect in correlations of importantly sex linked needs between higher self-esteem persons and their love partners as compared to the generic congruency effect that is found to obtain in general. But this magnification of the GCE would be especially marked in terms of the variables just mentioned in comparisons between higher and low self-esteem groups. Further, the magnification of the generic congruency effect should obtain most strongly for the correlations between the most importantly sex linked need of the male, dominance, and the most importantly sex linked need of the female, affiliation.

Again, it is expected that the differences revealing the magnification of the genderic congruency effect will be smaller in the comparisons between higher and low self-esteem female groups than will be the case in the comparisons of males. This would be expected for the same reasons as those noted with reference to the previous hypotheses examined in this chapter.

In order to make the necessary and somewhat complex comparisons, Table XXVI has been prepared. In the table are indicated the cross need correlational values for the three most important gendericly linked needs of the male (excluding aggression because of its special hostility property), namely dom, ach and aut, with the three most importantly sex linked needs of females (excluding abasement because of its special property and also because there is an artificial restriction of range of its variation here); namely, aff, nur, and suc. The exclusion of aggression is simply a convenience, because of the desirability of not complicating the comparisons by the negative correlational values it characteristically is identified with. The inclusion of aba in the comparisons would seem entirely inappropriate since it is the variable that is being "held constant" in the separate groups it has been employed to distinguish, and thus has an arbitrarily restricted range of variability in each such group.

As explained in a previous chapter, what is referred to here as the genderic congruency effect is the diminution in correlational value revealed whenever a pair of sex linked need variables is correlated in a direction counter to their respective sex linkages; thus, m aff-f dom, m suc-f aut, etc. As noted previously also, a meaningful and appropriate index to its magnitude is derived from subtracting the incongruent correlational value from the congruent one; e.g., m aut-f aff = .60 minus m aff-f aut = .20 gives a genderic congruency value of .40. In Table XXVI in rows C of each comparison this difference in genderic congruency value is given. To facilitate comparisons between the higher and low self-esteem groups, columns MZ and FZ respectively have been provided. The underlined values in these columns at their intersection with each row C reveals the net difference in magnification of the genderic congruency effect for each of nine comparisons within the male higher and low subsamples and also the net difference in magnification of the effect in the nine corresponding female comparisons. Column MF at the extreme right of the table is installed in order to afford comparisons between male and female subsamples in the magnification of the genderic congruency effect. The values recorded in it are arrived at by subtracting the difference in differences between higher and low females from the difference in differences between higher and low males. Finally, at the base of the table are net values for the genderic congruency effect summed for all nine comparisons in each case, and the net outcome for the nine comparisons between male and female samples.

As predicted the greatest difference in magnification of genderic congruency occurs in both male and female higher self-esteem and low self-esteem comparisons for the correlation of m dom-f aff, but it is closely seconded in value, again in comparisons within both samples, for the pairing m aut-f aff.

In the higher self-esteem male group the genderic congruency effect is great enough for the seven largest of the nine correlational differences to achieve conventional significance levels, while none of those in the low group do so. In the low sample the genderic congruency effect in the ach-nur correlations vanishes, while in four other cases, namely aut-aff, aut-suc, ach-aff and ach-suc we find the anomaly of a *negative* value genderic congruency effect. The differences in differences (col. MZ) between male groups are in each of the nine cases in the predicted direction, favoring the higher self-esteem group.

Within the higher self-esteem female group the effect is consistently in evidence, although typically sufficiently reduced in magnitude to be smaller than the effect in the corresponding male group in eight of the nine comparisons. Still, in all nine comparisons of the higher self-esteem females with the low self-esteem female group it is consistently larger and usually substantially so. Within the latter group, again, there are two instances; those of dom-suc and ach-suc, wherein there appear negative values for the genderic congruency effect.

Although there appears to be no statistical technique, other than the one which has been previously employed, by means of which the outcome of these higher-low self-esteem comparisons could be said to support the hypothesized difference at some stated significance

TABLE XXVI

CROSS NEED CORRELATIONS ON SOME IMPORTANTLY MALE-LINKED AND FEMALE-LINKED NEED SCORES OF LOVE PARTNERS, WITH MALES AND FEMALES DIFFERENTIATED INTO HIGHER AND LOW SELF-ESTEEM CATEGORIES IN THEIR RESPECTIVE SAMPLES

Needs by Sex and Difference in Generic Congruency Effect	MALES			FEMALES			
	MX Higher Self-Esteem N=35	MY Low Self-Esteem N=36	MZ Difference in Differences H-L	FX Higher Self-Esteem N=36	FY Low Self-Esteem N=35	FZ Difference in Differences H-L	MF Difference in Differences for Male-Female and Direction
A M Dom-F Aff	.67*	.40†		.51*	.33‡		
B F Dom-M Aff	−.14	.34‡		−.12	.26		
C Diff. in GC	.81•	.06	.75	.63•	.07	.56	.19M
A M Dom-F Nur	.48*	.39†		.27	.23		
B F Dom-M Nur	−.10	.11		−.15	.21		
C Diff. in GC	.58•	.28	.30	.42•	.02	.40	.10F
A M Dom-F Suc	.42†	.33‡		.36‡	.08		
B F Dom-M Suc	.05	.07		.10	.17		
C Diff. in GC	.37•	.26	.11	.26	−.09	.35	.24F
A M Aut-F Aff	.63*	.09		.34‡	.34‡		
B F Aut-M Aff	−.04	.12		−.11	.23		
C Diff. in GC	.67•	−.03	.70	.45•	.11	.34	.36M
A M Aut-F Nur	.60*	−.10		.35‡	.09		
B F Aut-M Nur	−.02	−.05		.01	−.01		
C Diff. in GC	.62•	.05	.57	.34•	.10	.24	.33M

A	M Aut-F Suc	.40†	.01		.16	.23		
B	F Aut-M Suc	−.04	.09		−.01	.12		
C	Diff. in GC	.44•	−.08	.52	.17	.11	.06	.46M
A	M Ach-F Aff	.62*	.05		.39†	.27		
B	F Ach-M Aff	.20	.26		.12	.16		
C	Diff. in GC	.42•	−.21	.63	.27	.11	.16	.47M
A	M Ach-F Nur	.60*	.05		.43*	.15		
B	F Ach-M Nur	.37‡	.05		.11	.07		
C	Diff. in GC	.23	.00	.23	.32•	.08	.24	.01F
A	M Ach-F Suc	.40†	.07		.25	−.11		
B	F Ach-M Suc	.15	.28§		.11	.16		
C	Diff. in GC	.25	−.21	.46	.14	−.27	.41	.05M
	Totals, i.e., Net Differences in GC:			4.27	4.27		2.76	1.51M

Significance levels of *rs*: * = .005; † = .01; ‡ = .025; § = .05.

level, the possibility of the patterning exemplified in Table XXVI
having occurred by chance seems quite remote. Assuming the null
hypothesis and applying the cumulative binomial sign test for the
eighteen positively predicted differences in differences (Columns
MZ and FZ) out of the eighteen opportunities the probability of
such an accurrence by chance is .0005.

The hypothesis appears to be clearly supported, even if not unequivocally confirmed.

The predicted sex difference in the difference in differences of the
generic congruency effect, it is notable in Table XXVI, in examining the values entered in column MF, is somewhat inconsistently
manifest, being in one third of the instances shown there in the female direction. The net magnification effect is, however, very definitely greater in the male sample.

SUMMARY

The data of this chapter have been ordered to test as effectively
as possible three points of importance to the theory advanced here;
namely that:

1. The culturally standardized sexual identities and roles assigned
to and socialized into the respective sexes in our society equip them
with differentially patterned motivational forces. These, in order to
be maximally gratified by them, lead them to be attracted to and
form love relationships with those of the opposite sex whose patterning of motivational forces tends to complement their own. Although, obviously, there is wide variation in the perfection with
which the complementary matching is achieved between couples,
the over-all patterning of choices indicates that those who have
formed love relationships with each other and chosen each other as
"life partners" have on the whole approximated the complementary
condition in doing so.

2. But it is not a pattern wherein similarity of needs plays no role.
For, on the contrary, it has been hypothesized, in effect, and veri-
fied, that the greater the self-esteem possessed by either male or female the more likely either will have been to have been attracted to and to
have formed a love relationship with someone whose motivational animus
is more similar to his own than will have been the case with individuals of low self-esteem. This is true for both the self assertive and

affectional drives as well as for implemental ones. Behavioral and motivational tendencies devolving upon self-esteem were seen as the causal agents in producing the effects described, and it was in terms of the supposed operation of their dynamics that the effects were predicted to obtain.

3. But, it was hypothesized further that the existing feeling of self-esteem of the individual might well be in some large part a function of the gratification achieved in the existing love relationship for the individual's sexual identity need, itself an aspect of the need for self-esteem. The sustenance to feelings of self-esteem thus received have been theorized to be of important determinative value in intersexual attraction and love. It was deduced that if such gratifications as those supposed to be influential were being received, it would have consequences that would be identifyable in the correlational data. It would require a more fully complementary patterning between the need structures of individuals with higher feelings of self-esteem and those of their love partners than that which would obtain between individuals of low self-esteem and their love partners. This would, it was argued, be manifested in a magnification of the genderic congruency effect in correlations of the most importantly sex linked needs of partners in the higher esteem group as contrasted with this same effect in the low esteem group. The expected magnification of the effect was, in fact, found.

CHAPTER THIRTEEN

SUMMARY AND CONCLUSIONS

RESUME

THE MAIN BURDEN of the arguments in this work has been that interpersonal attraction, liking and loving are derivatives of the condition of human interdependence, but more particularly of the fact that the behaviors of each of us come to be instrumental to the gratification rather than the punification of the needs of another or others. A male or female, it has been asserted, is attracted to one of the opposite sex whenever one of them sees the other as an important source of need gratification, although rarely would a person thus attracted verbalize it quite in this way. Most likely he or she would speak of the beauty, sexiness, strength, affectionateness, etc. of the other as the source of and raison d'etre of his attraction. Intersexual dyads are formed and endure under conditions wherein there is, other things being equal, a surplus of gratifications reciprocally exchanged as compared with whatever punifications are incidental to the relationship and interaction.

In Chapter One it was pointed out that the instrumental theory of interpersonal attraction was mostly congruent with rather than in opposition to hitherto existing reinforcement and exchange theories of this phenomenon. But it was later asserted that instrumental formulations seek to go beyond existing theoretical statements both in providing a more complete understanding of the underlying motivations involved as well as by identifying the mechanisms by which the behaviors instigated by the needs of one partner could become instrumental to the gratification of particular needs in the other.

In Chapter Two was presented a somewhat detailed review of previous theory and research specific to intersexual attraction. Particular attention was addressed to the complementarity theory of Winch, which holds that the need patterns of those attracted to each other are different rather than similar, and it was pointed out that the data accumulated from several studies relating to this difference theory had quite clearly failed to confirm and support it. Indeed, the data were seen as indicating varying degrees of similarity in measured strength of almost all of the motivational variables which had been investigated in correlational studies of the motivational patterns of married or engaged couples. Similarity, it was noted, in itself has little or no explanatory value, however; and, in the attempt to go beyond the mere surface finding of its existence and to account for its being, a set of mechanisms was postulated and their supposed effects described. These mechanisms served as a basis for predictions of outcomes of a projected reexamination of the relationships of 15 motivational variables of engaged couples. Then, with the supplementation of these mechanisms with several additional postulates concerning the patent and latent consequences of the properties of the behaviors instigated by the several needs, predictions were extended so that the nature and magnitude of the correlation of each of the 15 needs with every other need (a 225 item matrix) was more or less successfully predicted. To accomplish the foregoing task required an intensive examination of the nature of the needs under consideration and a more or less comprehensive realization of the interactive consequences each would have for members of the respective sexes. Since the work alluded to in the foregoing constituted support for or confirmation of the basic propositions and postulates of the instrumental theory, it is fitting to summarize at this point by listing and restating these formulations.

1. A first proposition was that concerning interpersonal dependency for interpersonal need gratifications. Individuals are dependent upon each other for specific gratifications of certain motives, which for that reason are referred to as interpersonal needs.

2. A second proposition was the postulate of gratification and punification as the functional antecedents (or causes) of attraction and repulsion (effects). Because the behaviors devolving upon the interpersonal needs of one person directly or indirectly gratify or punify the needs of those persons (or gratify or punify the *persons*) with whom he interacts, feelings of attraction and liking or repulsion and disliking are produced toward or with reference to him as object.

These ideas are restated in a more general way in the following:

3. Social interaction and interpersonal behavior may be conceived of as a process wherein we seek to use and do use each other for the gratification of our needs. When there is mutually gratifying use of each other it results in attraction and love. When there is mutual or one-sided punification of needs the result is repulsion and hate. Where no exchange of gratifications or punifications results from our encounters and interactions we experience merely disinterest and apathy.

4. As part of the instrumental theory, a theory of love, identifying it as a response was proposed. Sexual love was itself defined specifically as follows: "Love on the part of one individual for another is the response or responses evoked in the first individual through his experiencing of rewards, pleasures, or need gratifications as products of his interactions with the other. If the gratifications experienced are sexual in nature, or, more specifically, if there is gratification of the sex need, then it is sexual love." This definition, of course, encompasses both heterosexual and homosexual instances of love, but it is in no sense diminished in meaningfulness because of the inclusiveness. It refers specifically and explicitly to sexual love. But it should be understood to imply and acknowledge the existence of non-sexual love as well; the latter term being conceived of as a referent for all those instances where there is no involvement of the sexual motivations of the persons concerned, although gratifications of other motives are present and, in fact, constitute the basis for the resulting feeling state.

5. A theory of initial attraction was proposed as follows. Initial attraction to one of the opposite sex, sexual attraction, physical attraction or, for that matter, simply attraction without involvement of sex impulses is a resultant of the perceived, subceived, imagined or unconsciously anticipated gratifyingness of the other.

6. A theory of sexual attraction in particular was also proposed. It was stated, in effect, that what we experience as sexual attraction, which has both conscious and unconscious components, is essentially merely a product of the exteroceptive, interoceptive and proprioceptive feedback from our incipient responses to the stimulus person and especially from the fractional anticipatory consummatory responses of a sexual nature with him or her.

7. The central thesis of the instrumental theory of interper-

sonal relations as applied to intersexual dyad formation was formally stated as follows:

In intersexual dyad formation each person seeks among his circle of acquaintances within the compass of his self-acknowledged compeers to form a relationship with that person or those persons whose behavioral and other resources provide (or are perceived or expected to provide) maximum gratification and minimum punification for his needs.

8. It was seen that such a statement as the foregoing was inadequately explanatory or specific; hence it was supplemented with a theory of a hierarchy of determining needs in intersexual attraction and love. The theory, in brief, assigned priority to sex as the most prepotent determining drive, with this followed by the need for affectionate intimacy, the need for maintenance and enhancement of sexual identity and role, the need for interpersonal security and the need for self esteem, in that order.

9. The needs of males and females differ, not only in degree but to some, as yet incompletely determined extent, in kind as well. Yet, accepting the rather convincing findings of studies (e.g. Banta and Hetherington) already accomplished as a factual starting point, and noting that males and females already established as attracted to each other by virtue of their engagement to be married manifested similarity rather than difference in needs, a theory of intermotivational mechanics was developed to explain this. A set of several mechanisms were proposed as the means by which the reciprocal gratification supposed to underlie their attraction might have been accomplished.

A. One of the simplest and most important of these mechanisms was that of *reciprocality*, best exemplified in the interactive functioning of needs like sex and affection. Herein are instances where the behaviors instigated by the needs of one partner are not only directly gratifying to him or herself but directly to the other partner in the exchange as well. Two persons each with high strengths of such needs, especially as they are measured by the EPPS items wherein they are needs to both produce and consume the respective kinds of behaviors, would have great likelihood of being able to reciprocally provide gratifications to each other. Hence such persons would be expected to experience strong feelings of attraction.

B. Behaviors motivated by needs such as dominance and aggression, it was noted, may be expected to be in varying degrees punifying in social interactions, yet interattracted partners are revealed to have sufficient similarity of need strengths on these variables for positive correlations to obtain between them. In explanation for the apparent paradox, the supposition was advanced that interactions of a conflictful and possibly punifying nature could still result in a net balance of gratification by virtue of the behaviors engaged in being productive of outcomes gratifying to *other needs* simultaneously in operation in the interactive episode. The mechanism was named *adjuvance* (for one way effects) and *coadjuvance* for two way effects). Included as a special case of this mechanism was a subvariety of it which was labelled *procreance* and *coprocreance*, the former for unidirectional action, the latter for reciprocal operation.

C. Still another mechanism called *vicariousness* was invoked to help explain the attraction found to exist between partners both fairly high in motivations instigative of competitive and conflictful behaviors. For it was recognized that humans are prone to identify with others in many behavioral contexts, but especially so in assertive, dramatic, combative and achieving ones. One could be gratified by vicariously experiencing the gratification of the other through such identification. Since, it was pointed out, each partner could be gratified in such a way in interaction episodes, this two-way phenomenon was called covicariousness.

D. An achieving partner, it was observed, may by his accomplishments directly or indirectly benefit an associate. Hence a mechanism called *agentiality* (for single direction work) and *coagentiality* (for reciprocal execution) was postulated as playing a role in the effecting of the mutual need gratification of attracted pairs.

E. Not involved as a mechanism for effectance of gratification of the *same* need in interacting partners, but rather of paramount importance as a means through which *different* needs accomplished this result, was the instrumentality referred to as *complementarity*. This mechanism was, nevertheless, found to be operative in accounting for the fact of positive correlations existing between particular *same* needs because the correlation in question was, in effect, an artifact of the simultaneous functioning of unrecognized but 'logically necessary' *different* needs in the interacting parties. This particular variety of complementarity was named *reciprocal complementarity, or cocomplementarity*. An example of its operation was described in a situation where two persons, both motivated by exhibition take turns in entertaining and amusing each other, thus alternately gratifying not only their needs for showing off, but their needs to be entertained as well.

10. It was stressed that these mechanisms were in themselves insufficient as a basis for predicting interpair need correlations,

for also required was necessity for taking into account both the patent and latent properties of the needs and those of the behaviors instigated by them in interactive episodes, including perceptually mediated and imagined ones. This, in confrontation with the desirability of predicting hitherto unknown correlations among a set of fifteen interpersonal needs, led to an attempt at stating the properties of the relevant motivated behaviors. This was followed by the setting forth of a set of postulates (or hypotheses) as constituents of a theory of intermotivational dynamics from which, in combination with the mechanisms, particular correlational predictions were derived and later tested.

The properties identified as most salient and relevant for the fifteen EPPS needs were (1) strength-weakness, (2) beneficence-suppliance, (3) affection-hostility and (4) excitement-sameness. Of these, the strength-weakness characteristic was, because of its intimate association with masculinity-femininity, given outstanding importance.

Implicit but heretofore unrecognized as a dynamic factor in previous correlational analyses of interpartner need strengths was a motivational force which herein has been postulated and referred to as a *sexual identity and sex-role maintenance drive.* Its effects were seen as permeating and thus as crosscutting and compromising the relationships that might be expected to be found between particular need pairings of male and female dyadic partners. A statement embodying the relevant aforementioned postulate follows.

The postulate of a sexual identity and sex role maintenance drive: Individuals of the respective sexes are strongly motivated to behave in ways congruent with the cultural definitions of their sexual identities and roles as these, together with the needs which are generative of behaviors expressive of them, have been embodied in their personalities. And, ceteris paribus, in intersexual dyad formation each will seek a relationship with that partner whose own needs instigate behaviors most facilitative of and promotive to the gratification of this motive.

This was more particularized in a restatement as *the postulate of intersexual attraction arising from generic congruency of needs and resources:* In intersexual interaction the behaviors instigated by those most distinctively sex-linked needs will have high attraction value if found in a person of the sex they are associated with most strongly in the social-cultural definition of sex type, but less attraction value if found in a person of the sex with which they are popularly regarded as less congruent or incongruent.

A theory of the interactive functioning of behaviors devolving upon the general and common properties of needs together with the involvement of these with the generic congruency factor was elaborated and the integrant proposed as the *theory of intermotivational dynamics* referred to previously.

Two additional important assumptions which were seen as necessary for the theory to be predictively effective were (1) the postulate of isomorphism of motive and behavior and (2) the postulate of need—resource resonance.

In the postulate of isomorphism of motive and behavior it is assumed that the needs of a person as indicated by his test scores have each instigated responses more or less isomorphic with them or at least meaningfully congruent with them in his past interactions and exposures to the person known to be attracted to him, and that the other person's needs have, fulfilling this same principle, done likewise.

The postulate of need-resource resonance assumes that each person in the interactive relationship is more or less able to accurately interpret the others' behaviors and to respond more or less appropriately to them in interactions with the other. Persons are additionally assumed to be particularly sensitized by their own needs in such a manner as to respond to reduced and subtle cues as to the possession or nonpossession of the relevant resources for their gratification in the behaviors of others.

The principles involved in the theory of intermotivational dynamics in combination with those of intermotivational mechanics were subsequently employed (in Chapter Ten) to predict all of the cross sex-cross need correlations in the 210 item matrix.

In Chapter Six the research methodology and the sample of 71 couples whose responses were employed to evaluate the theories of intermotivational mechanics, intermotivational dynamics and the theory of the hierarchy of determining needs were described. In Chapter Seven an analysis of the data was presented and interpreted as strongly supportive of the body of theoretical formulations constituent to the theory of the order of primacy of particular needs as determinants of attraction and love as well as of those constituent to the theory of intermotivational mechanics. In Chapter Eleven a similar appraisal was made with respect to both the theory of intermotivational dynamics and to the instrumental theory as a whole. It was concluded in both cases that the predictive power was indeed high. In the same chapter comparisons with complementarity theory were also presented and from these it was concluded that the instrumental formulations were far more effective than those of the aforementioned one.

A following chapter was devoted to testing two important additional formulations. The first of these was the conception of intersexual dyadic complementarity in patterning of need strengths as an effect of the respective drives of the partners for sexual identity and sex role maintenance. Data were ordered to the demonstration that the reciprocal choices of intersexual dyadic partners were highly congruent with the postulated operation of this drive.

A second set of ideas was embodied in a series of hypotheses drawn from the implications of instrumental theory regarding the involvement of feelings of self-esteem in the formation of intersexual love relationships. The data testing these were interpreted as supporting the idea that the sexual identity drive, which is conceived of as being at the same time a primal aspect of the need for self-esteem, functions in such a way as to both sustain feelings of self-esteem and to express them in intersexual love relationships.

CONCLUSIONS

In conclusion, with respect to all that has been considered and examined in the intensive analysis of motivational forces which constitutes the substance of this work, the following points are of primal salience.

In intersexual dyad formation each person seeks as a partner that person whose abilities and attributes (or behavioral and other resources) provide, or are perceived or are expected to provide, by interactions with him, maximum gratification for his or her needs for sexual satisfaction, affectionate intimacy, including emotional support and understanding, maintenance and enhancement of sexual identity and role, of interpersonal security and of his self-esteem. It is as a response evoked primarily by the experience of gratification of these needs, mentioned in their order of priority, that love is born in the feelings of the respective interacting persons.

Not all of the needs enumerated in the above were directly measured in the research reported herein, and, in fact, perhaps only n sex could with obvious justification be claimed to be. The others were indicated as to their nature and degree more or less indirectly; namely, either as they were represented in some variable under a different name, such as affiliation, intraception, or succorance, or inferred as operative as an underlying causal condition in accounting for the complex interrelations found to exist between pairs and larger groupings of needs. This latter was exemplified, specifically, in the case of the posited need for maintenance and enhancement of sexual identity and role.

Even though the list in the foregoing has had a perhaps uncommonly thorough documentation through this research and the attendant analysis, it is still to be regarded as tentative in certain respects, but in particular with regard to the validation of the positioning in it of a posited need for interpersonal security. It remains for future research to determine the accuracy of the position theorized to exist for it in the earlier portion of this enterprize as well as, of course, to fix the finality of the list itself.

Whether the needs and need strengths of partners are similar or different was seen as a question demanding a more sophisticated phrasing and, in the face of hitherto existing confusion as to facts, a better devised answer. The data of this research make it quite clear that both similarity *and* difference obtain. And those aspects of instrumental theory which are referred to as intermotivational mechanics and intermotivational dynamics, employed in combination, provide an explanation in terms of both the causes for this state of affairs and their modi operandi.

The aggregate of principles which constitutes instrumental theory, while already large, may itself be expected to become larger with continuing study; for the theory, even if woefully lacking in simplistic elegance, has a comprehensiveness of conception that loses nothing in meaningfulness by the addition of new and compatible particulars and extensions. Additional research guided by deductions from its postulates may, moreover, possibly succeed in an economy of reformulations and reconceptualizations which will improve it; a consummation hopefully aspired to by its author.

REFERENCES
Adams, R.: *Interracial Marriage in Hawaii.* New York, Macmillan, 1937.

Aristotle: *The Rhetoric.* New York, Appleton-Century, 1932.

Aronson, E. and Linder D.: Gain and loss of esteem as determinants of interpersonal attractiveness. *Journal of Experimental Social Psychology, 1,* 156-171, 1965.

Backman, C.W. and Secord, P.F.: The effect of perceived liking on interpersonal attraction. *Human Relations, 12,* 379-384, 1959.

Backman, C.W. and Secord, P.F.: Liking, selective interaction, and misperception in congruent interpersonal relations. *Sociometry, 25,* 321-335, 1962.

Banta, T.J. and Hetherington, M.: Relations between needs of friends and fiancés. *Journal of Abnormal and Social Psychology, 66,* 401-404, 1963.

Barclay, A.M.: Information as a defensive control of sexual arousal. *Journal of Personality and Social Psychology, 17,* 244-249, 1971.

Barron, M.L.: *People who intermarry.* Syracuse, Syracuse University Press, 1946.

Bass, B.M.: Famous sayings test: General manual. *Psychological Reports, 4,* 479-497, 1958.

Becker, G.: The complementary need hypothesis: Authoritarianism, dominance and other Edwards Personal Preference Schedule Scores. *Journal of Personality, 32,* 45-56, 1934.

Beier, E.G., Rossi, A.M. and Garfield, R.L.: Similarity plus dissimilarity of personality: basis for friendship? *Psychological Reports, 8,* 3-8, 1961.

Bendig, A.W. and Martin, A.M.: The factor structure and stability of fifteen human needs. *Journal of General Psychology, 67* (2), 229-235, 1962.

Benedek, T.: *Insight and personality adjustment.* New York, Ronald, 1946.

Berger, E.M.: The relation between expressed acceptance of self and expressed acceptance of others. *Journal of Abnormal and Social Psychology, 47,* 778-782, 1952.

Bergler, E.: *Unhappy marriage and divorce.* New York, International Universities Press, 1946.

Bergler, E.: *Divorce won't help.* New York, Harper and Bros., 1948.

Bergler, E. and Kroger, W.S.: *Kinsey's myth of female sexuality: The medical facts.* New York, Greene and Stratton, 1954.

Berkowitz, L.: *Aggression.* New York, McGraw-Hill, 1962.

Berscheid, E. and Walster, E.H.: *Interpersonal attraction.* Reading, Mass., Addison-Wesley Publishing Co., 1969.

Bixenstine, V.E., Potash, H.M. and Wilson, K.V.: Effects on level of cooperative choices in a prisoner's dilemma game. Part I. *Journal of Abnormal and Social Psychology, 66,* 308-313, 1963.

Bjerstedt, A.: A field force model as a basis for predictions of social behavior. *Human Relations, 11,* 331-340, 1958.

Blau, P.M.: *Exchange and power in social life.* New York, John Wiley and Sons, 1964.

Bonney, M.E.: Popular and unpopular children: a sociometric study. *Sociometry Monographs*, No. 9, 1947.

Bossard, J.H.S.: Residential propinquity as a factor in marriage selection. *American Journal of Sociology, 38*, 219-224, 1932.

Bossard, J.H.S.: Nationality and nativity as factors in marriage. *American Sociological Review, 4*, 792-798, 1939.

Bossard, J.H.S.: Marrying late in life. *Social Forces, 29*, 405-408, 1951.

Bowerman, C.E.: Assortative mating by previous marital status: Seattle. *American Sociological Review, 18*, 170-177, 1953.

Bowerman, C.E. and Day, B.R.: A test of the theory of complementary needs as applied to couples during courtship. *American Sociological Review, 21*, 602-605, 1956.

Broxton, J.A.: A test of interpersonal attraction predictions derived from balance theory. *Journal of Abnormal and Social Psychology, 66*, 394-397, 1963.

Burgess, E. and Wallin, P.: *Engagement and marriage*. Chicago, Lippincott, 1953.

Burma, J.H.: Research note on the measurement of interracial marriage. *American Journal of Sociology, 57*, 587-589, 1952.

Buss, A.: *The Psychology of aggression*. New York, John Wiley and Sons, 1961.

Byrne, D.: Interpersonal attraction and attitude similarity. *Journal of Abnormal and Social Psychology, 62*, 713-715, 1961.

Byrne, D.: Response to attitude similarity-dissimilarity as a function of affiliation need. *Journal of Personality, 30*, 164-177, 1962.

Byrne, D.: Attitudes and attraction. In Berkowitz, L. (Ed.), *Advances in experimental social psychology, 4*, 36-89, 1969.

Byrne, D. and Clore, G.L. Jr.: Predicting interpersonal attraction toward strangers presented in three different stimulus modes. *Psychonomic Science, 4*, 239-240, 1966.

Byrne, D., Clore, G.L. Jr. and Worchel, P.: Effect of economic similarity-dissimilarity in interpersonal attraction. *Journal of Personality and Social Psychology, 4*, 220-224, 1966.

Byrne, D. and Ervin, C.R.: Attraction toward a Negro stranger as a function of prejudice, attitude similarity, and the stranger's evaluation of the subject. *Human Relation, 22*, 397-404, 1969.

Byrne, D., Ervin, C.R. and Lamberth, J.: Continuity between the Experimental study of attraction and real-life computer dating. *Journal of Personality and Social Psychology, 16*, 157-165, 1970.

Byrne, D. and Griffitt, W.: A developmental investigation of the law of attraction. *Journal of Personality and Social Psychology, 4*, 699-702, 1966.

Byrne, D., London, O. and Reeves, K.: The effects of physical attractiveness, sex and attitude similarity on interpersonal attraction. *Journal of Personality, 36*, 259-271, 1968.

Byrne, D. and Nelson, D.: Attraction as a linear function of proportion of positive reinforcements. *Journal of Personality and Social Psychology, 1,* 659-663, 1965.

Byrne, D. and Rhamey, R.: Magnitude of positive and negative reinforcements as a determinant of attraction. *Journal of Personality and Social Psychology, 2,* 884-889, 1965.

Cattell, R.B.: *Personality.* New York, McGraw-Hill, 1950.

Cattell, R.B. and Nesselroade, J.R.: Likeness and completeness theories examined by 16 personality factor measures on stably and unstably married couples. *Journal of Personality and Social Psychology, 7,* 351-361, 1967.

Centers, R.: Motivational aspects of occupational stratification. *Journal of Social Psychology, 28,* 187-217, 1948.

Centers, R.: *The psychology of social classes.* Princeton, Princeton University Press, 1949(a).

Centers, R.: Marital selection and occupational strata. *American Journal of Sociology, 54,* 530-535, 1949(b).

Centers, R.: Evaluating the loved one: the motivational congruency factor. *Journal of Personality, 39,* 303-318, 1971.

Centers, R. and Granville, A.C.: Reciprocal need gratification in intersexual attraction: A test of the hypotheses of Schutz and Winch. *Journal of Personality, 39,* 26-43, 1971.

Clarke, A.C.: An examination of the operation of residential propinquity as a factor in mate selection. *American Sociological Review, 17,* 17-22, 1952.

Combs, A.W. and Snygg, D.: Individual Behavior: A perceptual approach to behavior. New York, Harper and Row, 1959.

Corah, N.L., Feldman, M.J., Cohen, I.S., Gruen, W., Meadow, A., and Ringwell, E.A.: Social desirability as a variable in the Edwards Personal Preference Schedule. *Journal of Consulting Psychology, 22,* 70-72, 1958.

Davie, M.R. and Reeves, R.J.: Propinquity in residence before marriage. *American Journal of Sociology, 44,* 510-517, 1939.

Davitz, J.R.: Social perception and sociometric choice of children. *Journal of Abnormal and Social Psychology, 50,* 173-176, 1955.

Day, B.R.: A comparison of personality needs of courtship couples and same sex friendships. *Sociology and Social Research, 45,* 435-440, 1961.

Deutsch, M. and Solomon, L.: Reactions to evaluations by others as influenced by self-evaluations. *Sociometry, 22,* 93-112, 1959.

Dickoff, H.: Reactions to evaluations by another person as a function of self-evaluation and the interaction context. Unpublished doctoral dissertation, Duke University, 1961.

Dittes, J.E.: Attractiveness of group as a function of self esteem and acceptance by group. *Journal of Abnormal and Social Psychology, 59,* 77-82, 1959.

Dollard, J. and Miller, N.E.: *Personality and Psychotherapy.* New York, McGraw-Hill, 1950.

316 *Sexual Attraction and Love*

Dreikurs, R.: *The challenge of marriage.* New York, Duel, Sloan and Pearce, 1946.

Edwards, A.L.: *Edwards Personal Preference Schedule.* New York, The Psychological Corporation, 1959.

Ellsworth, J.S.: The relationship of population density to residential propinquity as a factor in marriage selection. *American Sociological Review, 13,* 444-448, 1948.

Faunce, D. and Beegle, J.A.: Cleavages in a relatively homogeneous group of rural youth: An experiment in the use of sociometry in attaining and measuring integration. *Sociometry, 11,* 207-216, 1948.

Farber, B.: An index of marital integration. *Sociometry, 20,* 117-134, 1957.

Feldman, M. and Corah, N.L.: Social desirability and the forced-choice method. *Journal of Consulting Psychology, 24,* 480-482, 1960.

Festinger, L.: Informal social communication. *Psychological Review, 57,* 271-282, 1950.

Festinger, L.: A theory of social comparison processes. *Human Relations, 7,* 117-140, 1954.

Flugel, J.C.: *The psychoanalytic study of the family.* London, Hogarth, 1921.

Flugel, J.C.: *Man, morals and society.* New York, International Universities Press, 1945.

Fordyce, W.E. and Crow, W.R.: Ego disjunction: A failure to replicate. Trehub's results. *Journal of Abnormal and Social Psychology, 60,* 446-448, 1960.

Freud, S.: *Group psychology and the analysis of the ego.* London, Hogarth, 1922.

Freud, S.: *On Narcissism: an introduction in collected papers.* Vol. IV. London, Hogarth Press, 1925.

Glick, P.C.: First marriages and remarriages. *American Sociological Review, 14,* 726-734, 1949.

Glick, P.C. and Landau, E.: Age as a factor in marriage. *American Sociological Review, 15,* 517-529, 1950.

Gocka, E.F. and Rozynko, V.: Some comments on the EPPS ego disjunction score. *Journal of Abnormal and Social Psychology, 62,* 458-460, 1961.

Golden, J.: Patterns of negro-white intermarriage. *American Sociological Review, 19,* 144-147, 1954.

Gray, H.: Jung's psychological types in men and women. *Stanford Medical Bulletin, 6,* 29-36, 1946.

Gray, H.: Psychological types in married people. *Journal of Social Psychology, 29,* 189-200, 1949.

Gray, H. and Wheelwright, J.B.: Jung's psychological types, their frequency of occurrence. *Journal of General Psychology, 34,* 3-17, 1946.

Hahn, M.E.: *The California life goals evaluation schedules manual.* Los Angeles, Western Psychological Services, 1966, 1969.

Havighurst, R.J., Robinson, M.Z. and Dorr, M.: The development of the ideal self in childhood and adolescence. *Journal of Educational Research,*

40, 241-257, 1946.

Heider, F.: Social perception and phenomenal causality. *Psychological Review*, *51*, 358-374, 1944.

Heider, F.: *The psychology of interpersonal relations*. New York, John Wiley and Sons, Inc., 1958(a).

Heider, F.: Perceiving the other person. In Tagiuri, R. and Petrullo, L. (Eds.), *Person perception and interpersonal behavior*. Stanford, Stanford University Press, 1958(b).

Heider, F.: Consciousness, the perceptual world and communications with others. In Tagiuri, R. and Petrullo, L. (Eds.), *Person perception and interpersonal behavior*. Stanford, Stanford University Press, 1958(c).

Heilizer, F.: A note on the scoring of ego disjunction. *Journal of Abnormal and Social Psychology*, *63*, 438-439, 1961 (a).

Heilizer, F.: A scale of compatibility and incompatibility of pairs of needs. *Psychological Reports*, *9*, 565-572, 1961 (b).

Heilizer, F.: Conjunctive and disjunctive conflict: a theory of need conflict. *Journal of Abnormal and Social Psychology*, *68*, 21-37, 1964.

Hoffeditz, E.L.: Family resemblances in personality traits. *Journal of Social Psychology*, *5*, 214-217, 1934.

Hollingshead, A.B.: Cultural factors in the selection of marriage mates. *American Sociological Review*, *15*, 619-627, 1950.

Hollingshead, A.B.: Age relationships and marriage. *American Sociological Review*, *16*, 492-499, 1951.

Homans, G.C.: *Social behavior: its elementary forms*. New York, Harcourt, Brace and World, 1961.

Horney, K.: *Our inner conflicts*. New York, W.W. Norton, 1945.

Hoyt, M.F. and Centers, R.: Ego disjunction as a factor in intersexual attraction. *Journal of Personality Assessment*, *35*, 367-374, 1971.

Hunt, T.C.: Occupational status and marriage selection. *American Sociological Review*, *5*, 495-504, 1940.

James, W.: *Principles of Psychology* (2 vols.). New York, Holt, 1890.

Jennings, H. H.: *Leadership and isolation*. New York, Longmans Green, 1950, 2nd Edition.

Jones, E.E.: Authoritarianism as a determinant of first impression formation. *Journal of Personality*, *23*, 107-127, 1954.

Jones, E.E., Hester, S.L., Farina, A. and Davis, K.E.: Reactions to unfavorable personal evaluations as a function of the evaluator's perceived adjustment. *Journal of Abnormal and Social Psychology*, *59*, 363-370, 1959.

Kamano, D.K.: Relationship of ego disjunction and manifest anxiety to conflict resolution. *Journal of Abnormal and Social Psychology*, *66*, 281-284, 1963.

Kennedy, R.J.R.: Pre-marital residential propinquity and ethnic endogamy. *American Journal of Sociology*, *48*, 580-584, 1943.

Kennedy, R.J.R.: Single or triple melting pot? Intermarriage in New Haven, 1870-1950. *American Journal of Sociology*, *58*, 56-59, 1952.

Kerckhoff, A. and Davis, K.E.: Value consensus and need complementarity in mate selection. *American Sociological Review, 27,* 295-303, 1962.

Kidd, J.W.: An analysis of social rejection in a college men's residence hall. *Sociometry, 14,* 226-234, 1951.

Klineberg, O.: *Characteristics of the American Negro.* New York, Harper, 1944.

Ktsanes, T.: Mate selection on the basis of personality type: a study utilizing an empirical typology of personality. *American Sociological Review, 20,* 547-551, 1955.

Landis, P.H. and Day, K.H.: Education as a factor in mate selection. *American Sociological Review, 10,* 558-560, 1945.

Leary, T.: *Interpersonal diagnosis of personality.* New York, Ronald Press, 1957.

Levinger, G. and Senn, D.J.: Progress toward permanence in courtship: A test of the Kerckhoff-Davis Hypotheses. *Sociometry, 33,* 427-443, 1970.

Levonian, E., Comrey, A., Levy, W. and Proctor, D.: A statistical evaluation of Edwards' Personal Preference Schedule. *Journal of Applied Psychology, 43,* 355-359, 1959.

Locke, H.J. and Wallace, K.M.: Short marital adjustment and prediction tests: their reliability and validity. *Marriage and Family Living, 21,* 251-255, 1959.

Lundy, R.M., Katkovsky, W., Cromwell, R.L. and Shoemaker, D.J.: Self acceptability and descriptions of sociometric choices. *Journal of Abnormal and Social Psychology, 51,* 260-262, 1955.

McClelland, D.C., Atkinson, J.W., Clark, R.A. and Lowell, E.L.: *The achievement motive.* New York, Appleton-Century-Crofts, 1953.

Marches, J.R. and Turbeville, G.: The effect of residential propinquity on marriage selection. *American Journal of Sociology, 58,* 592-595, 1953.

Marcson, S.: Predicting intermarriages. *Sociology and Social Research, 37,* 151-156, 1953.

Martinson, F.M.: Ego deficiency as a factor in marriage. *American Sociological Review, 20,* 161-164, 1955.

Martinson, F.M.: Ego deficiency as a factor in marriage: a male sample. *Marriage and Family Living, 21,* 48-52, 1959.

Marvin, D.: Occupational propinquity as a factor in marriage selection. *Journal of the American Statistical Association, 16,* 131-150, 1918-1919.

Maslow, A.H.: Dominance—feeling, behavior and status. *Psychological Review, 44,* 404, 1937.

Maslow, A.H.: Self esteem (dominance feeling) and sexuality in women. *Journal of Social Psychology, 16,* 259-294, 1942 (a).

Maslow, A.H.: The dynamics of psychological security—insecurity. *Character and Personality, 10,* 331-344, 1942 (b).

Maslow, A.H.: A theory of human motivation. *Psychological Review, 50,* 370-396, 1943.

Maslow, A.H., Hirsh, E., Stein, M. and Honigman, I.: A clinically derived test for measuring psychological security—insecurity. *The Journal of General Psychology, 33*, 21-41, 1945.

Merton, R.K.: Intermarriage and the social structure. *Psychiatry, 4*, 371-374, 1941.

Mittleman, B.: Analysis of Reciprocal Neurotic Patterns in Family Relationships. In Victor W. Eisenstein (Ed.), *Neurotic Interaction in Marriage*. New York, Basic Books, 81-100, 1956.

Moreno, J.L.: *Who shall survive?* Washington, D.C., Nervous and Mental Disease Monographs, No. 58, 1934.

Mosteller, F., Rourke, R.E.K. and Thomas, G.B. Jr.: *Probability with statistical applications*. Reading, Mass., Addison-Wesley Pub. Co., 1961.

Murray, H.A.: The effect of fear upon estimates of the maliciousness of other personalities. *Journal of Social Psychology, 4*, 310-329, 1933.

Murray, H.A.: *Explorations in personality*. New York, Oxford University Press, 1938.

Murstein, B.I.: The complementary need hypothesis in newlyweds and middle-aged married couples. *Journal of Abnormal and Social Psychology, 63*, 194-197, 1961.

Murstein, B.I.: The relationship of mental health to marital choice and courtship progress. *Journal of Marriage and the Family, 29*, 447-451, 1967.

Neugarten, B.L.: Social class and friendship among school children. *American Journal of Sociology, 51*, 305-313, 1946.

Newcomb, T.M.: The prediction of interpersonal attraction. *American Psychologist, 11*, 575-586, 1956.

Newcomb, T.M.: *The acquaintance process*. New York, Holt, Rinehart and Winston, 1961.

Nimkoff, M.F.: Occupational factors and marriage. *American Journal of Sociology, 49*, 248-254, 1943.

Ohmann, O.: The psychology of attraction. Chapter 2 in H.M. Jordon (Ed.), *You and marriage*, New York, Wiley, 1942.

Omwake, K.: The relationship between acceptance of self and acceptance of others shown by three personality inventories. *Journal of Consulting Psychology, 18*, 443-446, 1954.

Osgood, C.E., Suci, G.J. and Tannenbaum, P.H.: *The measurement of meaning*. Urbana, The University of Illinois Press, 1957.

Panunzio, C.: Intermarriage in Los Angeles, 1924-1933. *American Journal of Sociology, 47*, 399-401, 1942.

Perrin, F.A.C.: Physical Attractiveness and Repulsiveness. *Journal of Experimental Psychology, 4*, 203-217, 1921.

Plato: The symposium. In *The Works of Plato*, B. Jowett (Translator). New York, Tudor Publishing Co., pp. 293-358, 1933.

Preston, M.G., Peltz, W., Mudd, E.H. and Froscher, H.B.: Impressions of personality as a function of marital conflict. *Journal of Abnormal and Social Psychology, 47*, 326-336, 1952.

Reader, N. and English, H.B.: Personality factors in adolescent female friendships. *Journal of Consulting Psychology, 11*, 212-220, 1947.

Reik, T.A.: *Psychologist looks at love.* New York, Farrar and Rinehart, 1944.

Reik, T.A.: *Of love and lust.* New York, Farrar, Straus and Cuhady, 1957.

Rodgers, C.R.: *Client Centered Therapy.* Boston, Houghton Mifflin Company, 1951.

Rokeach, M.: *The Open and Closed Mind.* New York, Basic Books, 1960.

Rosenberg, M.: *Occupations and values.* Glencoe, Ill., The Free Press, 1957.

Schacter, S.: *The psychology of affiliation.* Stanford, Stanford University Press, 1959.

Schellenberg, J.A. and Bee, L.S.: A re-examination of the theory of complementary needs in mate selection. *Marriage and Family Living, 22*, 227-232, 1960.

Schutz, W.C.: *FIRO.* New York, Rinehart & Co., 1958.

Scodel, A.: Heterosexual somatic preference and fantasy dependency. *Journal of Consulting Psychology, 21*, 371-374, 1957.

Scott, W.A.: Social desirability and individual conceptions of the desirable. *Journal of Abnormal and Social Psychology, 67*, 574-585, 1963.

Sears, R.R.: Experimental studies of projection: II. Ideas of reference. *Journal of Social Psychology, 8*, 389-400, 1937.

Secord, P.F. and Backman, C.W.: *Social Psychology.* New York, McGraw-Hill Book Co., 1964.

Shaw, M.E.: Implicit conversion of fate control in dyadic interaction. *Psychological Reports, 10*, 758, 1962.

Shostrom, E.L.: Personal Orientation Inventory, San Diego: *Educational and Industrial Testing Service*, 1966, 1968.

Sinha, S.N.: A psychometric study of selected dimensions of vocational maturational motivation—life goals. Unpublished Ph.D. dissertation. University of California, Los Angeles, 1964.

Skolnick, P.: Reactions to personal evaluations: A failure to replicate. *Journal of Personality and Social Psychology, 18*, 62-67, 1971.

Slotkin, J.S.: Jewish-gentile intermarriage in Chicago. *American Sociological Review, 7*, 34-39, 1942.

Smuker, L.L.: Human encounter, personality types, and implicit theory of personality. Dissertation Abstracts, *20*, 3873, 1960.

Spinoza, B.: *Philosophy.* R.H.M. Elwes (Translator). New York, Tudor Publishing Co., 1936.

Stock, D.: An investigation into the intercorrelations between the self concept and feelings directed toward other persons and groups. *Journal of Consulting Psychology, 13*, 176-180, 1949.

Stroebe, W., Insko, C.A., Thompson, V.D. and Layton, B.D.: Effects of physical attractiveness, attitude similarity and *sex* on various aspects of interpersonal attraction. *Journal of Personality and Social Psychology, 18*, 79-91, 1971.

Sullivan, H.S.: *Conceptions of modern psychiatry.* Washington, D.C., The William Alanson White Psychiatric Foundation, 1947.

Sullivan, H.S.: *The interpersonal theory of psychiatry.* New York, Norton, 1953.

Taguiri, R.: Social preference and its perception. In R. Taguiri and L. Petrullo (Eds.), *Person perception and interpersonal behavior.* Stanford, Stanford University Press, pp. 316-336, 1958.

Taylor, J.A.: A personality scale of manifest anxiety. *Journal of Abnormal and Social Psychology, 48,* 285-290, 1953.

Thibaut, J.W. and Kelley, H.H.: *The social psychology of groups.* New York, John Wiley & Sons, Inc., 1959.

Thomas, J.L.: The factor of religion in the selection of marriage mates. *American Sociological Review, 16,* 487-491, 1951.

Thompson, W.R. and Nishimura, R.: Some determinants of friendship. *Journal of Personality, 20,* 305-314, 1952.

Trehub, A.: Ego disjunction and psychopathology. *Journal of Abnormal and Social Psychology, 58,* 191-194, 1959.

Walster, E.: The effect of self-esteem on romantic liking. *Journal of Experimental Social Psychology, 1,* 184-197, 1965.

Walster, E.V., Aronson, V., Abrahams, D. and Rottman, L.: Importance of physical attractiveness in dating behavior. *Journal of Personality and Social Psychology, 5,* 508-516, 1966.

Walster, E., Walster, B., Abraham, D. and Brown, Z.: The effect on liking of underrating or overrating another. *Journal of Experimental Social Psychology, 2,* 70-84, 1966.

Weatherly, U.G.: Race and marriage. *American Journal of Sociology, 15,* 433-453, 1919.

Wiggins, J.S., Wiggins, N. and Conger, J.C.: Correlates of heterosexual somatic preference. *Journal of Personality and Social Psychology, 10,* 82-90, 1968.

Willis, R.H. and Joseph, M.L.: Bargaining behavior I. "Prominence" as a predictor of the outcome of games of agreement. *Conflict Resolution, 3,* 102-113, 1959.

Willoughby, R.R.: Neuroticism in marriage: IV, Homogamy. V. Summary and conclusions. *Journal of Social Psychology, 7,* 19-33, 1936.

Winch, R.F.: The theory of complementary needs in mate selection; a test of one kind of complementariness. *American Sociological Review, 20,* 52-56, 1955.

Winch, R.F.: The theory of complementary needs in mate selection: final results on the test of the general hypothesis. *American Sociological Review, 20,* 552-555, 1955.

Winch, R.F.: *Mate selection.* New York, Harper & Brothers, 1958.

Winch, R.F.: Another look at the theory of complementary needs in mate selection. In R.F. Winch and L.W. Goodman (Eds.), *Selected studies in marriage and the family*. Holt, Rinehart and Winston, Inc., 3rd Edition, pp. 529-539, 1968.

Winch, R.F., Ktsanes, T. and Ktsanes, V.: The theory of complementary needs in mate selection: an analytic and descriptive study. *American Sociological Review, 19,* 241-249, 1954.

INDEX

A

Abrahams, D., 56, 321
Adjuvance, mechanism of, 106
Adlerians, 19
Agentiality, mechanism of, 111
Agreement effect, 82
Aristophanes, 15
Aristotle, 14, 313
Aronson, V., 56, 321
Attitudes and interpersonal attraction, 7

B

Backman, C. W., 8, 313, 320
Balance theory, 9
Banta, T. J., 31, 38, 96, 149, 160, 175, 178, 179, 180, 220, 222, 246, 273, 307, 313
Barclay, A. M., 51, 313
Bass, B. M., 31, 313
Becker, G., 32, 160, 313
Bee, L. S., 29, 30, 158, 320
Beier, E. G., 17, 313
Bendig, A. W., 146, 313
Benedek, T., 16, 313
Berger, E. M., 290, 313
Bergler, E., 16, 18, 313
Berkowitz, L., 199, 313
Bixenstein, V. E., 12, 313
Blau, P. M., 11, 313
Bonney, M. E., 7, 314
Bossard, J. H. S., 21, 22, 314
Bowerman, C. E., 22, 28, 158, 314
Breast size preferences, 54, 55, 56
Broxton, J. A., 8, 314
Buss, A., 199, 314
Buttocks, size preferences, 55
Byrne, D., 9, 10, 11, 36, 37, 82, 83, 84, 107, 128, 314, 315

C

Cattell, R. B., 17, 315

Centers, R., 21, 33, 44, 47, 182, 275, 315, 317
Clarke, A. C., 22, 315
Clore, G. L., 10, 314
Coadjuvance, mechanism of, 104
Coagentiality, mechanism of, 110
Cocomplementarity, mechanism of, 115
Comparison level, 11, 125
Comparison level for alternatives, 119
Complementarity
  Freud and, 15
  general and specific, 121
  idea of, 15
  mechanism of, 113
  theory, 13
  varieties of, 123
Complementary neuroses, 18, 19
Completion principle, 15, 16, 17
Comrey, A., 146, 318
Conger, J. C., 54, 321
Consensual validation, 8, 192, 223
  need for, 37
Constantine, P., 281, 282
Coprocreance, mechanism of, 108
Corah, N. L., 146, 315, 316
Covicariousness, mechanism of, 109
Cromwell, R. L., 17, 318

D

Davie, M. R., 22, 315
Davis, K. E., 32, 33, 35, 160, 318
Davitz, J. R., 8, 315
Day, B. R., 28, 30, 71, 72, 158, 160, 314, 315
Day, K. H., 21, 318
Deserts stance, 40, 208
Difference principle, 35
Diffuse complementarity, concept of, 121
Dorr, M., 24, 316
Dreikurs, R., 20, 316

Dyad formation, 5, 29, 59, 60

E

Edwards, A. L., 28, 71, 72, 152, 192, 280, 285, 292, 316
Edwards Personal Preference Schedule, 28, 31, 38, 54, 55, 71, 72, 77, 78, 79, 91, 96, 97, 144, 182, 188, 201, 316
Ellsworth, J. S., 22, 316
English, H. B., 17, 320
Euclid, 14

F

Feldman, M., 146, 315, 316
Festinger, L., 8, 83, 84, 107, 192, 316
Flugel, J. C., 15, 16, 24, 316
Freud, S., 4, 15, 50, 53, 54, 316
Froscher, H. B., 8, 319

G

Game theory, 11
Garfield, R. L., 17, 313
Genderic congruency, 124, 129, 135, 164, 166, 182, 212, 214, 221, 224, 227, 228, 229, 230, 233, 309, 310
and threat property of various needs, 78
degrees of, 77
postulate of, 70
types of, 76
Genderic congruency effect, 167
magnification of, 297
Glick, P. C., 21, 316
Granville, A. C., 33, 315
Gray, H., 16, 20, 316
Griffitt, W., 10, 314
Group formation, 5

H

Havighurst, R. J., 24, 316
Heider, F., 8, 9, 317
Hetherington, M., 31, 38, 96, 149, 160, 175, 178, 179, 180, 220, 222, 246, 273, 307, 313
Hollingshead, A. B., 21, 317
Homans, G. C., 11, 317
Hunt, T. C., 21, 317

I

Initial attraction, theory of, 49
Instrumentality, concept of, 3

Instrumental theory, components of, 42, 43
Intermotivational mechanics, summary of principles, 138
Intermotivational mechanisms
Adjuvance and Coadjuvance, 104
Agentiality and Coagentiality, 110
Complementarity and Cocomplementarity, 113
Procreance and Coprocreance, 108
Reciprocality, 97
Vicariousness and Covicariousness, 109
Interpersonal deception, 203
Intersexual dyad formation, 63
Intrapsychic costs, 202
Intrapsychic inhibitions, 202
Irrelevance, postulate of, 103
Isomorphism of motive and behavior, 201, 310

J

James, W., 291, 317
Jennings, H. H., 7, 218, 219, 317
Joseph, M. L., 12
Jungians, 19

K

Katkovsky, W., 17, 318
Kelley, H. H., 11, 12, 290, 321
Kennedy, R. J. R., 21, 22, 317
Kerckhoff, A., 32, 33, 35, 160, 318
Kidd, J. W., 218, 318
Ktsanes, T., 21, 178, 318, 322
Ktsanes, V., 21, 178, 322

L

Landis, P. H., 21, 318
Levinger, G., 33, 318
Levonian, E., 146, 318
Levy, W., 146, 318
Lewin, K., 7
Limit of tolerance for punification, 119
Locke, H. J., 31, 318
Los Angeles Times, 282
Love at first sight, 61
Love, theory of, 45
Lundy, R. M., 17, 318

M

McClelland, D. C., 199, 318

McDougall, W., 4, 15
Marches, J. R., 22, 318
Martin, A. M., 146, 313
Martinson, F. M., 16, 318
Marvin, D., 21, 318
Maslow, A. H., 81, 82, 237, 290, 318
Mate market, 207
Mittelman, M., 16, 19, 319
Moreno, J. L., 6, 7, 218, 319
Mosteller, F., 288, 319
Mudd, E. H., 8, 319
Murray, H. A., 4, 22, 28, 38, 66, 115, 134, 145, 188, 192, 200, 319
Murstein, B. I., 30, 31, 160, 161, 319

N

Need conflict, 102
Need-resource resonance, 206
    postulate of, 195, 310
Needs, 3, 4
    items defining
        abasement, 133
        achievement, 110
        affiliation, 99
        aggression, 105
        autonomy, 129
        change, 135
        deference, 127
        dominance, 105
        endurance, 137
        exhibition, 124
        intraception, 133
        nurturance, 115
        order, 136
        sex, 98
        succorance, 114
Nelson, D., 10, 315
Nesselroade, J. R., 17, 315
Neugarten, B. L., 8, 319
Newcomb, T. M., 7, 8, 10, 11, 36, 37, 82, 107, 128, 319
Nimkoff, M. F., 21, 319
Nishimura, F., 17, 321

O

Ohmann, O., 16, 319
Omwake, W., 290, 319
Osgood, C. E., 190, 319

P

Pavlov, I. P., 50
Peltz, W., 8, 319
Physical attraction, 52
Physical attractiveness, 56
Plato, 15, 319
Potash, H. M., 12
Preston, M. G., 8, 319
Procreance, mechanism of, 108
Proctor, D., 146, 318
Profit, 211, 219, 222
Punification
    definition of, 38
Punification avoidance, principle of, 102, 103

R

Reader, N., 17, 320
Reciprocal Compatibility, 35
Reciprocal complementarity (or Cocomplementarity), mechanism of, 115
Reeves, R. J., 22, 315
Reik, T. A., 16, 320
Reinforcement theory, 9
Robinson, M. Z., 24, 316
Rossi, A. M., 17, 313
Rottman, L., 56, 321
Rourke, R. E. K., 288, 319

S

Schachter, S., 115, 188, 191, 192, 199, 216, 320
Schellenberg, J. A., 29, 30, 158, 320
Schutz, W. C., 32, 33, 42, 66, 182, 320
Scodel A., 53, 54, 55, 320
Scott, W. A., 146, 320
Secord, P. F., 8, 313, 320
Self esteem
    and assertive drives, 130
Senn, D. J., 33, 318
Sexual Attraction, specific theory of, 49
Sexual style, 41, 73
Shaw, M. E., 12, 320
Shoemaker, D. J., 17, 318
Similarity principle, 35
Smuker, L. L., 8, 320
Spinoza, B., 14, 15, 320
Stock, D., 290, 320
Suchi, G. J., 190, 319

Sullivan, H. S., 8, 19, 66, 80, 83, 84, 107, 192, **321**
Supply and demand in the mate market, 207

T

Taguiri, R., 8, 321
Tannenbaum, P. H., 190, 319
Taylor, J. A., 192, 321
Thibaut, J. W., 11, 12, 290, 321
Thomas, G. B., 288
Thomas, J. L., 21, 321
Thompson, W. R., 17, 321
Threat property of needs, 165, 215, 217
Turbeville, G., 22, 318

U

Unit formation, 9

V

Vicariousness, mechanism of, 108

W

Wallace, K. M., 31, 318
Walster, E., 56, 321
Wheelwright, J. B., 20, 316
Wiggins, J. S., 54, 321
Wiggins, N., 54, 321
Willis, R. H., 12, 321
Winch, R. F., 13, 16, 21, 71, 73, 75, 90, 91, 92, 93, 109, 116, 144, 158, 178, 179, 182, 275, 304, 321, 322